A Nation Unaware

The Canadian Economic Culture

By Herschel Hardin

J.J. Douglas Ltd., Vancouver, 1974.

ISBN (cloth) 0-88894-030-0

J.J. DOUGLAS LTD.
132 Philip Avenue
North Vancouver, British Columbia

Design by Ben Lim
Typesetting by B.C. Monthly Typesetting Service
Printed and bound in Canada by the Hunter Rose Company

Contents

If the country is to be saved, the saviours will not be found in the haunts of capital, nor will they come from the seats of the mighty, but such salvation as may be will find its birth in the hearts and minds of the great mass of the common people of the Dominion.

SIR HENRY THORNTON, president of Canadian National Railways, 1922-1932, in his final letter to Canada shortly before his death in 1933.

Preface

This book was begun three years ago. Some of the contemporary imagery dates back to that period and before, through to 1968, when I began to read background material and to collect clippings.

Ken Dryden, for example, was playing goal for the Montreal Canadiens in those days. Polymer was a crown corporation. W. A. C. Bennett was premier of British Columbia. The United States was a more dominant power in the world than it is now. (Canadians were thoroughly cowed by the American economic presence; how much has that changed?) The Expo summer was still in some of our minds. So was terrorism in Quebec, especially, of course, the events of October 1970. René Lévesque had yet to fail for the second time to be elected to the Quebec National Assembly as leader of the Parti Québecois.

I have updated the economic detail, excluding however the current energy question (western oil and natural gas) and its ramifications with regard to Canadian federalism. The introductory section on identity and ideology, with its many reference points, I have largely left alone, as also the historical argument which is the core of the book.

I am still collecting images and miscellaneous facts, in files and in my own mind. I hope interested readers will add to this work, and the work of the book, in their own way.

My wife Marguerite has been of particular assistance to me. I would also like to thank the people in the business and economics department of the Vancouver Public Library whose help in tracking down details and turning up files was much appreciated.

Herschel Hardin

West Vancouver, B.C.
December 15, 1973

PART I

Introduction

CHAPTER 1

The Old Identity Riddle

It is a peculiar anthropological puzzle that Canadians don't know who they are, although they have been trying to find out, by introspection, almost from the beginning of their history.

Not that they suffer from a lack of imagination. The search for a Canadian identity, and for a definition of Canadian nationalism, has gone on for so long, and is so gloriously rich in idiosyncrasy, that it constitutes one of the wonders of the world.

At one time, for example, people really believed in the myth of the true north, strong and free. One such observer saw Canada, in 1889, as "a young, fair and stalwart maiden of the north," as if Canada were a character in a 19th century melodrama — which their Canada probably was. A country of "unseizable virginity" is how Rupert Brooke described it. "Lady of the Snows," wrote Rudyard Kipling.

None of the romanticism has fallen off. Some metaphors are better, like Gilles Vigneault's *"Mon pays, ce n'est pas un pays, c'est l'hiver."* Some metaphors are worse, like the newspaper disclosure that "there is a tide in the affairs of nations which, taken at the flood, leads on to fortune . . . yet few Canadians seem fully aware that their national ship of state has set sail on just such a voyage of destiny in the Arctic Ocean." Even Irving Layton's "A dull people, but the rivers of this country are wide and beautiful" puts down the people and underlines the emotional impact of the countryside.

Perhaps the only substantive change since the turn of the century has been the movement of the symbolism farther north a few parallels of latitude to take in Ungava Bay, the

Northwest Territories and the Arctic Ocean. (And probably, says the cynic in me, it will keep on moving until the Canadian imagination settles the Arctic islands with figures of speech, crosses the North Pole and moves down the other side.) A social science professor writes, "The farther north one goes, the more truly national the setting becomes. The north is now inextricably tied up with the Canadian identity. It is like a vast screen upon which our being as Canadians is projected." It is already happening.

This is not to mention, either, the North's out-and-out magical qualities. According to a syndicated Ottawa columnist, the best way to make good Canadians out of Quebec separatists would be to take them on a trip through the Northwest Territories where they would be transmogrified by the pan-Arctic-Canadian landscape — "My suggestion to the politicians: launch a program of Arctic tours for separatists with all expenses paid." (Or maybe he has one-way tours in mind.)

The list of Canadian modes of self-identification, of course, only just begins with this myth of the land and vision of the North.

Canadian identity, for example, is seen as taking its rise in anti-Americanism, as "the product of a victorious counter-revolution" which "in a sense must justify its *raison d'être* by emphasizing the virtues of being separate from the United States"; such at least is the thesis of Seymour Martin Lipset, the American sociologist, as elaborated in *Revolution and Counterrevolution.* This is something like saying that the identity of modern Poland is a product of its refusal to be annexed by Russia and Germany. It begs the question. Why have the Poles struggled to remain a separate sovereign nation? Why are Canadians "the world's oldest and continuing anti-Americans?"

The charitable answer usually given is that we are, or have been, royalists — British North Americans. We are told, although it doesn't square with history, that Canadians accepted a national purpose based on the principle of the "indivisibility of the Commonwealth." "The Crown-in-Parliament is the supreme symbol of our nationhood," wrote Vincent Massey, "and our greatest defense against absorption into a continental state."

British nativism and transplanted French loyalist reaction do help to explain the dynamic of the counterrevolution in the past, but now that real allegiance to the crown hardly exists among French Canadians, and is variable among other Canadians, we are led to the conclusion that the Canadian identity does not exist any more. We don't, any longer, identify as Canadians, or at least we're not supposed to. So funeral rites are in order, and many years ago were in fact prepared and delivered by the Reverend George Grant in his celebrated book *Lament for a Nation.*

But Canada is alive and kicking as usual. And Canadians are as anti-American and as nationalist as ever. *Lament for a Nation* is now a museum piece, valuable in insight but eclipsed by events.

The picture of Canadians as an identifiably unique counterrevolutionary people, to the right of the United States, has now been overshadowed by a self-image on the left. Lipset suggests that in the long run this may "contribute strongly to eliminating the relatively small differences between the values of the two countries . . . for a democratic leftist ideology is synonymous with the social content of Americanism." And he quotes Frank Underhill that "if we are eventually to satisfy ourselves that we have at last achieved a Canadian identity, it will be only when we are satisfied that we have arrived at a better American way of life than the Americans have."

There are all kinds of perverse American assumptions in that suggestion. First of all, it implies that "a populist democratic culture" is a unique American characteristic, definitive of the American character, whereas in fact the impetus towards mass democracy is a widespread phenomenon, across which countries show their differing characteristics

just as much as ever. Left alone within Lipset's framework of
national identity and values, it could be argued without any
trouble that Canadians, in shifting to the left, are becoming
more Chinese than American, or that the Chinese, in pushing
forward with the Communist Revolution and becoming a
mass egalitarian society, are Americanizing themselves.

The similarity between China and the United States, for
example, is inescapable. There is, to start with, a startling
resemblance between the intolerant egalitarian pressure to
conform ideologically in China, and the same pressure towards conformity in American history, of which Tocqueville
remarked, "I know of no country in which there is so little
independence of mind and real freedom of discussion . . . ."
The mass enthusiasm and economic creativity released by the
Chinese revolution also have close counterparts in the U.S.
past. So does the anti-bureaucratic, anti-feudal thrust of
Maoism, and the resort to mass demonstrations and occasional
violence to assert the people's inalienable rights. Chinese
proletarian art, in its naturalistic portrayal of the myths of
the citizenry and its elimination of the ornate, heavy artistic
forms created for the rich pleasures of a small, well-educated
minority, reminds one of American mass culture. The ballet
The Red Detachment of Women is a Maoist West Side Story.
But skin colour and the formal structures of government
aside, nobody would suggest that between the Chinese and
Americans there are only "small value differences."

In lesser, and less noticeable, but nevertheless profound
ways, Canadian identity is separate from American identity.
In fact, as it happens, Americans are becoming, and will
become, more Canadian rather than vice-versa.

The "revolution and counterrevolution" framework also
fails to explain why Canadians still consider themselves more
conservative than Americans, and are so considered by others,
while their self-image has moved to the non-conservative left
side of them. Or why an emigré American professor should
exclaim with exasperation, "Why are you Canadians so
feudal?" in a part of the country, British Columbia, which

embodies some thoroughly unAmerican progressive ideas.

What Underhill has proclaimed, and what Lipset, reading the texts, has brilliantly elaborated, is, in effect, that there is no Canadian way of life, other than American-envy. "Canada is a different kind of American society," declares William Kilbourn, "an American alternative to what has happened in the United States." "What is true of American identity is *a fortiori* true of Canadian identity," Northrop Frye expounds. Canada is the Americans' "misallocated resource," says Dalton Camp, and again, Canada is "the natural accessory after the American fact."

From there it is not much further to the citizen's judgment, in the *Toronto Star*, that only "an invisible line . . . makes some of us Americans and others Canadians," or to the agreement by hardware merchants from Redondo Beach (California), Cincinnati (Ohio) and Brownsville (Texas), at a convention in the Royal York Hotel, that Canada isn't a "foreign country," that the idea is "inconceivable."

Other descriptions are less charitable. Canada, observed a New Yorker, is "that gray neutral zone that you flop into if you step off the northern edge of the United States."

"To those who do not know the country," reported *Newsweek*, "there has often seemed to be something faintly irrelevant about Canada," and then went on to describe the country as "a minor power militarily, an appendage of the U.S. economically and of limited interest culturally."

Canadians, nevertheless, persist in their search for Canadian particularisms. Canadians are less violent than Americans, everybody concurs, which is like saying that we are less violent Americans. The central difference is that "in the United States, social groups make greater demands on the individual than do equivalent groups in Canada," according to a political science professor, which makes Canadians . . . more private Americans. And both peoples talk through the nose, observed Sir Francis Bond Head in the 1830's. Hence they must be the same, although the Yankees are more so.

In the same way, we have come to see ourselves as sluggish, easy-going Americans, or less pushy Americans, although our early speculators and traders, even our early Montreal establishment — they in particular in fact — encouraged brutality and pursued bribery with extraordinary vigour, in quest of the native Canadian dollar. Back in 1891, the *Saturday Review* concluded that in the field of corruption, Canada could "modestly challenge comparison" with the United States. "Her opportunities and means are not so great as those wielded by the lobbyists and log-rollers of Washington, or the bosses and wire-pullers of New York, but the most has been made of them . . . ."

The myth of the Canadian mosaic, and of a multicultural Canada, falls short too. The historian Kenneth McNaught inadvertently put his finger on the weakness of the myth when he wrote that "tradition has planted firmly in the minds of English-speaking Canadians the idea that their national loyalty is to national diversity" but "unhappily this seems trite only to English-speaking Canadians." French-speaking Canada is sceptical, for good reason, and turns to its own mythology. Nor does it help to cite the fact that a considerable part of Canada speaks French and has an absolutely distinctive unAmerican past and personality. That only makes English Canadians in search of an identity depressed and envious, and French Canadians slightly smug. ("Canadian patriotism," writes a literary critic in *Le Devoir*, "is the most ridiculous of all patriotisms because it's not rooted in a homeland, at least not yet: even the nationalists speak in the future tense.")

Roughly at this point in the argument, frustration gives way to humour, fantasy, exotica. . . .

Harry G. Johnson, an economist who left Canada but still likes to preach to Canadians, observes that Canadians at a seminar he attended, characteristically quoted the Bible to make a point (instead of Adam Smith's *Wealth of Nations*, perhaps), which made him wonder why Canadians wanted to be different anyway.

Then there's the joke, claimed by John Colombo, that Canada was meant to be a combination of French culture, British government and American know-how but ended up a mixture of French government, American culture and British know-how.

Harold Horwood, a novelist from Newfoundland, thinks of Canadians as "a people who are non-lineal, non-violent, coolly involved, relaxed, and at home with the idea of their electronic nerve-endings reaching out to Vietnam and Biafra and the backside of the moon. . . . Among 'western' countries at least, Canada is the first truly 20th century nation . . . Our revolution concerns the innerness of society, its soul, its essences and values. . . . I dare to hope that what we are achieving in Canada is not just a new nation, but a new species: a spiritual mutation such as Nietzsche dreamed about when he wrote of the superman . . . it is happening in Nanaimo and Lloydminster and Brandon and Orillia and Mont Joli and Sussex and New Glasgow and Corner Brook. . . ."

And so on.

It's no good, of course. Everybody has his own list, at least in his head, and they're all, probably, equally useless. None of it evokes that immediate self-recognition which identity is. "Debating nationalism is the great Canadian pastime," writes the historian, and finding out that common language, religion and ethnic origin, and the other ordinary characteristics of nationality aren't available, but that Canadians still compulsively and laboriously attempt to define "the Canadian identity," he decides that "Canada has asserted its nationalism by looking for it."

Or in the words of a foreign correspondent of the *New York Times*: "Your very nationality consists of an identity crisis with which you have a national love affair."

That's a nice turn of phrase, but the "identity crisis," as we know, has mostly hollowness and barrenness in it, and the kind of love that makes the heart go dead.

There is even a kind of comic, existential perplexity about it. "This country," writes a young journalist in 1970, "has no sense of being" (although Canada in fact has had a continuous existential quality for just about as long as the history of the United States). "Canadian identity might be not much more at the moment than a cough or harumph barely heard in the howlings of U.S. culture," writes another. ". . . This country does not exist. . . . Whenever I sit down and think about this country it seems to disappear," writes another.

A letter writer in the *Toronto Star* reports that "some time ago, the host of an American late night talk show briefly mentioned the term [Canadian identity] and asked why Canadians should have an identity problem; I immediately began a letter to him explaining the 'Identity Crisis' and what it really means to be a Canadian; that letter remains unfinished; I have no idea what it is to be a Canadian or why there should be any problem being identified . . . or whatever."

According to the newspapers, even the Minister of Citizenship, in 1970, was looking for the Canadian identity, hoping "to tap a deep stream of Canadian consciousness, running through all regions, linking English and French. . . ." How does a man who doesn't know what the Canadian identity is get to become Minister of Citizenship in the first place? Because of the nature of the riddle. And by the nature of the riddle, he is not likely to find it.

He is not likely to find it because, like almost everybody who has tackled the riddle, he seems to be looking for common characteristics and for a common emotional rootedness which aren't there. Otherwise they would have created common symbols long ago, and the whole question of identity would not arise. There are no common symbols that can summon up absolute loyalty in all the pockets of the community, and there may never be. Yet there *is* a community. And Canada *has* acted as a nation for a hundred years, and with historical antecedents that go back from 1867 probably just as far.

Canada exists, but is invisible. There must be something wrong, then, with the way we look at ourselves.

There is no hope for it but to go at the riddle backwards — to identify Canadians in terms of the root circumstances and forces of the country rather than in terms of individual feeling; and once having explored those circumstances, to find out why a former Minister of Citizenship and most other Canadians relate so weakly to them.

CHAPTER 2
_____

Canada as a Series of Contradictions

To get at the Canadian circumstance, and through it, to identity, and to escape from riddles with no answers, is above all to see the country in terms of its *contradictions* — the contending forces that underlie the character of the people. The same methodology of contradictions can also provide luminous insight into certain societies with strong common symbolism, like China and the United States, or into historical characteristics shared by a group of countries (western Europe, and so on) that lend themselves to such an approach.

The central contradiction of Chinese civilization, for example, is the one between the educated elite and the masses of the people — a contradiction rooted in the ancient circumstances of the Chinese people.

From the earliest days of settlement of the Yellow River Valley, the Han people realized that only a strong, central authority could maintain and synchronize the necessary diking and canal systems over long stretches of the river. This centralized control, in turn, was impossible without an administrative class. Chinese civilization, the unique Chinese mentality, the codes of behaviour (Confucianism, Maoism) which are characteristic of the Chinese, are the products of the contradiction between this class (mandarins, Communist Party cadres), without whose consent no dynasty could govern, and the peasantry — the mass of society — without whose consent no dynasty could survive.

One could almost say that only in terms of that fundamental age-old contradiction does Maoism, in its anti-bureaucratic thrust, the Cultural Revolution, the particular route by which China has become a modernized mass democracy . . . only in those terms does any of it become intelligible, do the Chinese become visible as Chinese rather than as inscrutable Europeans with yellow skins.

In the same way, not the only, or the most useful, but the richest appreciation of American character comes not from celebrating or deploring Americans' legendary materialism and violence, or from observing them worshipping their myths and demonstrating their patriotism, but from exploring the contradictory phenomenon of an America irrationally, intolerantly absorbed in the myth of rational, liberal freedom.

This is the contradiction which Louis Hartz illuminated with such gusto in *The Liberal Tradition in America*. "Here is a doctrine [liberalism]," wrote Hartz, "which everywhere in the West has been a glorious symbol of individual liberty, yet in America its compulsive power has been so great that it has posed a threat to liberty itself." The mark of Hartz' originality was that he gave this "compulsive power" such bold and suggestive names that they encapsulate in a few words the particular psychic, parochial dilemma which is America — names like "colossal liberal absolutism," "the national irrational liberalism," "the grip of Locke," and the "Americanistic mechanism" of terrifying dissenters. But part and parcel of the American contradiction, with its Red scares and its absolutist intolerance in the name of freedom, is a quality of individual freedom and creative energy unknown to the rest of history, but again, an individualism and a creativity of a special kind — the American kind.

Contradictions also inform the industrial European experience — the contradictions of class. Merely to mention them is to write a footnote to Marx, to all of the European Marxists, to all the European anti-Marxists, and to all the non-Marxist, non-anti-Marxist appreciations of European class differences. Whatever the strength of class contradictions in

Europe now, modern European society has evolved by the elaboration of those contradictions, and I doubt if there is any European who does not have fragments of that elaboration embedded in his psyche.

What are the basic contradictions of the Canadian experience? There are three of them: (1) French Canada as against English Canada; (2) the regions as against the federal centre; and (3) Canada as against the United States. The second one incorporates much of the first, Quebec being both the thrust of French Canada and the most centrifugal, psychically, of the regions. It is across these contradictions that Canada has defined itself.

That these three contradictions are at the centre of the Canadian experience, that they have been the forcing ground of our identity, is obvious. But Canadians have exquisite ways of missing the point.

One poignant case sticks in my mind, because it illustrates the leading Canadian contradiction at work on a man whose identity as a Canadian was still in the process of formation. It was during the St. Léonard controversy over whether all schools should be French-language, or whether there should be English-language instruction available as well. An ethnic spokesman caught in the crossfire protested with quiet emotion to CBC Radio that his group was an innocent victim of an inexplicable quarrel, all the more innocent because they had no ingrained hostility against French Canadians. We're not against the French Canadians, he said. And we're not against the English Canadians. We just want to be Canadian.

It never occurred to him that having to explore this linguistic conflict, having to get behind it in order to understand it and cope with it, and in intensely passionate, practical circumstances, would give him more insight into what it meant to be a Canadian than most Canadians would gather from a lifetime. Even while he was protesting, he probably had already realized there was no total escape from the contradiction other than by leaving the country. Wasn't that why he was protesting in the first place? And after going through that experience, would he ever agree that being a Canadian and an American involved more or less the same thing?

Here is where the Canadian character is working itself out in passion, and even in blood. By contrast, the dispatch of available search parties on exotic missions into the tundra and muskeg and the land of stunted conifers, where few Canadians actually live or have visited, in search of identity, is escapist fantasy.

Canadian identity is in the guts of the physical and psychological settlement, not on the periphery of the hinterland.

On top of that familiar Canadian syndrome of "identification with the subhuman" — the northern subhuman now — and tied into it, we now perceive, also, the self-demeaning habit by which a once confident people has been conditioned to look at itself through the narrowing eyes of other peoples infected with other contradictions — to search after other peoples' kinds of mythology — which habit is the colonial mentality.

In other words, if you ask an American, or a European, or a Chinese question, you won't get a Canadian answer.

"There is no great national hero who cut down a maple tree, threw a silver dollar across the St. Lawrence and then proceeded to lead a revolution and govern the victorious nation wisely and judiciously," we are told. Nor are there any "great Canadian charters of freedom or independence expressing the collective will of the people," which we can put behind glass in our post offices or tack onto the walls of our offices and workshops, we are told. Then, when we are told that "Canadians have both thought and acted like contemporary nationalists" by throwing up tariffs and building the CPR, we still wonder why John A. Macdonald couldn't have thrown a silver dollar instead of giving away 25 million paper ones. The assiduously researched fact that Macdonald was an alcoholic is good stuff, but as we know in

our bones, it's a poor substitute for George Washington's
encounter with a cherry tree. It would never survive, if it
weren't for the tariff on history.

But any Canadian substitutes for the War of Independence and the other objects in the American museum will be
poor myth because they will be weak in Canadian contradictions. They will be the symbolic outcroppings and residue
of nothing at all. The languishing after a common symbolism,
in the way that the national mythology of Britain or China
or France or the U.S.A. is common to the citizenry, is a
sorrowful wild goose chase — a Canada Goose chase. It is the
uncommonly Canadian, uncommon symbolism we should be
trying to uncover, and it is here, because we are.

The colonial wives' tale that, being a country of
immigrants, Canada is "a land with little common civilization," also misses the point — misses several points — and in
the same way. It begs the question: What kind of immigrants
and in what historical context? It ignores the powerful effect
which indigenous influences and circumstances can have on
immigrants, if the new country is politically and economically
free. A spirit of independence abroad in the land is crucial if
the indigenous circumstances are to have an impact.

The United States is also a country of immigrants. Yet
was there any doubt, even from the earlier days of settlement
before the War of Independence, that life in America was
different in kind from life in Europe, that it functioned by a
different ethic and in a different spirit, quite apart from the
novel economic demands of the frontier? An immigrant, from
out of the class contradictions of Europe, came to America,
a land of immigrants — and nothing else except the belea-
guered Indians — and he was a new man almost overnight.
And this new dimension which America brought out in him,
and which he shared in common with other immigrants, had
little to do with his own past loyalties or with shared
historical experience in Europe. The American way of life
was in the air of the new society, and having to breathe, he
breathed it in, and breathed it in freely, without a European

sack over his head — that was important to the exercise.

Nevertheless, there were scholars and commentators from "civilized" Europe who continued to see the United States as a country of immigrants with little common civilization other than economic techniques and the legal and parliamentary traditions and other cultural hand-me-downs inherited from Great Britain. James M. Minifie reminds us that in the early days of the Republic, Englishmen, when they wanted to be friendly, often expressed the view that between the two peoples there wasn't much difference — that Americans were just "transatlantic John Bulls" — and that they were amazed at the apoplectic reception they received. Tocqueville knew better. (In the same way, a correspondent of the *Washington Post* wrote recently that we are "undeniably similar," although "nothing annoys some Canadians more than to be told [as much] by well-meaning Americans.")

The "Canadian way of life," as seen in terms of its own contradictions rather than other peoples', is similarly different in kind from American civilization, and is roughly just as old, dating back at least to the Conquest, when French Canadians began to realize that their only chance of survival was inside a state dominated by English-speaking power and later English-speaking numbers, and when English-speaking Canadians began to realize that the French Canadians existed in a body and might even endure. Then, and ever since, that contradiction has infected everything.

Now, if you consider common civilizations in their European sense only, and look to them for national identities, you are forced to conclude that immigrants become Canadians by joining one of the two sides. But that way, in fact, they just become English Canadians or French Canadians. It is only when they are caught up in the elaboration of the primal Canadian contradiction between the two groups that the inescapable, dense, bewildering sense of what it means to be a Canadian rather than a transplanted European, or American, hits home, as many an immigrant parent in Montreal can testify. Newcomers become transformed into natives almost overnight, and without common histories, in Canada too.

Two hundred years and more of the elaboration of a constant set of defining contradictions is not a long time as some civilizations go. But it is not a short time either. It parallels, for example, the entire duration of the industrial age, with its antecedents in the mercantile glories of England and France.

Canada is not a young country. Canada is not "a land without real history . . . rootless, cut off, out of touch, and therefore barren." Canada is not "collectively youthful." Canada is not "culturally immature." Canada is a country of immigrants only incidentally. The notion that "the Canadian reaction to life is a strictly contemporary one," that we can "escape history," not having had a continuous history which has formed our characters, holds true only outside the Canadian contradictions, which means that it doesn't hold true at all. There is a thick continuity in us, as a collectivity, which has been deeply felt when Canadians have been in an independent mood.

*   *   *

The more independent the mood, the greater the self-definition. In that most independent of Canadian times, the 1830's, when Canada was actually and obviously young, there were nevertheless binding psychological roots put down in the country, in Lower Canada among the French Canadians, but in English Canada as well. Since then — since the failure of the rebellions in 1837 — we have been conscientious colonials. Over the years, little by little, our identity has gone begging.

But look back to the 1830's.

When Lord Durham, Canada's Tocqueville, came to the country from the outside to look at the anatomy of the anti-imperialist rebellions, he noticed immediately the "two nations warring inside the bosom of a single state." This was so peculiar, and so unlike the American experiment, that Durham's solution was to assimilate the one side — a solution which had no practical application. Being liberal and perspicacious, he was able to analyze the social forces giving definition to Canada. But being an outsider, he was not able to identify with more than an incomplete part of them, and then only from a psychological distance.

Compare this to the appreciation of an equally articulate liberal, but one infected with the indigenous spirit — William Lyon Mackenzie. Mackenzie, as a journalist and politician living in the colony, was too closely tied to the particular circumstances of the country to mistake it for another one. His sensitivity to the reality that is Canada was so uncanny that, passionately put down on paper in the 1820's, long before even Confederation, it still, save for the details, speaks for the native soul. . . .

If there is, *and I begin to imagine that you have some shadow of cause for saying so* (for the Canadians have been very ill used and feel it), a French Canadian party who would wish to obtain the ascendancy in Canada, for the purpose of visiting on the heads of the population of your origin and mine the sins of the old tyrannical governments of unreformed England, believe me, for I say it most sincerely, I am the last Scotsman in Upper Canada who would be their tool or their slave — but in as far as it is sought by the House of Assembly of Lower Canada to educate all and give all equal rights, why should there be two opinions?

As to the friendship of the Canadians of French origin towards the English, Scotch and Irish — perhaps it is less warm than I had supposed — but, be this as it may, it is us who are to blame. England conquered their country — turned their *colleges into a barrack* — kept their people in ignorance — insulted their leading men — neglected their best interests — forgot to conciliate and trust in them — preferred strangers to their language, manners and customs — *appeared to* give them popular institutions forty years ago, and now declared them virtually unfit to enjoy them!

United to the States, the vast revenue raised at our seaports would go to swell the funds of congress; their southern and northern generals would be ours; their slave questions and immense territory might not add to our happiness; . . . .

> Greatly therefore, although I admire them as a people, and
> *I do admire their course as a nation, and glory in their success,*
> as affording a proof of the practical untility *of the representa-*
> *tive system of government,* yet do I believe that these colonies
> might be fully as happy separated from them; but if better
> measures are not taken, and a more statesmanlike policy
> pursued by us (by the colonists) disunion among ourselves
> will end only in making us conquered states, sneered at
> though received into the Union.

Everything is there to be wondered at — English as against French, region binding region, Canada versus the United States.

Instead of disunion among the colonies, Mackenzie recommended a "federal system" or a "federative union" — also uncannily farsighted.

Even with the cumulative insights provided by a century of federalism, nothing still has quite that lyrical sensitivity to French-Canadian grievances and, at the same time, to the dangers of unstatesmanlike disunity between the regions as against the thrust of the United States, as do the above passages. Mackenzie, though fiercely partisan in the debate between privilege and democracy, was one of the few able to perceive, and to sympathize with, both sides of the leading Canadian contradiction.

Settlement of Upper Canada west of Kingston had only really begun at the turn of the century. Mackenzie didn't arrive until 1820. The immigrant, pluralistic character of the peoples in the colony was self-evident, and celebrated often by Mackenzie. His rhapsodical account of the diversity of peoples at an election meeting in Niagara in 1824 is as delightful a description of man's variety as one could find anywhere. But taking in Canada directly, in travels, reportage and political activity, Mackenzie saw them above all as Canadians — a community with a bond, linked essentially to the other Canadians, including the French-speaking majority in Lower Canada, different from the Americans, different from the British, and as deserving of independence, as a people, as the Irish and the Poles whom he often cited as examples. Also, without *arrière-pensées,* and identifying spontaneously the way a Frenchman might identify with Joan of Arc, Mackenzie made mighty appeals to the Canadians' sense of history, although there were only 20 or 30 years of it, and although a good part of the people who responded to the appeals hadn't even been around that long, as Mackenzie hadn't either.

How is it possible that a century and a half later a young journalist should complain that Canada has no "sense of being," and, more peculiar, that most Canadians, including a Minister of Citizenship, would probably understand what he was getting at, and even more peculiar, that today's Canadians should make outsiders out of thoroughly native spirits like Mackenzie and his brethren, and should go on misreading their own situation?

The argument, in Mackenzie's case, is that because he was an egalitarian liberal, and a passionate democratic rabble-rouser, he was really an American in disguise, and that the definitive Canadian character exhibited itself in the elitism and conservatism which followed the failure of the rebellions. William Kilbourn, in his biography of Mackenzie, feels obliged to give him only a discontinued tangential line on the "main graph of Canadian history."

In fact, the conservative social structure is only a skin which has bound Canada in, the way it has restricted countless other countries. When it is shed, Canada will be as different from the United States as it always has been, and will see the difference more. Similarly, the egalitarianism, the work ethic, the economic dynamism of the Republic, no longer are distinctive to the United States, and were not considered as such by Mackenzie in his own time. Had the populist, democratic impulse triumphed in Canada in the early 1830's, before disunity was upon British North America, it is just as likely as not that a Canada would be in existence today.

The proof of Mackenzie's identity is in himself. He was

closely attached, intellectually and emotionally, to the British liberal reform movement and to the ideals of British justice. But when he visited Great Britain in 1832, only 12 years after he had emigrated to Canada, he was already the outsider, noticing more and more the great distance between his community and Europe. Exile in the United States, for all Mackenzie's admiration of the American yéoman, was also disillusioning.

Louis Hartz, to make a point about the absolute distinctiveness of the newly effulgent liberal America in the 19th century, imagines Andrew Jackson across the Atlantic, and the point is made. "Where would he have stood?" asks Hartz. "Would he have stood with Disraeli and the land, or with Cobbett and the workers, or with the petty enterprisers who scarcely had an independent leadership? The fact is, he would not have known where to stand. He would have wandered homelessly over the face of Europe, a lost giant from another world, finding parts of his personality in various places but the whole of it nowhere. Victorious in the liberal society of America, he would have been, precisely for that reason, a massive misfit in the old society of Europe."

Mackenzie was a massive misfit both in the old society and in the new, American one — and in the colonial Canada as well! Mackenzie was not an American in the wrong country. He was a Canadian at the wrong time.

English Canadians like to talk about Canada's age of innocence, meaning the whole of Canadian history, and how it was shattered by the events of October 1970. Mackenzie may have been utopian, but he never had any illusions about the innocence of his country. Creating a simulacrum of innocence is only a way colonials have of avoiding their condition.

If Canadians had an identity, then Riel and Mackenzie would be heroes, writes the poet, the idea not entering his head that they *are* heroes and that Canada does have identity, but that the colonial habit will not admit it. "America is all around us," proclaims an American immigrant, in his backward fondness for the Canadian difference, "and a psychic cartographer for this continent would place Canada somewhere around Kansas-Nebraska." Spoken like a true colonial, domiciled in post-rebellion, colonial Toronto. Mackenzie and Papineau would have scolded him into the Gulf of Mexico.

When the rebellions failed, all that indigenous self-perception — and it was just beginning — came to an end. Not the granting of self-government, nor the National Economic Policy, nor Laurier's pan-Canadianism, nor Mackenzie King's weaning of Canada from the wrinkled British imperial mother, nor French-Canadian attempts to encourage in other Canadians an equal commitment to a native outlook, nor all of the exegeses of scholars and speeches of politicians . . . none of it has freed the Canadian identity (as distinct from the French-Canadian identity alone) from its borrowed, frustrating, wrong-headed perspectives.

*　　*　　*

To explore contradictions further. . . .

Contradictions, as an analytical tool, lend themselves to a dialectical appreciation of social forces, and are rich in suggestion and capable of considerable subtlety. Most important for our purposes: when contradictions are internal to a single community, they express themselves best in paradoxes, and these paradoxes are often so unique in their absurdity that if we understand how they are absurd, we understand everything.

What could be more absurd, for example, than for Americans to form super-patriotic agencies to protect liberties, but whose sole function was to suppress them? The committee to investigate unAmerican activities was the most unAmerican turn of all. Senator Joseph McCarthy was, at one and the same time, the least American and the most typically American of public figures. To be "born equal," as Tocqueville remarked of America, and yet to be unequally imprisoned by a "tyranny of opinion" is a paradox on the face of it.

The ordinary Chinese Communist Party cadre, not being an American (which is the best way of putting it), would probably not be able to make head nor tail of that, just as the ordinary American libertarian activist would be altogether perplexed if confronted in his daily experience with a perfectly understandable, to the Chinese, Maoist imperative to show initiative and flexibility — to use one's own imagination and be responsive to the people — and yet, at the same time, to give unswerving obedience to the correct party line. What makes such a paradoxical lesson understandable to the Chinese, whereas liberal orthodoxy has judged it pernicious and mind-boggling, is indigenous experience. The contradiction is informed not just by Chairman Mao's elucidation of the paradox, in his theoretical work on internal (non-antagonistic) contradictions, but also by practical examples and public debate at all levels which, cumulatively, go to make up the native perspective.

Even with years, or centuries, of precedent, and intensive training, however, the practical application of a paradox can be excruciating. Young Communist Party cadres in China, in the late 1950's, were reported to have suffered an unusual incidence of nervous breakdowns, faced with the performance demands of the Great Leap Forward but without either themselves or the participants in the commune system having sufficient ideological preparation. The cadres did not have enough sensitivity to the paradoxical requirements expected of them.

The United States, based on individual liberty but restricting that liberty with an excessive ideological conformism, also suffers from a malaise of paradox, which has broken out in violent, brutal pathological symptoms, aside from the scandal of racism which is a chronic betrayal of that liberty.

And so is Canada continually bewildered by its own paradoxical character.

Salvador de Madariaga observed in *Spain: A Modern History* that Catalonia, being the most separatist (and in that sense, the most disloyal) of provinces, was also the most characteristically Spanish (and in that sense, the most loyal) of the provinces, by so being. So he saw nothing untoward about a strong central power in Madrid keeping Catalonia in check, and nothing regressive, either, about Catalonia checking that central power with its own autonomous thrust whenever it could. Madariaga's paradoxical definition of Catalan "nationalism" is totally absurd, and, to a Canadian, perfectly reasonable.

Madariaga, in turn, would have likely recognized as familiar Daniel Johnson's contention that the only way to save Canada was to give the Quebec government control over all decisions affecting the social, economic and cultural life of the people; in other words, the only way to save Canada was effectively to eliminate it. Jean-Jacques Bertrand, when he was prime minister of Quebec, doggedly advocated the same kind of autonomy. Also, he had "separatists" (at least, ultra-nationalists) in his cabinet, and he exclaimed at a particularly sensitive moment in federal-provincial relations that Canada was "the happiest land in the world."

W.A.C. Bennett, at the end of an era of rapid aggrandizement of provincial power — late 1969 — argued, as premier of British Columbia, that the federal government was too strong relative to the regions, and that was why Canada was weak. The implication was that if the regions were given more power, there would be less regional alienation and hence more national loyalty. Weaken the weak centre so that the excessively strong centre will hold! Madariaga would have understood.

Although the *raison d'être* of the Parti Québecois is *indépendance* — at least that — Bennett, at the time, told western Canadians that René Lévesque was not a separatist, but a nationalist, like all Québecois, and that the federal government, which at that period was trying to bring itself closer to Quebecers, was destroying Confederation, and therefore itself, by doing so. Two inferences can be drawn from Bennett's perceptions — one, that Lévesque, the separatist, was playing the Canadian game, and one of the few, along with Bennett, playing it fairly; and two, that the federal government is more representative when it represents less.

W.A.C. Bennett considers himself a Canadian patriot, and while an Englishman or a Peruvian or a parochial misfit in Toronto might find that astounding, what citizen informed by the Canadian paradox can deny it?

The contradiction is such that Lévesque is in fact a Canadian benefactor without intending to be one. Many French Canadians complain bitterly that the French fact in Canada was hardly recognized until the movement for more provincial autonomy, and then Quebec separatism, grew — which is finally, belatedly, to realize that history is the product of broad social forces rather than of abstract judgments about what is fair and what isn't. That, in any case, is how the Canadian dialectic works.

By the strange laws of Canadian federalism, a man campaigning among French Canadians in Quebec may end up having an equal influence on English Canadians outside Quebec, and by forcing an opening up of the federation to French Canadians — a policy which he considers a trap — may in the long run undercut his own movement.

Every political move taken by René Lévesque has within it the possibility that it will have an equal and opposite reaction. On the other hand, and from the opposite direction, the federal government, attempting to head off separatism, allocates large sums of money for regional development programs in eastern Quebec, and strengthens the textile quota to protect the province's textile industry, and builds an airport, and hands out subsidies, even for the Montreal region, airport, and hands out subsidies, even for the Montreal region, to help reinforce Quebec's economy, which, if fully successful, will give Quebec the economic infrastructure and entrepreneurial cadres necessary to make independence work in practice.

The two forces in the contradiction reinforce their opposites while reinforcing themselves. Canadian politics is the art of suffering gladly a horrible ambiguity in one's own actions. There is no way to overcome this and to get a grip on affairs by establishing a lineal cause and effect, because contradictions are irrational. They are fast in the blindness of history. Eventually the man of action just gets tired of trying to sort things out — of trying to straddle the contradiction from both sides, which would paralyze him — and inserts himself into the contradiction in a certain direction, dictated by his own past, and keeps on going.

Perhaps this is why so many Canadians — federalists and separatists — find Claude Ryan's stance in *Le Devoir* so maddening and ambiguous, and why it *is* so maddening and ambiguous. Ryan's role, as an analyst of the Canadian contradiction, is to make rational sense out of the irrational meeting of historical forces, which is impossible, and which leads his analysis to go on and on, growing increasingly tortuous and refined, in a vain attempt to tie the contradiction down. But Ryan's contribution is absolutely essential. Only through direct analysis does a reader's appreciation of the contradiction, by indirection, grow in sensitivity.

Following the Quebec election in 1970, a commentator on CBC English-language radio wondered how Ryan, an avowed "federalist" as he described him, and as he was then, could write so passionately of the political virtues of René Lévesque, and of the blow to Quebec of Lévesque's failure to win a seat. That was absurd, said the commentator. If you're a federalist, surely you want a man like Lévesque to lose. Why doesn't Ryan make up his mind?

The observation that Ryan's position was absurd was correct but irrelevant. Should French Canadians "concentrate on the territory of Quebec" or should they "take Canada in its entirety?" asked Pierre Elliott Trudeau. And the collectivity in Quebec, by producing a Trudeau and a Lévesque in the same generation, answered yes to both questions, and is satisfied by neither answer. Quebec, like Catalonia in Spain, has the whole of the contradiction within itself.

As if that weren't enough, chance arranged it so that

Trudeau, the champion of federalism, was formed inside the Quebec political hothouse, and fought the battle against Duplessis and centralism with autonomous instruments like *Cité Libre*, whereas Lévesque, the saint of separatism, came to be a public figure through Radio-Canada which, as one of the most distinctive and creative products of federalism, enabled him to animate French-Canadian society and broaden its viewpoint, at a time when the provincial government had drawn down the blinds.

The Canadian contradiction suggests another paradox — that the greatest Canadian nationalists are also the greatest internationalists. The more nationalist one is, the more one becomes involved in the phenomenon of cultural dualism, and, in turn, the greater the check on chauvinism and ethnocentric arrogance.

This paradox knows no bounds. The most militant Canadian nationalists, for the most part English-speaking, are sensitive to the ethnocentric blindness of the United States because, among other things, they have been taught to be sensitive by French Canada's defiance of a similar sort of arrogance in their English-speaking community. And they are so sensitive to French Canada's defiance that, militant nationalists and all, a good number of them cannot bring themselves to critically oppose the separatist movement, which subverts their nationalism. They are called chauvinists for their troubles.

Similarly, when an English Canadian in an English-speaking city wishes his French-Canadian colleagues a happy Saint Jean-Baptiste June 24, but absent-mindedly, out of habit, goes through July 1 like any other day off, he is acting out a covert nationalist ritual. Canadians do not assert their nationalism by looking for it, as the historian claims. They assert it by not finding it.

These contradictions across which a society defines itself are not solved, and are resolved only in some unimaginable utopia. The tension and conflict arising out of Canadian dualism, or out of Canadian regionalism, will not be settled, no matter how ingenious new constitutional formulas might be. If they were, Canada would no longer exist. It would be robbed of its dynamic.

Contradictions are not resolved, they are only elaborated on. And when the elaboration occurs on a large scale, or involves important social forces, it constitutes civilization.

In China, under the Empire, the civilization was codified as Confucianism. Now the code is Maoism. In both cases, a dense and complex social fabric has been maintained, involving a unique combination of interpersonal relationships, with an unmistakable character in the government and the arts of the people. The same can be said, and is said, of "American civilization" or the "American way of life," and of "European civilization" and "French civilization" and so on. Still, to the ear, "Canadian civilization" sounds a bit strange. Does the Canadian experience deserve it?

The question can be put another way: Does Canadian civilization represent a significantly instructive experiment in social relationships, as Maoism and American liberalism certainly do in their different ways, although Americans are blind to the first and the Chinese to the second?

On that scale, the coming together in one state of at least two ethnically contrary "nations," and maybe others if the native peoples assert themselves, and the simultaneous overlapping and coming together of powerful regionalisms, *has* been the making of a civilization in the commonly understood sense of the word.

It is because Canadian civilization is so vulnerable, because every once in a while it seems to be coming apart at the seams under the pressure of centrifugal forces, that it has been so fruitful, and has slowly developed a subterranean strength. Nothing has added to that strength, and to that vulnerability, more than the separatist movement, and English Canada's facing up to the possibility it symbolizes, and the attempts of René Lévesque and others to explain to English Canadians the logic behind the possibility.

Our historic rebellions, and our terrorism, and our

bizarre, passionate regional movements taken into account, the greatest argument against describing the Canadian system as "dull, grey federalism" is Lévesque himself. If Quebec were a North American Switzerland, or a Norway — a small nation of common values, in the words of a citation in *Option Québec* — there would be no Réne Lévesque with his sharp relentless insights into the contradictions between peoples, only a slightly eccentric, chain-smoking ambassador amusing his routinized counterparts with his misplaced enthusiasm.

The more one opens one's eyes, the more "the relatively stable, satisfied societies of squares" — an outsider's recent description of federal peoples — fits Swiss federalism, and West German federalism, and even Australian federalism, but the less it fits exasperating Canada, where the contradictions stretch over geographic and cultural chasms. And, after all, hasn't Lévesque himself called Canadian federalism a madhouse?

(Of course, if you have a civilization, you also have to have barbarians. To the ancient Chinese, anybody who did not belong to the Empire was a barbarian, no matter how knowledgeable and gentle he was, whereas presumably somebody, no matter how cruel, who wanted to reform or simply take over the Empire — nobody thought of changing it — was civilized. To the Americans, unAmericans are beyond the pale, and, in George Kennan's words, because of [Americans'] "inveterate tendency to judge others by the extent to which they contrive to be like ourselves," Americans have turned up just about as many barbarians in the world as the Chinese. As with the Chinese, the alien becomes identified with the unintelligible. To the archetypal Canadian, schooled by his country's dualism to beware of ethnocentric arrogance, the lack of similar sensitivity by the Americans or Chinese or anybody else, including his own countrymen, is barbarian, and is seen to have barbarous consequences, witness the rampage of the "absolute moral ethos" of Americanism in Vietnam. Grown men and women who wander around the Arctic looking for a national identity are barbarians. And

Canadians who categorize other people as barbarians may well be barbarians.)

That is the political dimension. Canadian civilization, like the Chinese and the American, as I am going to argue, has also produced by the force of its contradictions a distinctive economic culture and a distinctive artistic culture — a singular Canadian way of life — which has been only imperfectly perceived, or hardly noticed at all, and has often as not been scorned by Canadians themselves, because of their heretofore dogged colonial mentality.

The colonial mentality aside, there is the inescapable feeling that Canada is an artificial creature. If the United States did not exist, neither would Canada, because there would be no external threat to keep the diverse regions, particularly Quebec, inside Confederation. Canada is a marriage of convenience rather than of love. Manifest Destiny was the external threat which bound the parties into Confederation in the first place, and made loyal British subjects out of the French-Canadian elite even before that, and it is still invoked by English-Canadian and French-Canadian federalists alike when they want to underscore the perils of Quebec independence.

Unlike the United States, which was "born equal" — freely born into its own world without a constricting legacy — Canadian civilization, like the Chinese Empire in its formative days, is a civilization of necessity. The exigencies of the Yellow River forced on the Chinese the central administration of early Empire, from which everything else followed. The United States is our Yellow River.

Now, there are two ways of reflecting on that characteristic. Habitually, we have been negative. Canada is a defensive reaction against the United States, simply "the losing side of the American revolution," and nothing else, the "counter-revolution" school has told us; Canada is cursed with a hopeless, narrow-minded longing for an unAmerican identity. Most Canadians have probably sometime in their lives confessed as much to themselves. Or, as the separatists maintain, Canada is an unnatural alliance; English Canadians have everything in common with Americans and very little in common with French Canadians; Canada is an impossibility, a common market against nature. Again, not just among French Canadians, but among all of us, the urge to escape our maddening contradictions, to be reborn free, is always just under our skin. The mythical, spontaneous, dynamic, liberating phenomenon of the United States remains in sight, on the other side of the 49th parallel, throwing into the soul of Canadians a chronic anguish.

But civilizations born without restraints — and there may be only one, the United States — have their own terrible flaw. Without the experience of accommodating antagonistic classes and cultural assumptions, they never rise above shallowness. They never "come of age." They suffer fatally, as Louis Hartz put it, from "atrophy of the philosophic impulse." White Americans are hopeless romantics. When their romanticism has been challenged by realists at home and abroad, like the American blacks, or the native peoples, or the Vietnamese, they have turned on them with a violent, absolutist vengeance, which is the underside of romanticism.

That is the other way of looking at it. There is a certain profundity of feeling and experience in the Canadian personality which is absent in America. The reflective citizen whose identity, in the collectivity, has been stretched to the breaking point by the play of contradictions, may come out of that uncertainty in an angry despair and start planting bombs in mailboxes or shouting at public meetings, "No French spoken here!"; but he also may come out of it powerfully liberated by an understanding denied to his American brother. Civilizations of necessity can also be great and liberating civilizations.

Either way, there's no guarantee that any particular civilization will endure. Canadian civilization can bog down in its own machinery just as surely as Imperial China fell over into anarchy, with only a slight European push, because of the encrusted, corrupt, absolutist rigidities of an aging

Confucianism; or as America may well destroy itself by the compulsive, dogmatic pursuit of profit and property.

Canadians, in fact, almost always feel bogged down, as a matter of course. It's part of our civilized climate. It's the onerous burden of civilization upon us. Most of the weight is made up of discarded position papers from federal-provincial conferences, where the close, grating, bureaucratic, polite segment of elaboration usually takes place and, if agreement is reached, is codified. Protest and despair are common. A lead article in *Saturday Night* in 1970 angrily asked, "Can we go on arguing interminably about Dominion-provincial relationships and the constitution affecting them while cities become polluted, housing decays, trade opportunities are lost and the brain drain to the United States continues?" Their conclusion was that we can not. To Jacques Parizeau, Canadian federalism is so loaded down with federal-provincial committees (150 of them), with duplicated services (billions of dollars worth), and with tangled lines of responsibility, that the whole system will sink of its own weight, taking us down with it. "A sterile and tiresome game," is how Claude Ryan describes it. "An outdated, creaky, inefficient remnant of a 19th century colonial experiment . . . one of the most obsolete [systems] in the whole civilized world," says René Lévesque. And the fact is that civilizations have been known to sink into a morass of their own rules.

Canadian civilization may not only bog down in the centre, it may also unravel at the edges. Forced by regional pressures, particularly the pressure of separatism in Quebec, to create jobs and eliminate disparities, Ottawa has subsidized the intrusion of the American economy, which itself is undermining the civilization. Canada takes one contradiction in its teeth but has its tail bitten off by another. After the tail comes the body.

Or a civilization can simply lose its ideological steam, can simply have run its course; and unable to overcome a profound malaise in a vital part, it deteriorates, often with much bloodshed.

The key may be to let the elaboration of contradictions go on with the maximum of political freedom even if it means that the contradictions may be pulled apart.

Despite the War Measures Act, and not discounting less obvious curbs on free expression and politics, Canadian civilization does afford about as open an elaboration of contradictions as one could hope to find anywhere in history, not because Canadians are particularly generous or far-sighted, but because of their unique historical circumstances. Michel Brunet is right when he says that the English in Canada should be credited only with realism, not with generosity, because they didn't attempt to suppress the French, although what he doesn't say is that realism in itself is a great virtue. The federalism which René Lévesque attacks is also the federalism which enables him to attack it with such potency, by leaving him a special geographical area to build his appeal on and by allowing, or encouraging, in that area an economic base of its own making — concrete examples of collective achievement like Hydro-Québec — advantages which are denied dissenters in the United States, or parties of class in Europe like the communist parties of France and Italy. And again, it is not because of English-Canadian generosity, but because of the inevitable way Canada was put together.

Still, there are incidents whose realism and humanity are so acute that the adjective "civilized" applies to them in its universal sense. And the fact that nobody wonders at them, that nobody cries out "isn't that remarkable!," suggests that, although such incidents may be exceptional, Canadian civilization is an historical marvel.

To pick only one example among many: early in 1968, more than two years before the Parti Québecois' electoral inroads, *The Star Weekly* published a special section called "The View from Quebec," including an article by René Lévesque, "Why I believe a free Quebec is the best thing for you, too," and one about the young separatist elite, "We are fighting . . . fighting for a free Quebec!" The idea, according to the preface, was to present "the aims and aspirations of the people of French Canada . . . set down in their own words." The total effect was an eloquent argument for separatism. But the *Toronto Star* organization has been outspokenly committed to federalism and national unity.

What it comes down to is that a group of people committed to a collectivity — and love of country is no light-hearted whim — allows another group passionately committed to destroying that collectivity to present that commitment in the best possible light. *Le Devoir* is another example of such openness, from the direction of French Canadian nationalism. Here the paradox ceases to be mundane. It becomes wondrous.

A stranger coming to Canada, without any previous clues as to what kind of civilization it is, would likely be perplexed at finding citizens with a profound love of country who, at the same time, showed a natural sympathy for the man and the party who were intent on destroying that country. He would be even more puzzled that the apparent inconsistency of such contradictory feelings goes almost unnoticed by Canadians themselves. Trying somehow to make sense out of it all, he might also perceive, indirectly, that if Quebec decided to separate from Canada, *and if the rest of the country let it go peacefully*, it would be the greatest moment in the history of Canadian civilization. It would be. And, of course, also the most tragic.

CHAPTER 3

The Importance of Being Ideological

Our identity is there, in the long working out of the Canadian contradictions: French Canada as against English Canada, the regions as against the centre, Canada as against the United States. The question now arises: Why have we related so weakly to it, and felt so lacking in identity, while suspecting that we were caught up in a unique experience nevertheless?

The answer is in the way we have looked at ourselves, that is to say, in ideology.

Ideology is "a set of ideas and beliefs which provide an interpretation of social (economic, political) phenomena and a means for defining such situations." Ideology is perspective. Ideology is the looking glass through which contradictions are perceived, and conditions those contradictions, and is in turn changed under the historical force of those contradictions, in interaction.

If a sure perception of our identity comes out of the elaboration of the dominant Canadian contradictions, then what we are most in need of in Canada is ideological liveliness — a working out of native ways of looking at things, in terms of our own experience rather than in terms of other peoples' with other contradictions. Borrowed ideological habits distort and screen out the Canadian circumstance, leaving behind the uneasy feeling that while Canada exists because it is on the map, there is nothing else to it — which, as we have seen, is the problem. And this elaboration of a native ideology has to be seen for what it is, not as an exercise in narrow-minded irrationalism, but as the prerequisite for a practical understanding of ourselves.

Ideology, then, is not necessarily dogma, which rests fixed and inert until it is shattered by the pressures of a changing reality. Ideologies can be, and have been, brilliantly pragmatic, changing through debate and elaboration and evolution to adapt to circumstances. Generally speaking, the same set of circumstances can be interpreted through a whole range of ideologies and come out as altogether different realities all of them valid to the separate beholders, but not all of them equally appropriate to a particular situation or a particular country.

Nor can it be repeated too often that all societies have ideologies, and all thinking individuals within society are ideological.

The paradox of a successful ideological current is that over time, unless it is challenged, it makes its interpretation of reality seem to inhere in the very nature of things, so that what began as most ideological may come to be seen as least ideological. A man who denies that he is ideological, therefore, is liable to be the most dogmatic of people. On the other hand, anybody who is aware of the ideological element of social perceptions is least likely to become a prisoner of inappropriate ideology.

Dogma comes not from ideology, which is with all of us, but from a lack of ideological exploration and contention.

Our most famous example of invisible ideology comes from our own philosophic backyard, here in the West and North America — our economic ideology. Most of our basic ideas about economics are relics of the Industrial Revolution — that man by nature is an economic, acquisitive (capitalist) creature; that economic motivation comes from this acquisitiveness; that the market economy is natural to man and society, and to economic activity (and further, that only by the rules of the market can complex economies be made to function); and so on — all those ideas which make up economic liberalism. Looking back to their origin, we discover that, at the time, they ran against the grain of tradition and common sense, and everything that had gone before. Only with a vigorous ideological campaign, led by a radical vanguard, did the British people come to accept the doctrine.

As Karl Polanyi explained so lucidly in *The Great Transformation*, some of the premises of the doctrine were false by empirical test, for example the notion that labour and land (people and their environment) were commodities to be subjected to the workings of a market system rather than what they were, and are: essential elements of society that must be respected in their own terms if life is to be tolerable. And once the system was introduced, people did tenaciously fight back to break the doctrine by organizing trade unions and protecting their surroundings. (We are still fighting the battle, in our attempt to rescue our environment from the market system of values.) In the intervening 150 years, reality has changed to the point where the old description hardly has any application.

Nothing could be more ideological in its origins and its logic, and more obsolete today, than that mentality. But the old, doctrinal attitude is still implicit in much of our thinking, so that the people who invoke it to defend their own narrow experience consider themselves obviously empirical and stigmatize disbelievers as ideologically dogmatic theorists and scoundrels.

The American blindness to ideology is a variation of this, and is of particular importance to Canadians because it bears directly on our own colonial perceptions.

The American Dream of an individualistic society of economic men is the romantic, frontier distillation of that old and bygone British ideological revolution (economic liberalism). However, without the social antagonisms of Europe which created counter-ideologies, against which background the emotionalism and particularity of the American myth might come into focus, the ideological passion of the American way of life appears instead, to Americans, as dispassionate, exacting realism.

This is the root of America's continuing parochialism, what Louis Hartz has described as "a vast and almost charming innocence of mind." Americans are worshippers of the "fixed, dogmatic liberalism of a liberal way of life," in Hartz's words. They are slaves of the tyranny of Locke in America. But because they don't know it, because they have no "relative insight" into their own nature, they have come to consider themselves an altogether pragmatic people. They take their ideology so much for granted that "all problems emerge as problems of technique."

So that when Americans say of another people, of the Chinese for example, that they are ideological, whereas Americans are pragmatic, what they are really saying is that the Chinese have a different ideology than the Americans do. The Chinese, on the other hand, undoubtedly consider themselves highly pragmatic and the Americans the opposite, and can point to all kinds of American syndromes — like the competition fetish, like Americanism, like the taboo on class politics — to justify their opinion. For example, where advances in production and marketing techniques lead to an elimination of competition, what could be less pragmatic than to pretend that competition still exists, and to mount a drum-beating, flag-waving anti-trust bureaucracy to police violations, when the natural economic forces, and man's inclination, are all against it, and when the policing doesn't do any good anyway? What could have been less pragmatic than America's involvement in Vietnam? All peoples tend to underestimate their dogmatism and overestimate their pragmatism, out of habit of mind.

Ideology and pragmatism do not necessarily exclude each other in any case. A close reading of Mao Tse-tung's career shows him, with some exceptions, to have been remarkably shrewd and pragmatic in his political strategy, and he is so described by outside biographers. Basing the revolution on the peasant masses was the most pragmatic touch of all. Ideology can feed on pragmatism. It is exactly because of Mao's pragmatism, his native originality, that Maoist ideology has had such an impact on the Chinese people.

The ideologues of the American Revolution — Thomas Jefferson, the author of the Declaration of Independence, in particular — were also pragmatists in their time. "We hold these truths to be self-evident . . ." begins the explanation in the Declaration of Independence. Those "truths" were self-evident, for their time and their place. George III, who was less ideological, and less pragmatic at the same time, didn't see it, and paid the price.

The main point is that while an ideology generates an emotional commitment, it also has a perceiving, learning, cognitive, creative dimension which adds to knowledge and insight and should not be underestimated or neglected.

The habit of westerners, particularly Americans, of emphasizing the non-rational aspect of all ideology, and citing the more savage cases of such irrationalism among other peoples, is just a way of defending their own irrationalism from legitimate ideologies on the outside. The examples given in the Concise Oxford Dictionary are "Fascist" ideology and "Nazi" ideology, not "liberal" ideology or "American" ideology. When the American writer Daniel Bell prematurely signalled *The End of Ideology* in 1960, he had particularly in mind the "all-or-none," divisive, irreconcilable passions of class politics of western Europe and the Soviet Union, which faded gradually after World War II, but which, in any case, never had much of a place in his own society — the United States — whose native ideology of Americanism had just spawned the McCarthy era.

*   *   *

Bell concluded that the death of ideology would allow for a type of social analysis uncommitted to dogma, which could be detached and particularly realistic. Haven't Americans suggested much the same of their social analysis and their scholars before, by way of self-justification and putting down ideologically foreign schools? Any American, or Canadian, who says it again is taking his chances. For, dogma or not, there is no uncommitted social analysis. All social analysis is subjective. All scholarship requires choice — of method as well as intent — and all such choice is based finally on assumptions rooted in people's psyches and their historical surroundings, where the concept of objectivity no longer applies. And if you rid yourself of choice and direction going back to assumptions, you emasculate your scholarship. It becomes nothing more than mental roughage. It is to social analysis what crossword puzzles are to literature.

A Maoist social scientist in China might possibly condemn most of the "consensus" social analysis in the West as the opposite of inquiring, critical, hard-headed, realistic, uncommitted and undogmatic. He would do so with tried analytical tools, for dogma is considered just as much an evil in China as in any other change-oriented society. The evils of dogmatism, as well as the evils of misconceived empiricism, have both been scored by Chairman Mao, and elaborated on by Chinese writers. Is Daniel Bell right, or is Mao Tse-tung right?

In disciplines like political economy and sociology, quantifiable surveys and mathematical techniques have become the new tools of "uncommitted" or "value-free" study. Particularly in economics, this enables Americanist scholars to avoid dwelling on their own assumptions — to suppress their consciousness of them — which is the practice of ideological obscurantism. The growing gap between Americanist ideology and reality is comfortably lost in abstracts of technique. What is passed off as realism is in fact escapism. But to the economics scholar with an indigenous Canadian outlook, whose attempts to get beyond Americanistic technique to something more appropriate are dismissed as unscientific, and therefore suspect and useless to boot, the new economics is as arbitrary and schizophrenic as a Stalinist edict.

No Canadian with intellectual roots in his own civilization's experience can help but be struck by the American limitations of U.S. social science since Bell's book, both as it is expounded in the U.S. and as it is drummed into Canadians by other Canadians who have been trained in the U.S.

Bell's notion of the alienation of the intellectual from ideology, which was to make the new objectivity possible, was American romanticism with scholarly footnotes. People aren't alienated in a vacuum, but in directions dictated by experience, as Bell himself recognized. The idea that ideology died in the West, just because an ideological tension on the edge of the American consensus subsided, was an exquisitely parochial, ideological thought in itself. It was the dogma of its time.

Michel Brunet hit closer to home in writing that ideologies are the product of men engaged in historical evolution. Deny the legitimacy of ideology and you deny men a particular meaning to their own collective history.

The disintegration of identity follows, and has followed in Canada. This is one of the ways in which the influence of Americanistic social science has affected us. It looks down on any indigenous ideological exploration, while obliging us to function with its own limited assumptions and methods. The Death of Ideology is an American masquerade.

*   *   *

But is there any doubt that Canadians, pragmatic and not, are themselves an ideologically impregnated mass of contradictions? When a group of Japanese visited Vancouver and remarked that the buildings looked like the ones in Tokyo, a local journalist could write that Canada was just an indistinguishable minor member of the global village. But when, in a seminar in Tokyo, Japanese students were told that the main lines of political tension in Canada were between English and French Canadians and between the regional governments and the federal government, and that these contradictions had usually submerged class contradictions, they were incredulous that any nation could be so ideologically strange. They would be even more incredulous if they tried to follow the strange rites of federal-provincial conferences, which even Canadians can't figure out because they still have a poorly developed sense of paradox. And what would the Japanese, or the Chinese, say if somebody told them that a difficult, hair-splitting essay on federal contributions to universities was, in its time, an important theoretical document? (What is our own conditioned scornful reaction to difficult, hair-splitting essays on class contradictions put forward as important theory by other peoples?) Wouldn't they say that any country with any common sense at all would simply let its central government give the money to universities, and get on to important matters? And they would also wonder how a man who not only objected, but did so at considerable erudite length, and with a profound commitment to such a trifle, could become head of that central government and then be accused on all sides of over-centralizing.

If you can explain why that essay was included in the collected works of Pierre Elliott Trudeau, and what has happened subsequently, you can explain a lot about Canada. On the other hand, to see Trudeau as unideological, as Anthony Westell did in the *Toronto Star*, in writing about political types (April 27, 1970), is to look right past the Canadian ethic, and to treat the dense questions of the Canadian contradiction as simply problems of technique, in other words to see Trudeau as a clever, superficial technician, which Anthony Westell might be, but which Trudeau is not.

Trudeau's case is worth looking into. For all of his political difficulties and ineptitude (and by the time this book appears, he may no longer be in office), he remains one of the best examples of Canadians' ideological aptitude at work.

Much like Chairman Mao and any other incisive and successful ideologue in history, Trudeau seized hold of the unique circumstances of his society and, while borrowing small insights from elsewhere, built ideologically upon them. "The game is played in Canada: there are two ethnic and linguistic groups; each is too strong to crush the other" is the Canadian equivalent of Mao's pragmatic realization that only with the mass of peasantry was revolution possible, or of Jefferson's perception of life and liberty. Ideological elaboration, including moralistic homilies for the people, followed.

I have beside me as I write this a copy of the French-language paperback edition of *Federalism and the French Canadians*. On the bottom halves of the cover and the back cover are 20 quotations of Pierre Elliott Trudeau. Put those and a few others inside a leatherette cover, with a red maple leaf on it, and you have a little red book of full ideological value.

Similarly, when Trudeau acceded to the prime minister-ship, clues to his inner mind were looked for in the essays with the same assiduity with which China watchers tried puzzling out Mao's essays on contradictions in order to throw light on the Cultural Revolution. The comparison between Trudeau and Mao came naturally, especially to detractors. Allan Fotheringham referred to Trudeau as "Our Leader." A book of speeches was routinely described as "The Selected Sayings of Pierre Elliott Trudeau." Many intellectuals, trying to make room for the separatist impulse in Quebec in their own ideological cupboard, savaged Trudeau for his "federalist dogma" and his "fanaticism." Robert Fulford saw some of the Trudeau rhetoric as rivalling the Quotations for its "sheer mind-numbing obviousness." And, in fact, what could have been more obvious than to affirm the legitimacy of the French-English contradiction in the Canadian make-up, or to point out that federalism was one of the givens (*"chose donnée"*) of politics in Canada, a federal state after all, except that when Trudeau was putting these ideas forward, in the 1950's and 1960's, the implications of Canadian federalism were not so obvious, despite our long history. Trudeau's ideas represented an unusual awareness of what the character of Canada was. Their obviousness, and the fullness of their implications, have come upon us only later.

There has been a sequel. In 1971, Trudeau and his ministers opened up a new ideological front, "multicultural-ism," departing from his previous description of Canada as bicultural in an abortive attempt to sidetrack a basic perception which could not be shunted out of the way where the contradiction between French and English cultures in Canada had so much force. Ideology is contained and pummelled by reality.

As for Trudeau's electoral disaster in the West in 1972, it was not because of too much ideology but too little: the failure to integrate the regional pressures of the West into a practical frame of reference for the country as a whole. But that ideological work, in any event, will just be a coming to grips with Trudeau's own, earlier perception that the "people from various parts of Canada *do* hang together on a regional basis," except that in the case of the West, Trudeau comes in from the outside and is incapable of ideological leadership (his contribution has already been made).

Canadians, then, in their own way, can be as ideological as the next people, or should be. That is how things come together, out of our contradictions, even in the slow and unnoticed ways of day-to-day practice. "This country is ungovernable!" declares a member of Parliament, and with his colleagues, straining day in and day out against the country's contradictions, he elaborates frames of reference (ideological work) to make it governable.

We can also say that the more our ideological striving shows up, the surer our sense of identity becomes. Conversely, the more we dismiss others as hopelessly ideological (meaning by that, dogmatic), the less likely we are to notice our own unique ideological bent.

For example, the whole weight of sophisticated liberal opinion in the West poked ridicule at the Maoist campaign to make China's technical and administrative cadres both Red and expert. It was said to be folly to waste the valuable time of scarce professional personnel by obliging them to attend classes of political instruction and to help out on the local commune; and even worse, that ideological correctness should be considered an important qualification for technically demanding work in industry and university. Yet if we had seen that there were good *Chinese* reasons for doing so, we would also see now that Canada, in its own way, and for its own good reasons, is in the middle of a similar ideological campaign.

Obliging highly trained, highly paid, valuable administrators of the country to spend days and months away from the job learning French, or English, is nothing more nor less than a program of political instruction to make our leading bureaucrats Canadian and expert, with all of the friction and reformation that such a process involves. (Some of our civil servants would probably prefer a few months down on the commune to a few weeks in a language immersion course!) Bilingualism programs are also underway, at different stages, in some crown corporations and private companies. Language qualifications are slowly becoming important qualifications for professionally demanding work at the highest levels. The next step is the introduction of more French language units in the upper reaches of the civil service and elsewhere, to make structures as well as personnel "Canadian and Expert." It is our own cultural revolution.

But that, of course, is only part of the story.

The inability of powerful and involved outsiders to see another community's unique ideological value is intellectual imperialism; the inability of natives to see it is intellectual colonialism. The second is by far the more maddening. Scholars are not immune. In a book called *Agenda 1970: proposals for a creative politics*, on public policy and Canada's future, there is an introductory chapter on "Our Ideological Tradition" which nowhere discusses the ideology of biculturalism and touches on federalism only incidentally. The April 1969 issue of *Saturday Night* carried an article entitled, simply, "Ideology," about developments in the late 1960's, with no Canadian citation at all, although the late 1960's was a period of intense ideological quickening in the community. The article was about George Lukács and Herbert Marcuse and the Students for a Democratic Society and Czechoslovakia instead.

No wonder that a year later, in the same magazine, a young Canadian, schooled in the ideological categories of other peoples' contradictions, should be confessing sadly to herself that Canada was just the "peanut gallery" to other nations' happenings. Not being a part of those other nations, she wondered what she could possibly do with her idealism. It is no wonder either that Mordecai Richler should describe the differences between Canada and the United States as one of nuances — nuances worth struggling to preserve — and that an economist cited in the *Toronto Star* should prize the small Canadian differences that mark us off from the substantial North American homogeneity, and that the one should be an expatriate in Great Britain, still seeing no incongruity in moralizing at Canadians from afar, and that the other should be teaching at Yale University. Nuances are not worth struggling for, though they are nice for the refined aficionados (and literary promoters) to have around. As the French-Canadian part of us has already realized, once you're reduced to the folklorish concept of nuances, you have already lost the struggle.

And again: "Our differences from the rest of the world, from France, from England and from the U.S.A. . . . are subtle," writes Robertson Davies, "but what is subtle in Canada tends to be minimized." What else could he expect?

The disillusioned Canadian girl, who was everybody else's revolutionary but her own, came to realize fairly painlessly, as personal suffering goes, that ideologies are not transferable — that Canada is "no place for borrowed styles" — because ideologies grow out of history which is always lived in particular circumstances, and not out of the heads of theorists, which is not to say that one community has nothing in common with others and can't learn from their experiences.

Not all voyages of ideological error and discovery have been quite so painless.

To return to our Chinese example, the Chinese, in this century, went through two phases of borrowed ideological styles, both of them with disastrous results in the truly horrendous terms of starvation and bloodshed, before settling on an indigenous way.

The first phase was the attempt by Sun Yat-sen and other republicans to establish a modern liberal democracy, in imitation of the West — more particularly in imitation of the United States and France — although China had no tradition of economic individualism or parliamentary practice. Disintegration of political and economic life into corruption and warlordism was not long in coming. Famine and violent social dislocation followed. The Chinese called it the Age of Confusion.

The second phase was the adoption by the Chinese

Communist Party of the Marxist-Leninist doctrine of proletarian revolution, in imitation of the Russian example. In
terms of the doctrine, it was axiomatic that the peasantry
was too backward, too feudal and too conservative to lead a
movement for change. But the storming of cities, after the
storming of the Winter Palace in St. Petersburg, and the
collaboration with Chiang Kai-shek, *on Stalin's advice*, ended
in slaughter. Only Mao and later a military cohort, who
retreated to a mountain base *among the peasantry*, were
able to continue functioning. Their revolution then went on
to success, not as a European class struggle but as a familiar
Chinese peasant rebellion.

Without an indigenous appreciation of the community,
ideology will be inappropriate, and efforts at change will
founder whatever the goal of those efforts.

The early American constitutionalists also realized this.
One of the young republic's ambassadors to France, Gouverneur Morris, wrote home astringently that [the French]
"want an American constitution without realizing they have
no Americans to uphold it." Louis Hartz reminds us that only
a thoroughly bourgeois people, free from the legacy of
feudalism, and highly unified by their common addiction
to the liberal norm, could make such an ingenious constitutional scheme work. The genius was in the ideology, but only
as it reflected the people.

The American ideology of liberty *and property* was not
exportable. But the Americans didn't let themselves worry
too much about it. They were even proud of it. "The
yeomanry of the United States are not the *canaille* of Paris,"
Jefferson wrote to Lafayette, and was confirmed in his
prejudice that America was the chosen land. Now they do
care, but the ideology still is not exportable.

Similarly, Trudeau's signal contribution to Canadian
ideology, and a contribution which perhaps only a French-
Canadian federalist could make, was to look at Canadian
politics in terms of the Canadian contradiction itself rather
than, first of all, in terms of the ideological contradictions

between the left and the right, which is Europe's contribution to political thought. The European ideological legacy does have a direct application in Canada, as it has, in one way or another, in most places in the world. It also has roots in the political history of Canada. Undoubtedly also, without a politics of polarization between left and right, Canada is going to continue to suffer from its inegalitarian, limiting social structure. But polarization along that axis likely will occur only after an intensive ideological campaign of self-discovery of the Canadian community, as it may already be occurring on the back of the separatist movement, rather than vice-versa. And, as in China, when it comes it will take such an indigenous form that it will be different in kind from anything experienced in other countries.

But the nagging question still remains: Why in a country that is so ideological, with a prime minister who has made a major contribution to the native ideology, and with at least 200 years of continuous history along the same axes — contradictions which are unique to that country — why should Canada still be trying to puzzle out the riddle of its identity? Why should so many sensitive and patriotic journalists, writers and scholars damn Canada in their classrooms and their journals by faintly praising it as a different, nuanced America (New York has gone rotten; maybe there's something to Canada after all), and by exercising themselves ideologically as if they were somewhere else — which is the same as asking why they consider Canada such a marginal experience *even to its own people?*

Why is their perception of Canadian reality such a secondary, derivative one?

The hypothesis I am going to explore here is that Canadian ideology lacks an important dimension — the economic one — and that without it, Canadian identity necessarily seems marginal and weak in substance, not to mention the heavy, demoralizing price Canadians pay in economic practice.

Economic and quasi-economic activities play a large

part in the way Canadians define themselves. A working man or woman spends the biggest single part of his waking lifetime on the job. Off the job, he is also a consumer. Even in school, he begins to sense the practical economic demands of the community. The narrow task itself is neither here nor there. A man working a metal lathe in Hamilton is doing somewhat the same job as his counterparts in São Paulo and Novosibirsk. But in his job, and through his job, he is identifying himself differently.

If he is a member of a Chinese commune, the act of turning out precision parts on improvised machinery, when a party cadre from the city said it couldn't be done, may mean to him applying the thoughts of Chairman Mao, or asserting China's new self-confidence, or demonstrating that the modernization of China will come from the initiative of the masses rather than from the calculations of administrative cadres. The managing director of a machine tool factory in the United States may see, in its effective, automated operation, corroboration of the American way of life, as well as confirmation of his own status and role, over and above his actual salary. The same holds for economic man as consumer, when he buys a ball of string or an automobile. Modern man learns and interprets his world in good part through economic participation.

But the practical life is not, and never has been, neutral. There is, really, no such creature as economic man; a consumer or producer is social man involved in economic activity. Economic cultures are infused with the habits and symbolism of ideology, arising, usually, out of the contradictions of the community, but in the case of an ideological colony, arising out of the contradictions of another, dissimilar community. Like constitutional monarchy in China, and Americanism in revolutionary France, and Marxism in Nebraska, this is received ideology, a "borrowed style," and doesn't fit. The ultimate effect of such borrowed, or imposed, economic ideology is to obscure native identity, just as a more strictly political ideology received from outside would underplay the contradictions of Canadian federalism and also obscure native identity. And has obscured it.

Writing about the inescapable, particular realities of Quebec and Canada during the Duplessis era and shortly after, and elaborating his political philosophy in those terms — uniting theory with reality — Trudeau successfully subdued the European-ideology-in-Canada, the ideology of unitary government and homogeneous nationalism, in which class contradictions were the dominant axis of creative politics, and replaced it with the ideology of federalism. "The Practice and Theory of Federalism" is to Canada, in a sense, what Mao's "On the Correct Handling of Contradictions Among the People" is to the Chinese. That's the political facet of Canadian identity. But in the meantime, as regards the economic aspect of Canadian identity, Trudeau and his whole generation have allowed what I call the American-ideology-in-Canada, which also flows from an outside reality, and which is also inappropriate, to superimpose itself on the country with all the force of orthodoxy.

The effect of looking at Canada in terms of this inappropriate ideology is cumulative. Without a lively, native economic ideology of our own, absolutely essential to the resilience and dynamism of a democratic community, the practical creativity of Canada has fallen under the American shadow. And the more it has fallen under the shadow, the less a native ideology is discernible. Eventually that particular dimension of the Canadian experience disappears.

During a local controversy about Americans in Canadian universities, a Canadian lecturer suggested that it was too much to ask busy American teachers to acquaint themselves with Canadian reality, when the Canadians all around them seemed oblivious to it, and when all the practical symbols and popular propaganda — the popularized ideological expression of the economic culture — seemed to be American. We have to agree. The literati and the native scholars might notice nuances and pretend that they represent a distinctive community, but for the generality of Canadians, particularly the French Canadians who have a cultural uniqueness unto themselves, the nuances are lost. And it is in the natural sentiments of this general public that the identity of the community exists, and from which the community derives its sure sense.

Two additional points can be made about the American-ideology-in-Canada. First, because it comes from the nation which benefits by it, and which also incessantly expounds it in Canada through the presence and propaganda of its economic organizations, it is an imperialist ideology in the commonly understood sense of the word "imperialist."

Secondly, although the predominant dimension of the American-ideology-in-Canada is an economic one, since the American Dream is predominantly an economic ethic, its effect on Canada is pervasive, and for that very reason: it cannot explain Canadian contradictions and Canadian culture which are not based on the economic principles underlying the American Dream. So it effectively submerges them.

What happens when we do lay aside the received American-ideology-in-Canada, when we abandon the inappropriate dogma, and get back to Canadian practice — get down to cases — with a sceptical native eye? We discover a Canadian economic civilization based on powerful indigenous roots: first of all on the contradiction between Canada and the United States, or more precisely the contradiction between the small Canadian domestic market next to the large American one; and secondly on the contradictions between French and English Canadas and between the regions and the centre. Out of the first has grown a unique entrepreneurial style which might best be described as "Canadian public enterprise." Out of the internal contradictions has come the adoption, and the elaboration as a fundamental principle, of the unAmerican transactional mode of redistribution, as opposed to the American transactional mode of market exchange.

The more we investigate this Canadian economic civilization, the more exhilarating the excitement of self-discovery;

the more, also, it becomes discernible that Canadians and Americans are markedly different where we are supposed to be most alike — in our economic cultures. I don't mean by that differences in the physical properties of our railroad tracks or the plastic packaging of our foods or the serious faces of our economic administrators. These are the artifacts and professional habits which are generally common to industrial societies — to the Japanese and the Russians as well as to the North Americans. In that sense, we are all participants in a world phenomenon.

But the concept of an economic culture also covers the ultimate reason why the railroad tracks were laid down, the economic rules adhered to, where the entrepreneurial thrust came from, the spirit and social context of the enterprise, the way a community encourages such activity and how it enlarges its own character in doing so. And in that sense, we are all different, the Chinese from the Americans, and the Americans from us. (That distinction understood, if Canada's economic culture does liberate itself from the American-ideology-in-Canada, and follows its own logic, even some of the artifacts of the consumer society will undergo change.)

We also discover with what inventive cunning and scholastic dogmatism we have discredited our economic originality which, if I may labour the point, grew out of the Canadian context. By so doing, we have abused the Canadian context, and ourselves. Who is not convinced that when it comes to economic activity, Canadians are second-rate Americans, lacking in initiative and entrepreneurial spirit? It's the kind of self-depreciation typical of the colonial mentality — which does not make it any more acceptable.

PART II

The Canadian Public Enterprise Culture

CHAPTER 4

The Formative Years

The economic dimension of Canadian identity is weak. We look at ourselves through the inappropriate American ideology instead. And since most of us spend a good part of our lives in economic activity, as producers and consumers, we get the feeling that there's not too much to Canada after all.

At the centre of this fragility of identity is our inability to accept one of the most vibrant expressions of the Canadian character — Canadian public enterprise. It's usually taken for granted that Canada is a free enterprise country, after the United States and its Americanism, and that the native public enterprise tradition is therefore a somehow secondary or untrustworthy, even marginal, phenomenon, although it exists on a substantial scale and in most sectors of the economy. But citizens of an ideological colony cannot take anything for granted. They have got to make their own analysis. And when they do, they are liable to discover an unexpected originality in themselves.

In Canada's case, the explorer of the colonial ideology begins to feel like Alice in Wonderland. The more he pursues his investigation of the Canadian experience *in its own terms* — in this case, in terms of the contradiction between itself and the United States — the more it appears that Canada, in fact, is a *public* enterprise country, and that native *private* enterprise is a somehow secondary, untrustworthy phenomenon, although it exists on a substantial scale and in most sectors of the economy. So that the received colonial image of Canada as a free enterprise country must therefore be upside down. The American-ideology-in-Canada, with all of its phantasmagoric potency, stands Canadian reality on its head.

Public enterprise in Canada is the direct issue of the above-mentioned contradiction, more specifically, of the dilemma of Canadians with their small domestic market immediately next door to the Americans with their large market and manifest power. We did not choose public enterprise freely. It was forced on us by American expansion. But it happened in an age when the free enterprise ideology was the impelling doctrine (the new evangelism) in Great Britain, the mother country, and when its classic manifestation, the American republic, was producing the great middle class spectacular. No wonder that under that ideological avalanche, but in an inescapably contrary situation, we did things backwards, and got into the habit of seeing ourselves the wrong way around. Or that historian Arthur Lower should call Canada "a supreme act of faith." Or that Prime Minister Alexander Mackenzie, in the early days, should have denigrated the idea of building a railroad to the Pacific, which brought the country together, by condemning it as "an act of insane recklessness." How else could one explain the incomprehensible which lay outside the doctrinaire imaginations of Manchester and New York — when there was supposed to be nothing of rational value outside those boundaries — than to use the language of mysticism and damnation? But then again, what could be more comprehensible than the impulse of a community to survive, no matter how reactionary or counterrevolutionary it might be?

No nation ever grew up more absurd, and is taking so long to grow out of its absurdity.

It all started in 1821. In spite of generous purchases of stock by the imperial and provincial governments, the Company of the Proprietors of the Lachine Canal had made almost no progress in two years, and was taken over by the province, which did the job itself. The Rideau, Beauharnois and Cornwall Canals were also built by government. The Welland Canal Company quickly degenerated into a privately controlled vehicle for distributing public funds; in 1840, when the united provinces took the company over and began necessary enlargements and alterations, the two governments already had a majority of the shares.

Then came the railroads, and the cash grants, land grants, tax exemptions, bond guarantees and other forms of dispensation from all levels of government. From the first trunk lines, incorporated in the 1840's, through to the consolidation of the CNR beginning in 1920, it was government which provided most of the capital or the means of getting the capital.

An estimate made in 1913, evaluating land grants at $20 an acre, put the total value of cash and land grants at $1,320,113,173 or about $50,000 per mile. The privately built section of the CPR, which got the largest single chunk of the booty, came in at a final cost of about $51,600 per mile. (The *Ottawa Free Press* in 1880 put the value of government largesse in the CPR contract at $261,500,000 or $120,000 per mile.) Added to the total were $245 million in guarantees, plus tax and duty exemptions, mineral and timber rights, municipal terminal grants, water facilities and so on. Gustavus Myers was doing the exceptional only by pointing out the obvious when he wrote in 1914, in *The History of Canadian Wealth*, that while Canadian railroads were privately owned systems, "this is not to say that their proprietorship has come from the application of private cash. The funds that paid for their construction have come largely, if not fundamentally in whole, from the ever-accessible public treasury which the railway promoters early began to plunder, extending and elaborating the process with time and opportunity." And, it might be added, not without the occasional touch of graft.

In addition to the private systems were the two major government-built railroads: the Intercolonial and the National Transcontinental. If the willingness to invest capital is what makes for enterprise, then the construction of trunk railway lines in Canada was a halcyon public enterprise age.

It is possible to chart that whole series of nation-building episodes in terms of a strategic game against Manifest Destiny.

Step One: The Americans bring on the war of 1812. After it is over, the imperial government builds the Rideau Canal with military considerations in mind.

Step Two: In 1825 the Erie Canal is finished, drawing the commerce of the American midwest and parts of Upper Canada away from Montreal towards New York. So the Welland Canal is built. But by the time the Welland is functioning properly, American railroads have already robbed it, and the rest of the St. Lawrence system, of the traffic needed to make them prosper; so . . .

Step Three: The Grand Trunk is built from Sarnia to Montreal, although it doesn't succeed either in diverting American trade through Canada.

Step Four: The geopolitical power of the United States grows rapidly. Four of the British North American colonies join together in self-defence. Part of the price the Maritime provinces demand for joining the compact is an Intercolonial Railway.

Step Five: British Columbia joins Confederation, and all of the western colonies are tied to Canada, blocking American inroads into the British Northwest. The cost of that is also a railroad.

Not much after the National Policy begins to bear fruit — a policy made possible by the Pacific railroad, and making possible a broad range of Canadian manufacturing — American entrepreneurship and capital pass through the Great Tariff Wall, and take over and subordinate the most profitable sectors of the Canadian economy, effectively reducing our independence, which is where we are now, debating our next move.

In each case, the project was undertaken as a reaction to American initiatives, before markets were dense enough in Canada to justify them on a private enterprise basis. So private financing, even from the money markets of London and New York, was impossible. No matter how outrageous were the government grants to the CPR, for example, unless the government was willing to do the job itself (and it did build more than a quarter of the line) there was no other way of putting the railroad through, across Canadian territory exclusively. The role of the state was crucial.

There was even, in the old days, a certain amount of ideological exposition to explain and rationalize the astonishing Canadian behaviour. Spending large sums of public money, like spending large sums of private money, has to have a reason. The ideology, like the expenditure, had all of the force of local necessity behind it.

When William Hamilton Merritt said in 1834 that "canals ought never to be made, in any country, as objects of gain" — in itself a ringing public enterprise pronunciamento — he was, of course, rejecting the American ethic. He was also parroting the consensus of the Family Compact (although the members of the Compact, and fellow travellers like Merritt, weren't above making a private gain out of a public policy, if they could arrange it; Merritt's own original purpose in promoting the canal was "the value it will attach to my property"). He was also turning his coat on his profit-seeking American backers. Over and above that, however, he was describing how things in his neck of the Upper Canadian woods really were. If the Welland Canal were to be made as an object of gain, it wouldn't be made at all. Even Dr. Duncombe, a leading Reformer, whose party was rightly suspicious of large expenditures of public funds under Compact control, argued the case for public ownership, because the money had already been sunk into the project.

John A. Macdonald, when he condemned the syndicate proposing to build a western railroad through the United States *according to the soundest principles of free enterprise*, was still more eloquent. It would be "to the utter ruin of the great policy under which the Dominion of Canada has been created, the utter ruin of our hopes of being a great nation. . . ," he exclaimed in the House of Commons. "They would be relieved from running any portion of the road that would not pay. Canada might whistle for these connections . . . but the people would gradually see that the colonies would gradually be severed from each other; and we should become a bundle of sticks, as we were before, without a binding cord, and then we should fall, helpless, powerless and aimless, into the hands of the neighbouring republic."

Macdonald's unAmerican idea was to make the CPR build and operate uneconomic sections of railroad – an unjustifiable proposition except in terms of Canadian nationalism. But so was the tariff and the whole of the National Policy. So was Harold Innis' judgment of the Intercolonial, the railroad from Quebec to Halifax. "If the road must be regarded as an essential part of Confederation," Innis wrote, "its success is measured in terms of the value of Confederation." From which he inferred that a deficit – that epitome of failure in ideological America – "may be an indication of success inasmuch as it results from lower rates and a more satisfactory union between Canada and the Maritime Provinces." And, as Innis indicated, the proponents of the railway hadn't expected it to make a profit. That was not the point at all.

The American doctrine was laid aside.

Louis Hartz has pointed out that in the early days of the American republic "men began to be held together, not by the knowledge that they were different parts of a corporate whole, but by the knowledge that they were similar participants in a uniform way of life." This uniform individualism, this multitudinous, atomistic adherence to the same set of rules, coalesced to make of the United States a private enterprise nation, although the nation itself wasn't an enterprise.

Canada was just the opposite. Its economic reasoning was a product of nationalism, rather than the producer of nationalism, as in the American case. The large economic questions had nothing to do with celebrating and defending economic individualism – with the futile populist campaigns against the financial interests and the trusts, for example – but with bringing the parts into a whole. And in this making of a wholeness, the whole of Canada was a public enterprise. If the conformist commitment to the ideology of economic liberalism was the cement which bound Americans to each other — by which they defined themselves as Americans and stayed Americans, and in their rhetoric still do — and whose elaboration has given them those particular psychic characteristics which we recognize as the American mentality — what equivalent effect did the elaboration of Canada as a public enterprise nation have on our identity, and on how we see ourselves?

To answer the second part of the question first: We don't see ourselves, which is why we keep on searching for our identity and not finding it. The role of the state in Canadian economic history is an orthodoxy of political economy. The phenomenon of American move and collective Canadian countermove has even managed to inspire a particular, original name for itself — "defensive expansionism" — coined by Hugh G.J. Aitken. But the insights of our economic historians into the Canadian experience only get as far as a few students of a few professors in a few classrooms in a few universities. And they're only partial insights. All the rest is the American-ideology-in-Canada, which allows for the phenomenon of public enterprise, but which filters it through in terms of the American ethic, robbing it of its significance.

So that the CPR, for example, instead of being considered a glorious triumph of public enterprise, and the exciting work of a private syndicate only incidentally, is thought of as a glorious triumph of private enterprise, and a public undertaking only incidentally (the public money, the land, the monopoly, the tariff, and the economic imagination being the incidentals). General MacArthur was an earnest admirer of the CPR, as it demonstrated the American spirit at work in other peoples. And if the free enterprise culture constitutes the norm towards which everything is, or should be, moving, then it *is* the undertaking of the syndicate which has importance, because it is in that private profit-taking impulse and not in the collective impulse that entrepreneurial zest is found.

In that case, the nation-building era of laying down ties and hoisting up tariff walls was just a calculated, subsidized prelude to our own free enterprise extravaganza, with the privately owned CPR, running along efficiently and profitably, as the leading exhibit. Canadians, being full of grit and having a streak of masochism, could take public enterprise standing up, if they had to, but in our North American way of life, the public enterprise phenomenon was only a parochial anomaly (one of those nuances).

But there's another way of looking at the same nation-building era — a more indigenous way, I'm going to argue (because the free enterprise extravaganza never came; the Messiah didn't arrive to lead us into the American main-stream) — in which the Canadian experience itself is the norm, in which we do not bind ourselves down with the narrowing ideologies of other peoples. Then our perspectives are transformed. The railroad-building era, which put the nation together, ceases to be a vindication of the private enterprise way of doing things, and becomes a desperate, enormously costly and corrupt diversion of energy and resources into private hands, in the face of American expansionism, until the backward Canadian community evolves to the point where the nascent public enterprise tradition can take hold. Then the CPR syndicate is the anomaly, although even it too saves itself by exploiting the collective impulse.

And in trying to link up the past to the present, we notice that it is the public entrepreneurial style of a John A. Macdonald that has developed a continuous, creative momentum in Canada, and the private entrepreneurial culture of the Donald Smiths and the George Stephens that has wanted for dynamic progeny. When the nation-building era began in Canada, that private enterprise boldness and tenacity was lacking, and when it was finished — when the tariff and the eastern industries were in place — it was still lacking. Not all of the land grants and government loans and boomers' optimism could change one people into another.

That should come as no surprise. What makes for a dynamic free enterprise culture, or a private enterprise culture, is an habitual commitment to the rules and the game — an indefatigable zest of a compulsive kind — rooted deep in the popular consciousness, which at the same time creates an appropriate institutional pattern that will feed the compulsion instead of choking it. Greed and hard work and ambition are not enough. A great many peoples in history have had those. It was free banking, rough egalitarianism, practical education . . . and the relentless psychic push to keep up in the "Lockian race" that made the exceptional United States go.

But to expect that on this side of the border, out of a French Canada tied to its clerical, feudal past, and out of an English-speaking Canada which, although it inherited much of the spirit of liberal capitalism, was nevertheless an elitist, conservative, defensive colony — to expect it *without an intense ideological revolution* — was to dream a derivative impossibility. That still is the great Canadian illusion — that Canadians can escape from their unAmerican character — and it always will be an illusion because it is based on a false, received assumption about the nature of man: that the American capitalist spirit is natural to man, given his freedom, and all that Canadians have to do to make themselves free enterprise equals in North America is to be natural, to stop being so feudal, to stop being the way we are, to be the way we should be. And, of course, when we're not, there's never any satisfactory reason. Given that assumption about man, and given, as well, the obvious measure of freedom we enjoy, how can there be? The Canadian temperament appears to defy explanation.

Being an ideological colony, never having ourselves produced ideological counterweights to John Locke and Adam Smith and their American progeny, we have had no way of perceiving that liberal capitalist man is an historical oddity (along with the ideology that says he's the norm), and that the practical archetype, the American entrepreneur up to the end of the 19th century, was the product of unique historical circumstances. He had a psychic bearing all his own, which sensitive observers from elsewhere recognized immediately as one of the wonders of the world. Take away the unique circumstances, take away also the utopian romanticism of the American Dream, and the infallibility of the Horatio Alger myth, and in particular the dogmatic liberal absolutism of the American way of life, which keeps the dream intact and the myth whole, and which makes it a kind of treason to abandon the myth, to dismantle the Rat Race, and you take away the compulsive force behind that particular private enterprise energy.

In the colonial outposts of the Family Compact and the Chateau Clique, and in the Canada West and Canada East that followed, a different kind of man was being formed. When American energy had already settled New York State and was pushing westward, in the early 19th century, the Upper Canadian entrepreneur was still a man of sane, limited ambition, caught up only indirectly by the compulsive force of the American Dream, and whose contacts with the Family Compact weighed more in importance than his business acumen, at least if we can judge from the case of William Hamilton Merritt, the one outstanding example of the period. The imaginative Lower Canadian, for his part, was on the hustings or in the parish.

Nothing really changed later. There were, of course, exotic exceptions to the Canadian rule, and to the human rule, like Donald Smith, emerging out of Labrador in mid-career as he did, with his pathological acquisitiveness fastened to his consciousness like a psychic packsack — and that they were exceptions in Canada but not in the United States is an important clue in itself. But even they, in the end, had to cease being exceptions, and had to play the game according to the Canadian rules of public enterprise (which they could manage, because they could play it crookedly) and to be changed themselves by the playing, in order to get things done.

Their private enterprise side came to be the histrionic, impractical and impossible, Laurel and Hardy side of them.

Take the case of William Hamilton Merritt and the Welland Canal Company.

Four years after his entry into private business, Merritt was bankrupt. His original petition for the canal was framed in terms of government construction. Later, having been freed from the heavy weight of personal indebtedness, with the help of his relatives, Merritt set about organizing a private company. Still, he didn't conceive of the canal as the first building block of a capitalist empire, but only, as far as his personal interest went, as a means of increasing the value of that parcel of land of his.

H. G. J. Aitken, in his history of the company, writes that had the government undertaken the project from the beginning, Merritt probably would have gone along happily. This lack of capitalistic tenacity grew more marked as work progressed and debts rose. "Far more real and important for Merritt [than profits and revenue and the views of private stockholders]," writes Aitken, "were the opinions and beliefs which he encountered nearer home, in the newspapers, in legislative debates, and in the conversations and letters of his friends in Upper Canada. Here it was not the value of the stock so much as the canal itself as a physical entity and a political symbol which counted — the progress of construction, the number of ships which had passed through, whether the canal was just another piece of political jobbery or (as its protagonists claimed) truly a work of great national benefit. . . ." The other Canadian directors were of the same mind; "government purchase would constitute a natural and proper conclusion to their efforts."

John Beverley Robinson of the Family Compact recalled later how he became convinced of Merritt's "pure and disinterested and highly patriotic" motives — not exactly the motivation of free enterprise man, but, once the absolute moral tone is discounted, very much the motivation of public enterprise man. For practical reasons (extra funds were sought year after year from government) and for psychological reasons — and what other reasons are there that bear on the entrepreneurial psyche? — Merritt, as promoter of the Welland Canal, came to incorporate within his contradictory self the public enterprise spirit.

The Canadian public as a whole was equally removed from the private entrepreneurial challenge which the Welland Canal Company might have represented. By 1836, Canadian private investors (including New Brunswick) had only 7.2 per cent of the stock. Merritt himself owned only 38 of 20,024 shares. The major Canadian shareholders were the governments of Upper and Lower Canada, with 53 per cent of the stock between them.

Most of the private stock was held by Americans, led by John Yates, a New Yorker. Their interest in the company was totally different from Merritt's and the other Canadians', and so was their mentality and style. They were, truly, private enterprise people. Yates was a senior partner of a firm which managed lotteries (the paradigm of private risk and reward). He and his group fought tenaciously to keep the company under private control, and to make profitability a major rather than a secondary consideration. Otherwise, what was the point of investing in the company in the first place?

But if, in the minds of Upper Canadians, the construction of the Welland Canal came to be a public enterprise, the management of the company, until 1840, was a private enterprise. And it was a shambles.

In the early, promotional stage, Merritt illegally used the company seal to commission an incompetent member of the Family Compact as agent in England, and signed a draft to cover his expenses, on the mistaken belief that it had been approved by the directors. The new agent then took off to London without waiting for the plans and profiles. Once in England, he all but forgot about the project. Then panic struck the London market, and the sale of the shares reserved for England became impossible. "Deprived in effect of half its capital through laxity of organization and personal irresponsibility," Aitken writes, "the Company was crippled before ever its operations were fully begun."

Aitken also recounts that "rational bookkeeping and accounting, those hallmarks of capitalistic business organization, were nowhere to be found in the Welland Canal Company"; the lack of proper books, which, among other things, made cost accounting impossible, gave credibility to William Lyon Mackenzie's charges that "Economy and the Welland Canal are as far apart as earth and heaven" and that "the Welland Canal has been a hoax from first to last." By 1827, two years before the first two schooners passed through the canal, requests to the government of Upper Canada for capital had already become routine. Even after the canal had opened, thanks to the continuous public investment, the company by itself could not keep it operating; the wooden locks and unprotected dams and banks had been so cheaply built that the cost of maintenance was far out of line with revenue.

There were other engineering miscalculations. In 1828, in the middle of construction, the Deep Cut collapsed when an unsuspected layer of loose sand at the bottom of the cut was washed away by water, undermining the banks. It is unlikely that the Welland Canal Company would have been organized in the first place if Merritt hadn't underestimated the height of the ridge by half (and convinced himself the canal could be built), when he first measured it, fooling about with a spirit level, in 1818!

The private organization and construction of railroads in Canada was also a seemingly endless series of blunders, miscalculations, broken promises, and cutting of corners, not to mention the usurpation of public funds and the great long chronicle of corruption.

The first promotional attempts managed to raise enough money only for miniature railroads. Before the Guarantee Act was passed in 1849, bringing government aid into the picture, the St. Lawrence and Atlantic had managed only 40 miles, progress on the Great Western was also slow and the Northern, despite an ingenious attempt to raise money by means of a lottery, wasn't even able to begin construction. In the Maritimes, the Brassey firm of Britain failed twice to carry out its promises, and reneged on contracts.

The Northern Railway, running from Toronto to Collingwood when it finally did get started, was badly scamped by contractors. When the Commissioner of Public Works refused to sanction giving the company subsidy bonds until the contract was properly fulfilled, he was, according to a contemporary account, summarily dislodged from office by the accurate application of a bribe. The bonds were issued forthwith, which, of course, did nothing to improve the condition of the line.

More scandal of false and fraudulent representation, scamping, bribery and conflict of interest broke out over this and other, smaller lines in Ontario. "Railways are an oasis for the thirsty," said Samuel Zimmerman, one of the contractor-promoter-fixers of the time, and he and his associates, and their political associates and their associates, borrowing from U.S. practice (Zimmerman was an American), drank heavily.

The Great Western Railway, the second of the major lines built in the 1850's, and eventually absorbed by the Grand Trunk, was another entrepreneurial misadventure.

Construction costs for the first 24 miles west of Hamilton came in at more than five times the estimate, and overall costs at more than double the estimate. The right of way and other land for the Hamilton-Windsor section alone came to nine times what had been allocated under that heading for the whole main line extending to Niagara Falls. The brutal and dishonest behaviour of subcontractors and straw bosses added to the unsettledness of the labour gangs; special constabulary groups had to be organized to keep the lid on. Subcontractors came and went, underestimating costs, scamping their work, failing to meet payrolls, going bankrupt, and even, on occasion, decamping in the dead of night.

Early in the Great Western's operations, in 1854, there were 19 serious accidents, several involving fatalities, in the last one, 57 persons. A legislative commission investigating the accidents found "that at the opening of the road, the embankments and cuttings were in a dangerous state; that the ties or sleepers were without the stay or support of gravel on the surface; the road crossings and cattle grades were unfinished. The trestle works in some cases substituted for embankments were notoriously insecure, and in fact neither grading nor superstructure were in a fit state to hazard the prosecution of traffic in the face of the contingencies of the coming winter and spring in this climate and in this country." Employees were found to have been careless and criminally negligent. Three years later a Great Western train plunged off a bridge at Desjardins Canal, near Hamilton, killing 60 passengers. The provision of the railway act calling for the train to stop before crossing, because of the inadequate approach, had been waived after an appropriate bribe, according to a contemporary account. Moreover the bridge, planned originally to be built of oak timber, was constructed of pine, and was in a bad condition. Others attributed the accident to a mechanical defect. (The company, according to Gustavus Myers, declared that Providence was responsible!)

Notwithstanding government bond guarantees and government loans, the Great Western also illegally diverted large sums of money into projects beyond its charter, the most important of which, the Detroit and Milwaukee Railway, came a cropper. The Great Western, which had an overriding mortgage on the property, foreclosed, and then in effect sold the property to itself for a nominal sum, at the expense of less privileged or less useful creditors. The Commercial Bank, which had a large loan outstanding to the Detroit and Milwaukee, was ruined in the process.

But it was the Grand Trunk, the largest of the three major railroads benefiting from the Guarantee Act of 1849, which proved the biggest calamity. The railroad, incorporated in 1853, was already out of money and prospects by 1855, and virtually bankrupt by 1860, despite government guarantees and, from 1855 onward, government charity. Construction costs proved much higher than estimates. The great Brassey firm tried to save money by heavy grades, insufficient roadbeds, cheap iron rails and inadequate ballast — a practice in which they and other private contractors had considerable experience. But what they and the subcontractors saved by scamping, the Grand Trunk paid for many times over in maintenance and rebuilding costs. That was only the beginning of an incredible story of mismanagement, miscalculation, chicanery, misallocation of funds and special pleading — a state of organization which Edward Watkin, on assuming the supervision of the road in 1861, called "a sink of iniquity." Despite a period of good management towards the end of the century, the Grand Trunk's agony, and blundering, didn't really end until Ottawa finally let it go into receivership in 1919.

Even the Canadian Pacific, with the Hudson's Bay connections of Donald Smith and the Bank of Montreal connections of George Stephen — the best imaginable double whammy of the time — had to be rescued twice by Ottawa, at one time involving an illegal advance, *over and above the massive grants and other lucrative considerations of their contract*, because of slipshod estimating and lack of corporate muscle. At the time the contract was drawn up (actually a few months later), George Stephen projected the cost of the section to be built privately at $45 million. Estimates were soon revised upwards. The actual cost came to $112 million. Van Horne's engineering triumph was also Stephen's financial nightmare. As Pierre Berton documents so well in *The Last Spike*, Stephen went through emotional hell during the building of the road. He never did get over it.

The CPR syndicate, taken as a group of private financiers, had no way of escaping from this dilemma. It is true, of course, that they were victims at the end of malicious Grand Trunk propaganda in the London money market. But weren't they, themselves, expected to muster whatever malicious cleverness was necessary? They had made their reputations by parting the St. Paul and Pacific Railroad from its Dutch bondholders — with the aid, it appears, of the bondholders' representative. Unscrupulous cleverness and intrigue was where their strength as promoters supposedly lay. The essence of that game is not to let yourself be victimized.

They rode well, and they rode hard, but they rode mostly on the government's back.

Add the agonizing bankruptcy of the Grand Trunk, and the simultaneous bankruptcy of the third transcontinental line (the Canadian Northern), add also that had the government not paid the Canadian Northern $10.8 million for worthless shares, its creditor, the Canadian Bank of Commerce, might have been in trouble, and that in the 1860's the Commercial Bank did eventually go under when it got caught up in the Great Western's Detroit and Milwaukee machinations . . . put it all together and you have a quite dismal entrepreneurial record.

(In the United States, which we have come to consider a free enterprise model, railroad construction and financing, with few exceptions, like the Great Northern, were colossally corrupt, wasteful, manipulative and cannibalistic from beginning to end. By 1872, 30,000 miles of railways in the U.S. were virtually insolvent. The sensational collapse of Jay Cooke's financial empire, including the Northern Pacific, occurred the following year. After a subsequent shaking out in 1893, nearly half the railroad mileage in the country, representing 155 railroads, 39,000 miles of line and $2,500,-000,000 capitalization, was in receivership.)

One of the most astounding outcomes of all this, as it went along, was that *government* construction got a bad name for itself. It was a double irony, because what detractors looked down on as government construction was more often than not a case of private contractors battening on to a weak, embryonic, ideologically beseiged public enterprise culture, in other words, battening on to a helpless citizenry by a kind of blackmail. Even the upright stone-mason, Alexander Mackenzie, the Liberal prime minister in the 1870's, who was in charge of letting tenders for government sections of the Pacific railroad, and determined to prevent favouritism and block graft, was no match for the elaborate plots of private contractors and their political friends.

But this corruption didn't inhere in government undertakings. Just the opposite was the case. The dense corruption and manipulation which assaulted "government" construction in the 1870's was a carryover from the previous period in which not only private railroad companies cheated on government and the people, but also private contractors cheated on private railroad companies, and private sub-contractors, in effect, cheated on the whole chain of organization.

The logical alternative was for the government to build the railroads itself through its public works department. But the administrative resources available to government in the backward colony were slender and inexperienced. More than that, public works construction would have cut off the greater profit opportunities of private construction; the business class in Canada had more than sufficient influence to stop that from happening. The public enterprise culture was not yet strong enough for the Canadian public to draw on.

Even under the assault of private contractors, however, "government" construction held its own, and was too easily maligned. The government-built sections of the CPR, with their fair share of engineering difficulties, came in at a cost of $52,400 per mile compared to $50,300 per mile for the sections built by the syndicate. The much-abused Inter-colonial, whose high quality construction has been judged economically unwise by historians (a large extra expense being assumed), cost $43,180 per mile for the all-steel rail, iron bridge main section built by Sandford Fleming (Rivière-du-Loup to Truro) and $48,129 for the whole line in place in 1876, compared to $63,800 for the faultily built, poorly designed, high-cost Grand Trunk, and $66,000 for the mixed quality of all the private lines built in Canada before 1867 (excluding the Maritimes).

By comparison, in the United States, the Central Pacific came in at almost $100,000 per mile, and the Union Pacific at from $80,000 to $96,000 per mile.

The National Transcontinental in Canada, built in a higher cost period (labour and materials) after the turn of the century, and plagued by a lack of cost controls, and excessive spending on low grade, came to somewhere between $79,250 and $88,600 per mile, depending on how the estimate is calculated.

These various figures may not be exactly comparable in terms of what they include, so the comparison is only an approximate one. In any case, all of the fiddling of all of the private contractors to take outsized profits at the expense of government projects does not touch the massive cost to the public of grants of public money, land, tax exemptions and other rights to the private companies. (W.T. Easterbrook and H.G.J. Aitken, in their standard textbook *Canadian Economic History*, refer to the "cost of excessive waste, with excessive drains on the public treasury, and with excessive damage to Canada's credit on the world capital market," in summarizing the first period of railway building, up to 1867. They cautiously suggest "that a policy of direct government construction would have proved more effective." It is hard to come to any other conclusion.)

That wasn't the end of the price Canadians paid for doggedly sticking to an inappropriate economic ideology throughout the railroad-building era. Something inherent to the very spirit and definition of free enterprise proved to be the ultimate folly — competition. Was there ever any point to it here?

The first unnecessary charge on the country came when the Grand Trunk extended its line from Toronto to Sarnia instead of using the Great Western to Windsor as originally planned. This split the insufficient through traffic, and hurt both lines, and everybody else.

The second, greater mistake occurred when, in a mood of general optimism, both the Canadian Northern and the Grand Trunk built across Canada to provide competiton for the CPR. This meant three lines running east from Winnipeg, two lines running northwest side by side to the Yellowhead Pass where, for a few miles, they ran almost on top of each other, two lines from North Bay to Ottawa, and two lines running through the difficult section from Kamloops to Vancouver, when one line would have done in each case, and this at an enormous, crippling charge on the country's economy from which we did not recover until World War II. A second, pioneering line opening up new territory north of the CPR just made sense, but the construction of two extra lines never fails to amaze historians.

Nobody has yet explained, in non-ideological terms, why Laurier acceded to the Canadian Northern's transcontinental program. Laurier did in fact try to bring the Grand Trunk and the Canadian Northern together. They would not come to terms because each had its own ambitions. Laurier mystifyingly declined to force the issue.

The inappropriate free enterprise myth, which, in the vastly richer market of the United States, half a century before, had still resulted in grievous waste and overbuilding, won out over the public enterprise reality that was eventually to prevail.

But how private were the private entrepreneurs in the first place? Six of the twelve Canadian directors of the original Grand Trunk were cabinet ministers. Allan MacNab, president of the Great Western, was also in the Legislature, and for a while prime minister. In Gustavus Myers' *The History of Canadian Wealth*, the list goes on and on, along with the details of how the members in their public capacities voted charters and grants to themselves in their private capacities. It was, as Myers realized, a remarkably easy process of taxing the people — public enterprise in a weird, indigenous Canadian form — done so openly, and so unlike anything in the United States, that Myers, who was an American, saw it only as corruption in the extreme, and was flabbergasted. He missed the historical point: that unless railroads were political by one means or another, railroads would not be built.

Looking back into the anthropological evidence, we discover that the railroad entrepreneurs in this early period, as entrepreneurs, had their own peculiar style. Their private roles, as underwriter-promoters, were dull and trivial. Their public acts, as politician-promoters, constituted superb entrepreneurial cunning. When Allan MacNab unabashedly confessed that railways were his politics, he was not only baring his larcenous soul, he was also inadvertently indicating that railways were a public rather than a private business.

The building of the Pacific railroad was more public while seeming to be less so. Political pressure from British Columbia forced the issue, not a competitive struggle for the rewards of the contract. Macdonald had been looking for a syndicate for the best part of a year. (The original subsidy offer had been made eight years before the CPR group came forward.) Then there was the national doctrine, as enunciated by Macdonald. And, of course, the financing. And in the end, it was a political event, the Saskatchewan Rebellion, which emboldened Macdonald to force a final, decisive loan through the House of Commons and rescue the imperilled project.

Again, the "political power and social connections to create the security essential to large-scale investments in continental development" (W. T. Easterbrook's phrase) were the conclusive factors. It was the syndicate's political and social connections to Macdonald and Tupper that held; and their business connections to London and New York that failed. Even in the actual execution of the contract, the private profit-taking impulse which had brought the syndicate together in the St. Paul and Pacific caper was infiltrated, and perhaps even finally overwhelmed by the collective impulse.

What, after all, would move a man more — the making

of a nation or the making of a profit? In Canada, at least the two could be separated. Pierre Berton writes how Donald Smith became petulant when his name was left off the original CPR board because "he wanted the honour and glory of publicly participating in great national deeds." When Van Horne became a Canadian citizen he is alleged to have remarked that "building that railroad would have made a Canadian out of the German Emperor." The Pacific railroad, had it been primarily a private enterprise, would have only confirmed Van Horne in his Americanism.

All this, of course, came to be seen backwards in Canada. The CPR, defined, underwritten and rescued by government, came to be known as a private enterprise triumph (how could any railroad built by monopoly on the backs of western Canadians be considered a private anything?) and the CNR, which took over two irresponsible, bankrupt private roads and other fragmentary lines, and made them into a viable system, came to be considered a public enterprise white elephant, and still is by a lot of people.

If we are to believe G. R. Stevens, the author of *Canadian National Railways*, Sir Robert Borden and his ministers were nearly heartbroken in having to get the government into the railroad business. "The only people to be really pleased," wrote Stevens, "were a modest but growing group of doctrinaires who had sucked the milk of collectivism from the Fabian Essays." Nationalization was, to the government, Stevens suggests, sound practice but unnatural doctrine. As for the much disliked, and deservedly disliked, Grand Trunk, and for the Canadian Northern, Stevens manages sentimentality. He describes them as "two great systems," one dying "grimly, with repercussions that have never quite died away," the other passing "gallantly," although the first, for much of its history, resembled comic opera, and the second was run by two master pickpockets of the public purse, as Stevens' account also makes clear.

D'Arcy Marsh, a journalist and editor of the period, and also an observer of the railroad scene, put the CNR's inheritance a bit more realistically when he described the piecemeal conglomeration of bankrupt, propped-up organizations which came together in the railroad "not as a noble experiment but as a compromise with disaster . . . the heaped-up follies of the years of uncalculated Western expansion . . . the burden of the first mistake that had been made, and the last."

A chronological account of this pervasive historical current, taken not from the American perspective of an ascendant free enterprise culture, but from the indigenous perspective, would therefore run something like this:

The given is the sparsely settled Canadian community next to the growing American giant. The only way it can keep within hailing distance economically is by large public investment, and Canada in theory not being a kingdom governed for the benefit of private clans, the natural form for this investment to take is public enterprise. Public enterprise is indigenous to the Canadian demography.

After a chequered private start, it does take this form, with the Welland Canal, and with the Lachine Canal. Other canals are also publicly built. This precedent points to public ownership of railways. In 1847, two of the Montreal papers, the *Courier* and the *Witness* make the case for public ownership. Joseph Howe, a leading figure in Nova Scotia politics, argues eloquently for government construction of lines within the province and, in 1855, the Nova Scotia government, under Howe's watchful eye, does begin railroad construction. An act passed by the Canadian Parliament in 1850 contains a conditional provision that the Grand Trunk Railway could be constructed as a public work by the government together with the municipalities. But lobbying, and what may have been bribery of Sir Francis Hincks, Canada's Inspector-General (with the English contracting firm of Peto, Brassey, Betts and Jackson implicated), and other ambiguous influences, induce Hincks to change his mind and the new Colonial Minister to change the Imperial Government's arrangement. The Brassey firm and the Grand Trunk management then make a mess of things. Important investors try to intimidate the government into bailing them out, by threatening to seize the rolling stock for debt. The government, having to keep the railroad going as an urgent matter of public policy, but not willing to take it over (although even the investors' agent envisages the possibility), finally gives in, and sacrifices the province's investment. Open scandal (or open swindle, if you like) marks this period of "private" enterprise; without the demand for government ownership, the public continues to be victimized. Government construction of the Pacific railroad begins but is overwhelmed by private corruption. The government underwrites the CPR, although at one point the majority of Macdonald's followers call on it to take over the road rather than to give it still more money, and one cabinet minister resigns over the issue. The western half of the country then suffers the CPR's monopoly. By this time, government aid to railroads has been abandoned in the United States, and the ideology of laissez-faire re-affirmed; the history of corruption associated with government participation reinforces the taboo on government entrepreneurship. The U.S. in any case has just come through a spectacular private enterprise period. But in Canada, where a different contradiction is at work, stopping public investment means stopping rapid expansion. Clifford Sifton, Laurier's Minister of the Interior, favours government ownership and operation of a second transcontinental line. R. G. Blair, Laurier's Minister of Railways, also prefers a government road, but his motives are suspect. There is still no mandate for public enterprise. Laurier draws the wrong conclusions from the Intercolonial, hands money out to both the Grand Trunk Pacific and the Canadian Northern, and the whole country pays for their competitive overbuilding when they go bankrupt.

Then the CNR is formed. "Towards the inevitable," is how G. R. Stevens put it. And Harold Innis: "Government ownership . . . rests ultimately on the Precambrian shield." The subterranean public enterprise thrust finally breaks through 70 years of ideological mystification and private use, and comes out into the open, pushed forward by the Canadian dialectic at work.

Not the administrative or the financial but the cultural evolution and strengthening is what counted most in this tangled series of events — the public enterprise current — in which the CNR was rooted.

All economic systems exist in a cultural context, a free enterprise system like any other. No economy functions automatically. Economic rules and habits do not fall out of the sky.

The liberal capitalist revolution in Great Britain, and the unnatural subordination of even man and his environment to a market system that went with it, would never have occurred without the radical social changes brought on by the intro-duction of factory production, and the intense ideological campaign of its secular prophets. And it would have never been sustained without an extensive government administra-tion to enforce the rules and to administer myriad new regulations.

At a more fundamental level, the Chinese Communists had to launch a flag-waving and drum-beating campaign to eliminate economic crimes like theft, embezzlement and conversion of public property before they could establish a modern economy. Without the Americans' complex inheri-tance of economic habits, social assumptions and political traditions, any kind of economic system is imaginable in what is now U.S. territory, except the present one.

Private enterprise, free enterprise, public enterprise, socialist enterprise, co-operative enterprise, tribal enterprise, feudal enterprise, municipal enterprise, commune enterprise . . . any kind of organized economic activity works only as well as the culture in which it exists is suited to it.

European-American economic liberalism was disastrous in China. Canada was able to develop its economy only outside the American ethic. And as I am going to suggest, the

Canadian public enterprise model may be impossible to transplant whole into the United States. Economic cultures overlap one another, but each also has at its centre a dense web of habits, assumptions, precedents, sensitivities and so on — a psychic bearing was the phrase I used before — tied into the whole fabric of society. No other people can recreate it because no other people has lived the same history. And if you look closely at the particularities of an economic culture, you may catch a glimpse of the identity of the people themselves.

No other nation on the face of the earth, or in any madman's imagination, has ever gone through anything akin to Canada's railroad experience. It left us with a unique cultural legacy.

When railroad charters with their land grants, and the corrupting of legislators to get them, were creating a privileged class in the United States and betraying the promise of Jacksonian liberal capitalism, a privileged class of corrupt legislators in Canada were creating railroad charters and, by taking on the worst characteristics of liberal capitalism, were betraying whatever promise there was in Canadian conservatism.

When, a generation later, J. P. Morgan and other important capitalists in the U.S. were wondering how to impose order on America's cannibalistic railroad jungle in the face of contrary prejudice by the federal government, Canada was building its Pacific railroad in an ordered monopoly situation legislated by the federal government.

And a generation later, when Woodrow Wilson in the U.S. was campaigning against the trusts and the scheming big money men, in an attempt to re-establish the spirit of free competition, Canada was about to pay for its government's failure to do the opposite, namely to unite the scheming big money men and to eliminate competition.

In the meantime, while these cyclical movements in the United States, with their political intensity and economic exuberance, were creating one culture, a noisy, acrimonious, episodic struggle was taking place in Canada — a coming to grips with the inescapable problem of how to eliminate corruption, extravagance and inefficiency from public investment without eliminating public investment — and creating another culture.

By the time the CNR was established, the public enterprise behind it already had a thick, kaleidescopic cultural history. All of the intrigues of all of the railroad scandals were part of it. The CPR monopoly was part of it. So was the Grand Trunk fiasco, and the other abuses of private privilege financed by public sacrifice. Alexander Mackenzie's anguish over the helplessness of public works, and his weary disgust with "government" construction was part of it, along with all the parliamentary rages, the street gossip, the newspaper copy for, against and indifferent, from William Lyon Mackenzie's passionate runs at the Welland Canal Company in the 1830's to Wilfrid Laurier's visceral suspicions of the promoters of the Canadian Northern. The alleged (by historians) legendary cynicism of Canadians was part of it, and so was their passiveness and their subdued alienation. Each legislative commission added to the culture. The practical experiences with the Intercolonial and the National Transcontinental added to it, and the regional demands and defences (which touched as far down as the bargain of Confederation itself), and the charges and countercharges, the hammering of opinions, the unresolved debates and the elections that went with them, the politics everywhere . . . all were part of it.

Then, in the early 1920's, when the CNR was organized, and when all of the component parts were absorbed, this long cultural evolution of antagonisms came together. It was astonishingly long and variegated when one looks back on it now. The corruption, which to Alexander Mackenzie and to Laurier had seemed nightmarishly, cruelly attendant on public enterprise (and on private enterprise with public finances, as the Americans had also learned), and which the Canadian public imagined and gossiped about even when it didn't exist . . . such corruption suddenly became hard to imagine. The apparently intractable problems of mediocre management and patronage which had hounded the Intercolonial, but which, on the quiet, were being solved, also disappeared, although the new railroad was faced with a confusing tangle of physical properties and responsibilities.

In a few years, the CNR turned this hopeless, costly jumble of steel and unreliable equipment into an aggressive unified system, almost delivering itself, and the country, from evil in the process — almost, but not quite, because of the depression.

The CNR's contribution to Canada's economic culture was profound.

It had two complementary parts. In the 1920's, Sir Henry Thornton, the CNR's president and chairman, criss-crossed the country promoting economic activity in general, and explaining the contribution the CNR was making. For the first time, a positive, creative construction was put on the railroad's public ownership. Thornton also demonstrated — had to demonstrate — how umbilically linked the CNR was to the life of the country as a whole. The viability of Canada and the viability of public enterprise became one. And a native faith did emerge, both in the railroad and the country.

Sir Edward Beatty, president of the CPR, was also touring the country and talking about the railroad, but although he was talking a private kind of sense, the connection wasn't there any more. Looking back on his style, and defensive position, one gets the impression now that the CPR had nothing to contribute to the country's self-definition, that as a private bureaucracy, freed from the Canadian dialectic which had created it, the CPR had become an outsider.

The CNR also became an entrepreneurial and social innovator. Network broadcasting in Canada was pioneered by the CNR. In 1928, CNR engineers in Montreal began seriously exploring the idea of using a diesel-electric system for locomotive power. By August, 1929, they had a test model built — the first in the world. Unfortunately, when Wall Street disintegrated, the CNR's innovative mandate went with it, along with the possibility of a valuable diesel locomotive export industry. Social welfare and worker participation in management was also pioneered by Thornton and the railway.

The next stage of cultural evolution occurred during the depression, when the CNR found itself buried underneath the fixed debt and uneconomic services which it had largely inherited from the past. Edward Beatty of the CPR enlarged on the attempt to stigmatize the Canadian National's operation with the cost of this debt structure not of its own making (although it was taken for granted by the CPR that if they took over the operation, they would not take the debt structure with it). There was another royal commission, and parliamentary intrigue, and another desolate bout of lacerating introspection. Thornton came out of it a broken man.

The worst year was 1931, when the net income deficit rose to $84 million. This was a huge burden for a Canada strapped by the depression. The public, however, refused to turn the system over to the CPR. Having been put on the rack for so long by private railroads, until that suffrance was impressed in the collective character, and then having loosened the shackles with the CNR, the Canadian people were not about to surrender again.

Shortly after Thornton died, in 1933, D'Arcy Marsh wrote his passionate biography of the man, which incidentally gives an indication of how close to the bone the politics of the day cut. But underneath the bitterness and vituperation, and maybe partly because of them, questions at the base of the culture, for which there were already many clues and practical illustrations, were being explored by the whole country. Could monopoly be the most efficient economic form after all, and how could it be managed? If self-destructive competition between the private sector (the CPR) and the public sector (the CNR) is replaced by co-operation (in effect, formally institutionalized duopoly), how is responsibility to the public to be maintained? What are the best ways of giving public enterprises maximum freedom from political interference without giving up ultimate parliamentary control (the check on irresponsible executives)? And the question that is implicit in all of these: *What is the ideal relationship between economics and political democracy?*

(Compare this to the fixedness of the private enterprise culture of the United States which, in the same period, boiled over while standing in the same place, the place where it had been standing since the concentration of economic power towards the end of the 19th centruy. In the 1920's, the lid blew off some incredible corporate scandals, involving members of the U.S. cabinet. When Canadians, because of their railroad problem, were grappling with the fundamental questions of political economy, Americans had gone no further than a trivial, because futile and backward, ritualistic repetition of anti-trust dogma, and then the expedient obscurantism of Franklin Delanor Roosevelt. Yet because those of us who read the papers rather than economic history always imagined ourselves a free enterprise country, we never realized how telling and creative our own indigenous debate had been. Our administrative elite worshipped Roosevelt instead.)

The CNR was not alone. There was also an intensive acculturation process occurring, during this period, in Ontario and in parts of western Canada, giving shape to and taking shape from other enterprises.

In Ontario, the government had launched the Temis-kaming & Northern Ontario Railway (now Ontario North-land) to open up the northern part of the province. The discovery of mines in the area added greatly to the road's traffic and to an appreciation of the road's usefulness. Then came the movement for public power, beginning in 1902, and the impressive success of Ontario Hydro in cheap rates and technical innovation, also in developing entrepreneurial and administrative talent, and equally important, in keeping operations free from government manipulation and patronage, thanks in part to its co-operative municipal ownership. Coincidentally, the main antagonist of the public power movement was a syndicate headed by William Mackenzie of the Canadian Northern.

Ontario Hydro was one of the first cases in Canada of public enterprise entering a field coveted by private interests, and where private capital was available. The cultural conflict lasted for 25-odd years, involving expensive and relentless propaganda from the Mackenzie syndicate and private power producers in the United States, on the one hand, but a pervasive, continuous, often person-to-person educational campaign by the supporters of public power on the other — the kind of campaign which, by its very intensity, has a lasting effect on the character of society.

The dormant Upper Canadian populism came to the fore again — that uniquely Canadian amalgam of radical protest against privileged, scheming promoters together with the counterrevolutionary Tory rejection of uncontrolled acquisitive capitalism. There was also a more materialistic logic: the conservative manufacturing interests of south-western Ontario wanted cheap power and many of them did not think they would get it from private enterprise. At the same time, the manufacturers themselves were being pushed to advance quickly with cheap electricity in order to meet the rapid increase in demand from the West created in turn, at its origins, by the federal government's underwriting of the Pacific railroad!

Ontario Hydro also had an explicit nationalist side, expressed in the power movement's rhetoric against any U.S. takeover of electrical generation in Canada, and against the "political subserviency that no Canadian can or will tolerate," in the words of Adam Beck, the Commission's founder-chairman.

After the Conservative victory in the provincial election of 1905, in which public power was an issue, the new premier, James Pliny Whitney, proclaimed that "the water power of Niagara should be as free as air, and more than that, I say on behalf of the Government, that the water power all over the country should not in the future be made the sport and prey of capitalists and shall not be treated as anything else but a valuable asset of the people of Ontario, whose trustees this Government of the people are." That could have been said by any uncompromising radical of the 1830's, but also, if we stretch our imagination a bit, by an undemocratic, privileged, Tory snob like John Beverley Robinson. The two would come together, as they had before over the Welland Canal.

Shortly after, in the period 1905-1909, the Manitoba and Saskatchewan governments took over the telephones of the Bell Company and other private companies. Alberta entered into competition with Bell. All three provinces began to push the lines of poles and copper wire into the country-side to bind their communities together, a priority in which Bell had been considered delinquent. Again, as with Ontario Hydro, but in a different way, widespread and rapid western settlement, touched off by government support of railway construction, created a demand for installations and transmission on a large scale; and private enterprise was inadequate to the task.

The premier of Manitoba at the time was Sir Rodmond Roblin, like Whitney a Conservative. His rhetoric was much the same also. "I believe that it is a good commercial proposition," he proclaimed, "and whatever profit there is will from this time on belong to the people of Manitoba. I am also proud of the fact that we have been able to secure for the people the first complete system of government-owned telephones on the continent of North America." Or as an English observer of the telephone phenomenon described the Manitoba decision: "A stroke of inspired statesmanship."

Also in the same period, Winnipeg City Hydro was formed and a hydro-electric project undertaken to supply power in competition with the privately-owned Winnipeg Electric Company. "The civic democracy of Winnipeg was at its strongest and best at this time," writes historian W. L. Morton. The pressure of public opinion was strong. The mayor had been elected on a public ownership platform. The advent of publicly owned power in 1911 immediately brought down the high rates of Winnipeg Electric, and gave the city the cheapest power on the continent.

Now let us work forward from these earlier provincial cases to their cultural linkages with the CNR.

Every investigation undertaken by the Borden government into creating a healthy transportation system out of the deteriorating railway situation led to some form of nationalization, so much so that even the president of the Canadian Pacific, Lord Shaughnessy, saw no other solution except government ownership. But a cultural block was in the way. G. R. Stevens writes that the cabinet was quite willing to do the obvious thing "as long as it was not given the obvious description; . . . the words 'government ownership' stank in their nostrils."

Eroding this cultural block were the nationalization of railroads in several countries of the Empire and western Europe, the wartime experiences of government control even in Great Britain and the United States — and at home, the concrete example of Ontario Hydro and the other provincial examples that the public had already fought for and committed itself to. By 1917, Ontario Hydro was in full entrepreneurial vigour, plunging into the massive Queenston-Chippawa project, and managing its affairs well (and Adam Beck, Hydro's chairman, was in the middle of his own campaign for the nationalization of railways and for booting out the "old crowd" and the "Big Interests"). The combination of these native enterprises, plus other factors like the growing labour and agricultural movements, gave such an impetus to nationalization that Donald Mann of the Canadian Northern would recall ruefully that although, in his opinion, a private ownership solution was possible, "most of the people west of the Ottawa River were in favour of government ownership."

Those were the root public enterprise experiences and antecedents by which the culture was established. Everything else followed more easily now: the federal enterprises of the 1930's and the war, like the Bank of Canada, Air Canada (Trans-Canada Air Lines), Polymer, Eldorado Nuclear (Eldorado Mining and Refining), the National Harbours Board, the Industrial Development Bank; the second generation, like Atomic Energy of Canada, Northern Transportation, Northern Canada Power, Canadian Overseas Telecommunication Corporation, Canadian Patents and Development, the St. Lawrence Seaway; the provincial infrastructure corporations (or commissions) after Ontario Hydro and Manitoba Telephones and Alberta Government Telephones and Saskatchewan Telecommunications and Ontario Northland, and then their successive generations — first of all the utilities and railways, like the B.C. Railway (Pacific Great Eastern), B.C. Hydro, Manitoba Hydro, Hydro-Québec, Saskatchewan Power, Newfoundland and Labrador Power, Nova Scotia Power, New Brunswick Electric Power, and more recently the Alberta Resources Railway; then the industrial, insurance, financial and development corporations, like Sydney Steel (Sysco), Sidbec, Société québecoise d'exploration minière (Soquem), Société québecoise d'initiatives pétrolières (Soquip), Manitoba Mineral Resources, Manitoba Public Insurance Corporation, the A.E. McKenzie Seed Co., Saskatchewan Government Insurance, Alberta Treasury Branches, Caisse de dépôt et placement du Québec, Ocean Falls Corporation, Insurance Corporation of B.C., Labrador Linerboard Ltd. . . .

The list goes on, through the development corporations in all of the provinces, into the enduring but small and now almost ideologically invisible crown corporations established by the early CCF in Saskatchewan, like Saskatchewan Transportation and Saskatchewan Minerals and Saskatchewan Forest Products, touching also the remote or exotic or little known or declining or trite, both federally or provincially, involving hotels, liquor sales, irrigation schemes, a beet-sugar refinery, a printing plant, a fur marketing company, food wholesale facilities, fish processing, pulpwood harvesting, and the farm credit corporations, and the ones whose names seem to be more imposing than their specialized functions, like The Seaway International Bridge Corporation Ltd. or the Crown Assets Disposal Corporation.

Almost all of these public enterprises, these crown corporations or crown companies, these *sociétés de la couronne* or *entreprises du gouvernement* or *sociétés d'état*, are engaged in the industrial or financial sectors of the economy. Leaving financial enterprises aside, but including manufacturing, petroleum and natural gas, mining and smelting, railways and other utilities, and construction and merchandising, crown corporations make up over one-third of all Canadian-controlled corporate assets.

Then there are the crown corporations in cultural fields, like the CBC and the Canada Council, and, in the same lineage, the National Arts Centre Corporation and the Canadian Film Development Corporation. There are trading agencies like the Canadian Wheat Board and the Canadian Commercial Corporation, and the Export Development Corporation which provides financing and insurance to facilitate trade. There are crown corporations involved in housing and urban development, like the Central Mortgage and Housing Corporation and the National Capital Commission, and the provincial companies in Alberta, Manitoba, Ontario, Quebec, New Brunswick and Newfoundland, the largest being the Ontario Housing Corporation and the Société d'habitation du Québec.

And there are crown corporations unique unto themselves, like the National Research Council.

(A different but related public involvement is direct government participation in "private" companies, like Saskatchewan's holdings in Interprovincial Steel and Pipe and in Intercontinental Packers; B.C.'s majority shareholding in Canadian Cellulose; Ottawa's dominant 45 per cent interest in Panarctic Oils, its 50 per cent in Telesat or its 99.8 per cent shareholding in Radio Engineering Products, etc. B.C. Ferries is part of a government department.)

Each of these enterprises has added to the culture of

the entrepreneurial form. Here is where there has been real indigenous creativity. The American psyche has all this time been tied down to the free enterprise myth, which has frozen the American corporate form, save some exceptions. Canadian public enterprise has proliferated in entrepreneurial variety.

There are, for example, four different categories of federal crown corporations — departmental corporations, agency corporations, proprietary corporations, and an unclassified group — with different kinds of mandates and different relationships to the owner (the crown).

But within each group there are also differences. The CBC, a proprietary corporation, is organically a different entrepreneurial specimen than Northern Transportation, also a proprietary corporation. Atomic Energy of Canada and the Canadian Film Development Corporation are both agency corporations.

Provincially, the definition of a public enterprise or crown corporation varies, and dovetails or overlaps the whole range of government agencies. Ontario Hydro, from its inception, for example, has been a municipally owned co-operative, although the Ontario government has announced its intention (November 1972) to turn it into a crown corporation. From the other side, several provincial crown corporations have cabinet ministers on the board; the premier of B.C. is the president of B.C. Railway.

Within specific forms there are variances. The Ontario Development Corporation dispenses special loans to private companies (in the North and East of the province, at low cost and with generous repayment conditions). Until recent legislation, it was also in the grant-giving business — some would say the gift-giving business — handing out money as "forgivable loans" even to large U.S. multinational corporations. The Manitoba Development Corporation, on the other hand, while also making loans, wholly owns a computer time-sharing company, a vegetable processing plant and a corporation charged with building a new city in the northern part of the province, controls a bus manufacturer, and participates in a variety of other companies, from airplane manufacturing to prefabricated housing.

The range and adaptability of this entrepreneurial device go further. A crown corporation was established to produce Expo (Canadian Corporation for the 1967 World Exposition). The Company of Young Canadians is a crown corporation. The form admits of such variety that the Confederation of National Trade Unions could advocate a crown corporation for the Lapalme postal drivers, separate from the Post Office, as the only way to solve their labour dispute with the Treasury Board.

The kinds of independence these crown corporations enjoy are only sketched out in the legislation; in reality, their independence is conditioned by dense cultural factors of precedent, habit and the history of endless public debate, so closely tied to particular, indigenous experience and so ramified that the whole cannot be categorized but can only be hinted at as a certain politically touched imaginative open-ness — a certain way, transmitted in the cultural flow. Yet the originality of Canadian public enterprise, as well as the historical momentum it has created (slowly, over a century and a half), has been so close to us — so much into us — that we have hardly been aware of it.

Note again the cultural multiplier effect typical of lively societies, sometimes even spilling over the border into the United States.

Without Ontario Hydro, for example, there might not have been a Tennessee Valley Authority.   Franklin D. Roosevelt, when he was governor of New York State, had become a close student of Ontario Hydro, and many of its features were incorporated in the enabling legis-lation for the Authority.   TVA inherited the entrepren-eurial mystique that went with Hydro's power-at-cost form-ula.   Hydro was the practical example against which the propaganda of American private power companies foundered.

In the late 1950's, when Pierre Elliott Trudeau, in an

article in *Vrai*, attacked the stifling clerical prejudice against
economic initiative by the state, he used Ontario Hydro as
a leading example. ("They told us that the Popes were against
state ownership, with the result that the Ontario Hydro got
fifty years' head start over Quebec.") René Lévesque's campaign for the extension of public power in Quebec, a few
years later, was fought on Ontario Hydro's back (just as, 50
years earlier, the fledgling Ontario Hydro example was available to the proponents of public ownership in Winnipeg; in
later years the Manitoba government would call twice on
T. H. Hogg, one of Ontario Hydro's foremost engineers and
its chairman in the 1940's, to draw up reports and advise on
Manitoba's hydro-electric structure).

Or, for the sake of comparison, we can start from the
early railroad days, when the culture was weak.

In the 1860's, when powerful English bondholders,
through American representatives, suggested they would
run the Grand Trunk's rolling stock into Maine and hold
it for debt, which would close down the railroad, unless
the Canadian government bailed the company out, the
government was brought to a more pliable state of mind,
and eventually conceded (thereby authorizing an abject giveaway), although, as the bondholders' agent himself admitted
privately, the government could counteract all their threats
by taking the railroad over. In the winter of 1902-1903, when
Laurier tried to bring the Canadian Northern and the Grand
Trunk together, for the creation of a second transcontinental
line, the railways refused, and Laurier inexplicably conceded,
plunging the country into its second generation of railroad
nightmares, although as everybody saw clearly later, he could
have united the two systems quite simply, by taking them
over. In 1961, when B.C. Electric refused to commit itself
to simultaneous development of the Peace and Columbia
Rivers, thereby voiding government policy, W. A. C. Bennett,
with the Ontario Hydro experience and the early Hydro-
Québec experience and the prairie telephone companies
experience and the B.C. Ferries experience and all the rest of

the tradition lurking in his mysterious political subconscious, took B.C. Electric over.

Some of these enterprises are not important to identity. The Crown Assets Disposal Corporation, for example, is simply an administrative device for selling off public property, although it too, in a backward way, is culturally significant, because it shows to what varied uses the crown corporation form can be put.

Others, like the CNR (and the CPR) and Ontario Hydro and Hydro-Québec and the CBC have all of our history in themselves. Compared to them, even giant multinational corporations like Massey-Ferguson or MacMillan Bloedel, and even private enterprises with constant contact with the public, and long Canadian histories, like the Bank of Montreal, appear culturally impoverished, although the chartered banks, in another way, take on an historical presence — in their conservatism, in their long history of chartered protection and as instruments of centralized control by a backward, self-serving elite. Eaton's is, or at least was, one of the exceptions, perhaps because of its catalogues. But as symbols which provide clues to the Canadian psyche, by representing the country's economic life, private corporations are feeble in image. (For the Hudson's Bay Company, see Part III, Chapter 8.)

General Motors and Coca Cola and the other great "private" corporations symbolize the American way of life. The great public enterprises in transportation and communication symbolize the independent, creative Canadian spirit. And the great public enterprises in electric power symbolize Canada's regional dynamism. Their logos are with us everywhere in our historical subconscious.

The same goes for our entrepreneurial history. We have no John Jacob Astor or Cornelius Vanderbilt or Andrew Carnegie or John D. Rockefeller or J. Pierpont Morgan or Henry Ford, whose legendary economic activities are part of the national catechism. Canada's great entrepreneurs have been politicians, like Sir John A. Macdonald, Adam Beck and

C. D. Howe, the members of the CPR syndicate notwithstanding. Our wild promoter was Wilfrid Laurier. William
Mackenzie and Donald Mann of the Canadian Northern had
glib tongues and unbridled ambition, but they never said
anything as extravagant and compelling as "the twentieth
century would be the century of Canada." As entrepreneurs
go, H. R. MacMillan was not in the same league as W. A. C.
Bennett. Compare Bennett, the private enterprise hardware
merchant, to Bennett, the public enterprise builder of a
region. It was René Lévesque, with help from Eric Kierans
and acquiescence from Jean Lesage, who gave French
Canadians their new entrepreneurial dimension, by the
extension of Hydro-Québec and the creation of other crown
corporations, and not Armand Bombardier, the inventor of
the snowmobile.

Correspondingly, the great ages of public enterprise in
Canada were times when the persistent uneasiness about
our identity disappeared, along with our nagging, colonial
inferiority complex. When we built the Pacific railroad, and
during World War II, when public enterprise and public
administration and public broadcasting flourished, we thought
we had come into our own — because we *had* come into our
own. We were ourselves. But when, after each of these
periods, we sat back to wait for our great age of free
enterprise — our great, untramelled, competitive storming
of frontiers — which was waiting for an American Godot who
would not come, and could not come, we fell back again into
a stoic abjectness, depending on a false messenger from Godot
for capital which we already had, or could raise on our own,
and for enterprise that was in us but that we would not
summon from ourselves.

Similarly, public enterprise in British Columbia and
Quebec has been accompanied by, or been the product of,
or been the instrument of regional self-assertion and self-
confidence.

The wrong-headed pursuit after symbolic free enterprise
folk heroes, or folk villains, in this epic public enterprise ter-

ritory, ends up only in demonstrating how thin free enterprise legend in Canada really is.

One of the few records we have of such an attempt is Peter Newman's book *Flame of Power*, published in 1959. The book consists of a series of 11 biographical sketches of, in Newman's words, "the businessmen [who] transformed Canada from a community of traders and land tillers into one of the world's economically most animated nations" . . . who demonstrated a "phenomenal mastery of the entrepreneurial art" . . . who "personify the evolution of this country's economic thinking" . . . heroic language enough.

But by the nature of the pursuit, Newman made two ruinous errors of method. First, he limited himself to what he took to be rigorous believers in the free enterprise system, thereby laying aside the symbolism and complex code of the public enterprise character. Then he went on to sketch their careers as if they really were in a free enterprise system, as "capitalists in the classic sense," which for somebody like Donald Gordon of the Bank of Canada, the Wartime Prices and Trade Board and the CNR, and even for Donald Smith and William Van Horne of the CPR, constituted anthropological mutilation.

What, for example, did Van Horne really mean when he told a visiting U.S. senator, "I am a Chinese Wall protectionist. I don't mean merely in trade. I mean everything. I'd keep American ideas out of this country."? Could any capitalist in "the classic [free enterprise] sense" say such a thing? That was a Middle Kingdom Confucian (Central Canada species) talking. It's not surprising that the American senator was startled. Newman reported the incident but did not stay for the real anthropological discovery.

That they were hard-working individualists is undeniable. That they were participants in free enterprise is a proposition Andrew Jackson would have laughed right out of the White House.

The others Newman discussed were Herbert Holt of the Royal Bank of Canada and Montreal Light, Heat and Power;

three mining men — Harry Oakes, Gilbert Labine, and Hans Lundberg; and James Dunn, Lionel Forsyth, the Steinberg brothers and E. P. Taylor. Macdonald and Howe, of course, who were thoroughly radiant from their flames of power (and in Macdonald's case, from something else as well) were excluded by the terms of the study. So was Henry Thornton (an epochal figure; a tragic genius and a giant of a man of which legends are truly made!). So was Adam Beck, the founder of Ontario Hydro — no more single-minded, prickly, visionary and bold an entrepreneur ever lived — although in 1959, Ontario Hydro's assets about equalled those of the CPR, both of them, along with the CNR, far outdistancing anything created by indigenous private enterprise. (A few financial corporations had higher assets, but these are calculated on a different basis and have a different meaning.)

Where are people like James Dunn and E.P. Taylor now, and even Herbert Holt, in the Canadian mythology? If minor figures like Harry Oakes and Gilbert Labine and Lionel Forsyth are classic prototypes of the heroic Canadian entrepreneur, is it any wonder we have such a dim view of Canadian enterprise, or that in a school program in this country specifically and officially allocated to Canadian history, blocks of time should have been spent on American folklore figures instead, among them the Robber Barons (the unscrupulous, legendary 19th century American tycoons), the reason given being the lack of enough interesting Canadian material?

Colonial, imitative inquiry suppresses the epic quality of public enterprise in Canada because it takes it as an aberrant phenomenon. But the epic of Canadian private enterprise has no epic quality to it.

As it was, so is it now today. Canada is still a small domestic market next to the large American one. Native private capital or the private capital under native control, is still not forthcoming on an adequate scale, for indigenous innovation and entrepreneurial adventure, although capital abounds, as it was not forthcoming for the Welland Canal or the Pacific railroad. Yet Canadians' entrepreneurial passion will not be denied.

CHAPTER 5

The Culture at Work: Technical Innovation, Efficiency, *Entrepreneurial Zest*

I want to return to the general question of economic cultures. The Canadian dialectic never allowed a dynamic free enterprise culture to take hold at the centre of the country's life. The last real glimpse we had of it here was the Montreal fur trade. (As if arranged by the gods, the year the North West Company of Montreal was absorbed by the Hudson's Bay Company, 1821, was also the year the government of Lower Canada took over the building of the Lachine Canal.) Ever since, those of us who have been caught up in the free enterprise mystique in Canada have kept ourselves going on nothing but romanticism.

We had this fixed belief that the forces of competitive free enterprise, and only those forces, made for entrepreneurial inventiveness and endurance, in spite of the exceptions all around us. Ideologically passive and imitative, we had no inkling this was only a superstition inherited from western Europe and reinforced by the powerful American myth — that in practice, the aggressive, acquisitive free enterprise spirit on the part of more adventurous entrepreneurs, but without an appropriate free enterprise culture, could have a self-cancelling or destructive effect.

Take the case of the corruption of politics by scheming business buccaneers. In the United States, it could be taken as an excess of exuberant acquisitiveness. Their brawling and cheating could be romanticized, after the fact, to serve the Horatio Alger myth. The burgeoning American giant could laugh at, and even celebrate, its outsized sinners. American government and American enterprise were deeply enough rooted among the masses to outlive them all. In China, the same phenomenon, but in an altogether different culture, ended up in warlordism, profound social dislocation and mass starvation, that is to say, in chaos. In Canada, the corruption of the railroad era has usually been treated as if it had happened in the United States — as something natural to frontier economies that was passed off as time went on. But there was no explosive free enterprise culture to leaven and offset the privilege it created. There was no uncontrolled frontier in which masses of newcomers could let go an untrammelled self-seeking acquisitiveness of their own. Is it possible then that the graft, and corruption of politics, that accompanied grants to private railroad promoters in Canada had a subtle demoralizing effect on the entrepreneurial spirit in the generality of Canadians?

But who can chart the myriad ways in which the free enterprise spirit of the Commercial Empire was dissipated? It *was* dissipated, and, watching the American success, we have spent a good century regretting our inability to revive it.

The recent work of ethnographers and economic anthropologists suggests that our regret was futile, because the American experience (the whole liberal capitalist experience) was too particular, and in the broad historical spectrum, too freakish to sorrow after. But if the ethnographers and anthropologists tell us how exceptional and fragile and passing that free enterprise culture was, they also tell us that non-economic, socially bound incentives, like competition, status, the joy of work, or collective welfare, can also provide a powerful impetus to economic creativity — that, in fact, economic activity, as a rule, takes place inside a social context, rather than as an individual quest for accumulating profit. So that the absence of the compulsive force of the American ethic does not necessarily mean the absence of excellence in entrepreneurial imagination and of tenacity in entrepreneurial will. It means only that, other things being equal, they would come out of a different impulse — in Canada, quite likely, if they came at all, considering the circumstances, out of the profound impulse to remain an independent nation. National independence being a collective quest, that impulse would produce a public enterprise ethic, as it has.

If economic creativity is culturally induced, in the United States and Japan and western Europe as well as anywhere else, and if Canada is essentially a public enterprise country, where public enterprise can draw on a stronger impulse than private enterprise, and if acculturation in that direction has been going on for 150 years, then it should show up in current economic performance and in the mentality of our entrepreneurs. There should be some kind of empirical verification. And there is. We have just never bothered to look for it, because we have generally taken it for granted that private enterprise means efficiency, and that crown enterprise is synonymous with bureaucratic torpor and waste, and that's all there is to it. Why bother putting the proposition to an empirical test?

This lack of even the most elemental empiricism is surely a sign of backwardness.

A student who helped me paint my house, for example, assured me that all government enterprise was inefficient, by its very nature; everybody else, he said, had told him so.

A young engineer at Expo 67 put the high cost of building Habitat to public enterprise, not to its experimental nature. My citation of a long list of contrary examples was acknowledged without rebuttal. His convictions didn't change.

A friend who is a business executive pointed out that while public enterprise appeared to be efficient where it was protect. i by monopoly, it couldn't stand up to private competition. My description of contrary cases had no effect, and could have no effect, despite his good-natured tolerance. Such examples came at him from an unknown, unassimilable world. The hypothesis that "mature" private corporations protect themselves from destructive competition by oligopoly arrangements never came up.

A politician cited the failure of the CCF shoe factory in

Saskatchewan in the 1940's as conclusive proof that public enterprise had an inherent flaw in it.

And so on. Surveys done in the past showed a heavy bias of opinion against public ownership. Even Canadian socialists have been cautious and defensive about the public enterprise culture. But isn't a lack of empiricism exactly one of the symptoms of the colonial condition? When wasn't public enterprise the whipping boy of imitative politics in this country?

Although attitudes are changing, Canadians still appear to be hemmed in by the American ethnocentric notion that economics is basically a matter of private ownership and the rules of free enterprise. And if the public enterprise culture doesn't come into it, how can a public enterprise work well? There is nothing behind it. The incentive of gain has been turned into straw. The undeniable success of a public enterprise comes to appear, then, as nothing short of magic. It works, but there's no explanation for it. The other possibility is to deny that it works, which is psychologically easier. There are some Canadians who would remain convinced that Air Canada's service was inferior to the service of private airlines even if the latter always flew in the wrong direction and served ground glass in their coffee.

The myth of public enterprise has also been ill-served by circumstance. Often, as with the CNR, public enterprise has been saddled with private enterprise's failures. Sydney Steel and Clairtone (now virtually defunct) are other examples. The enterprise is kept going to provide an essential public service or to maintain employment or to keep a region alive. Or an enterprise which is public in an aberrant sense only is speciously cited to condemn the entrepreneurial form, like Deuterium of Canada, where a provincial government found itself captive to a private entrepreneur who failed to deliver, first financially and then technically. In other cases, like the B.C. Railway (Pacific Great Eastern), which also took over from a private failure, the enterprise is established or expanded at a loss, or with little hope of profit, in order to strengthen the economic infrastructure. Theoretically, the deficit is more than made up by taxes on the increased economic activity produced. The last case of such an infrastructure railroad, however, the Alberta Resources Railway, has been a financial disaster.

In the past, the general attitude has been that where there is profit to be made, private enterprise should be given the job, and where profit is unlikely but something should be done anyway, public enterprise should be given the job. Not unexpectedly, the public gets the impression that public enterprises lose money and that private enterprises make money. Never was a game so well fixed.

Further, crown corporations cannot hide their mistakes the way a private company can. Not just large miscalculations but also small blunders can become matters of opposition attack and public interest. Nor are crown corporations in the same position as private companies to jettison creditors via bankruptcy and reorganize with a clear financial slate, as did U.S. railroads, which went through one series of investors after another; the CNR, on the other hand, is stuck with its inherited and past debts, so that it almost always ends up with a deficit after payment of interest.

Similarly, the closing of that crown-owned shoe factory in Saskatchewan — a curiosity in the long continuum of public enterprise — has served many a prairie politician for rhetoric. By contrast, little is said of what has happened, as a rule, in the model private enterprise culture, the United States, where, for example, in the period 1900-1939, 85 per cent (or 16 million) of all new enterprises went out of business (according to a monograph done for a joint Senate and Securities and Exchange Commission inquiry, cited in Ferdinand Lundberg's *The Rich and the Super-Rich*). Henry Thoreau, writing in an earlier age, the mid-19th century, put the failure rate at 97 per cent!

Bankruptcy is as American as cherry pie. In the legendary days of U.S. small entrepreneurship, the 19th century, some American observers went so far as to advance rules on the uses of bankruptcy (the proper course was to draw heavily on creditors on the way down and then conceal assets). Perhaps, even, bankruptcy was essential to facilitating the American entrepreneurial spirit. "Vigorous individual entrepreneurship may necessarily have a high ratio of miscalculation and failure, a high ratio of entries and exits," writes Thomas C. Cochran in *Capital Formation and Economic Growth*. "American entrepreneurs like R. H. Macy and Cyrus McCormick failed in their early ventures, and many successful companies have been through one or more bankruptcies. Managerial know-how, essential to ultimate capital formation, was learned at the expense of empty-handed creditors." But all that is lost in Horatio Alger mythology. Canadian public enterprise suffers an ideological stigma instead.

In addition, a large segment of public enterprise in Canada is in utilities, where the absence of market competition is obvious. Any large profit is ascribed to the benefits of monopoly. Publicly owned utilities have no mandate for profit anyway. The great engines of private enterprise, on the other hand, like the farm machinery companies or the oil companies, are able to disguise the lack of vigorous price competition by simulated competition. Their profits appear to be earned by superior performance.

Sometimes direct comparisons can be made easily. Ontario Hydro, when it began to distribute power, forced prices down dramatically in Ontario — in Hamilton, the charge for residential current was reduced 87 per cent — and maintained prices considerably lower than those in New York State, in some cases as low as a third or less of U.S. rates. Telephone rates in the prairie provinces are markedly lower than rates elsewhere, although here comparison is complicated.

A much better way to assess the relative strength of the public enterprise ethic, and finally to see clearly the economic dimension of Canadian identity (which is what we are after) is to look at the workings of the economic culture itself —

how it develops and applies technology, how it generates inducements to efficiency, and how it keeps alive in our corporate cadres a zest for the entrepreneurial game. In all three cases there are enough clues to suggest that in Canada public enterprise is strong and private enterprise is weak — exactly the opposite of what we have been led to believe.

(1)   As far as creating new technology, and new industry based on new technology, Canadian private enterprise has been a monumental failure. I don't think that's too strong a phrase or too simple a generalization. Most Canadians are not aware of the inventive imagination that has sprung up in their country in the past, because business enterprise has not built upon it, to give it practical embodiment.

The list of lost chances is heartbreaking. The variable-pitch propeller, which made economic air transport possible, was developed in Canada; the patent rights were sold, chiefly to an American company. The electronic microscope was developed at the University of Toronto but the three men who worked on it were all lured to the United States, where the microscope was eventually produced. The hand-arm machine (automatically controlled machine tools, or AMCRO), the basic instrument of automation, was invented in Toronto. After a fruitless search in Canada, the inventor, E. W. Leaver, finally got development support from an American engineering firm. More telling in the long run, Leaver's firm, although it had a clear lead in the field of about six years, did not have the capital to build a patent fence around the basic idea, leaving the way open for others to build on it and profit from the whole range of alternative applications.

The first commercial jet in North America (the second, by only two weeks, in the world) was produced in Canada, and was making sensational test flights when American pure jets were still at the drawing board stage. The other commercial jet, the British Comet, was eventually grounded. The Canadian plane had a 10 year lead on the next medium-range jetliner, the Caravelle. But the

second Canadian Jetliner was never finished, and the prototype was scrapped.

One of the pioneering commercial developments of
electronic computer technology was underwritten by an
order of 12 machines from the Canadian government, in the
face of indifference and initial opposition from Thomas J.
Watson Sr., the founder-president of IBM. More than 1,000
of these machines (the IBM 101 Electronic Statistical Sorter)
have been sold around the world. The entrepreneurial thrust
came from the Dominion Bureau of Statistics (with C.D. Howe
in the wings). But the project, and the rewards, automatically
went to an American company (Remington Rand had been ap-
proached as well as IBM) because Canadian private enterprise
was nowhere visible on the computer horizon.

Subsequently, a large and salesworthy computer, comparable to the best available at the time, was built in Canada.
The company, Ferranti-Packard, however, was a British
subsidiary. According to the *Toronto Star*, foreign exchange
controls in the period made it impossible to draw the
necessary resources from its parent for mass manufacture,
leasing and marketing, so the designs and technology were
sold to a British firm, now International Computers Ltd. By
1970, 1,500 of the machines, brought out in a new series,
had been sold by ICL, and had helped the firm to gain the
largest single share of the British market, despite competition
from IBM.

The same thing has happened to less important inventions. The Eastman developing tank was invented by a
Canadian, who then sold his patents to the Eastman Kodak
Company in Rochester. The wirephoto was invented in
Canada, but developed in Great Britain after the inventor
unsuccessfully tried to interest Canadian newspapers and
electrical companies. The first electronic organ was demonstrated by its inventor Morse Robb in Belleville in 1927. It
was also first in conception by about eight years. But for
various reasons, not least of which was the difficulty of
raising investment capital, Robb had to throw in the towel

in 1936. The Helava Plotter, which prepares maps by computer through translating electronic impulses from earth satellites into precisely detailed diagrams, developed at the National Research Council, could not find a Canadian manufacturer and had to be licensed to a company in Milan, Italy. Canadian textile manufacturers refused to have anything to do with manufacturing, under licence, an engineered yarn developed by the Department of National Defence. It is now being spun in Belgium and woven in Holland. The Levy automatic mail sorter is only a slightly different case. Canada had a long lead in time on the rest of the world, and an effective working model had been built by Canadian Arsenals, a crown corporation. But the Diefenbaker government shut off the post office laboratory in Ottawa and took the job of building the equipment away from Canadian Arsenals and gave it to Canadair. Levy quit in disgust. The project came to a standstill.

Jet airliners, automation, computers — some of the basic bones of current technology — elements of all three, in different ways, came out of Canada, and kept on going across the 49th parallel. Reading J. J. Brown's *Ideas in Exile, a history of Canadian invention*, from which most of the above examples are drawn, is like reading an unceasing lament for entrepreneurial and financial chicken-heartedness.

"Time after time we have gotten there first after a magnificent sprint," writes Brown, "and then stood around idly for years waiting to collect the risk capital required to get an industry going. Usually by the time we have solved the financial problem, other less torpid nations have caught up with and passed us. . . . Our inventors present us with a world's first and a clear head start. But because of our conservative bent, and chronic financial ineptitude, we were unable to do anything with it."

Quite likely this deadening entrepreneurial atmosphere has also contributed to the current lack of general interest in invention in Canada. In 1968, Canadians made eight patent applications per 100,000 inhabitants compared to 31 for the Americans, 76 for the Japanese and 98 for the Swiss.

Lots of inventive brain but no entrepreneurial brawn! Or in Brown's words, "The paradox that enlivens the history of Canadian invention is that Canada is a great producer of ideas, yet it has virtually no native technical industry." (Brown's book was published in 1967. A more recent study, *Innovation and the Structure of Canadian Industry*, by Pierre Bourgault, dean of applied sciences at the University of Sherbrooke, which appeared in 1972, indicates the situation hasn't changed and may even be deteriorating. Bourgault refers to Canada's "poor performance" in innovation, and parallel to that, in manufacturing. He writes that "on a relative basis Canadians are increasingly becoming 'hewers of wood and drawers of water.' " He points out that Canada failed to capitalize on its advanced consumer market after World War II to take leading technological positions, and that particular fortuitous advantage is now lost, and that in some areas like military aircraft, automotive engineering, computer design and chemicals, Canadian technical capability has declined or vanished. He cites outside industrial opinion that, in terms of technological capability, Canada is falling behind even some small industrialized countries, like Sweden, the Netherlands and Switzerland, to say nothing of the U.S., U.S.S.R., Japan, West Germany, France, etc.)

Brown rakes all parties over the coals for this lack of entrepreneurial imagination and boldness. C. D. Howe's withdrawal of support for the Jetliner, and the handling of the automatic mail sorter, and other examples, put governments in the dock. The abysmal lethargy and caution of private enterprise and private financial institutions put them in the dock. Over and above all this, however, Brown isolates two principle factors: a lack of "public education" to overcome our inherited conservatism, and a "chronic shortage of risk capital."

Canadian public enterprise — not always, but in its classic manifestations — has escaped these two crippling limitations, almost by its very nature. In our great public enterprise projects, like the Pacific railroad and the heavy water nuclear reactor, we have put together huge sums of capital quickly for risks on the technological frontier. But wasn't public enterprise exactly the culture we created to raise investment capital that wasn't available in any other way in peculiar Canada? Also, for the most part, public enterprise has been the product of public debate, which in its essence is a process of educating the public to shake off their inherited conservatism. But then again, giving concrete form to what is least conservative and most adventurous about us is what public enterprise in Canada is all about.

I have already mentioned the CNR's pioneering work in radio and the development of the diesel locomotive, both of which had to be given up during the depression. (The CNR again has a vigorous research and development department — its Technical Research Centre is the largest and best equipped rail transport laboratory in North America — but it appears more closely oriented to operations; manufacture of equipment developed and patented by the department is mostly licensed out.)

Air Canada (Trans-Canada Air Lines), as well as having a long list of world firsts in airline operation and aircraft technology (including the use of wing-tip slots, top and bottom flashing warning lights, modern de-icing equipment, and the hydromatic and reversible pitch propellers), was the first airline in the world to prepare a detailed specification for a commercial jet transport. (This was in 1946, for what became the Jetliner, in whose early development TCA was closely involved. Eventually TCA cancelled its order when four Derwent engines were substituted on the prototype for the envisaged two Rolls-Royce AJ65 engines, still in development. Brown suggests that TCA's requirements were unreasonable, and that it was partly responsible, along with the manufacturer — Avro — and the government, for the Jetliner's demise. On the other hand, no sales were made to any of the other airlines on the basis of the one modified prototype. For some of that complicated story, see again *Ideas in Exile*.)

I have put down those two examples first, because they also illustrate the kind of dilemma public enterprise has found itself in when developing new technology. Taking over from private failures, as in the case of the CNR, or inserted into the breach where profit possibilities were negligible or non-existent, public enterprise has been hamstrung by punishing economic circumstances, unusually susceptible to downturns in the economy. Brown calls the CNR's decision to suspend the deisel locomotive program a "fiasco," but the pressures on the CNR, and on the country's finances, were so great at the time that to do otherwise would have required superhuman blockheadedness. Even among companies entering the 1930's with a backlog of profits and security, only rare exceptions like Ontario Hydro and the Pulp & Paper Research Institute maintained extensive laboratory facilities.

A more constricting factor, crown corporations have, in the past, been kept out of the manufacturing mainstream where technological innovation can become a technologically prolific industry. Had there been a crown corporation in calculating equipment to work with the Dominion Bureau of Statistics in its search for a quicker way of processing census data, the electronic statistical sorter might have been developed in Canada instead of by IBM, with explosive repercussions for Canadian invention. The process of applying technology in manufacturing also provides a rich climate for technological spin-off, which goes missing when manufacturing rights are licensed out.

The establishment of the CNR, and its intense rapport in the 1920's, under Henry Thornton, with the Canadian people and Canadian circumstances, opened up an unsuspected native reserve of technological creativity. In the 1930's, this creativity had to be closed off. Ontario Hydro, in a better position to sustain its inventiveness — in fact having to do so to survive — went from one technological triumph to another.

In 1908, under two young graduates of the University of Toronto, Ontario Hydro began construction of a 110,000 volt transmission line (which was its first construction of any kind!) when current dogma had it that 60,000 volts was the highest voltage practicable. High-voltage transmission soon became standard everywhere. Along with the 110,000 volt line, Hydro introduced ball-and-socket joint suspension insulators and steel core aluminum cable, which also soon became standard equipment around the world. Improvement of tower and cable design followed. Hydro also introduced electrical standards and a comprehensive inspection system to North America. By this time, Hydro's engineering team had become well known for solving unprecedented problems with improvised solutions — one of the surest criteria of a technologically dynamic culture.

In the 1920's, Hydro engineers invented and installed a remote control system, actuated by electrical impulses, which enabled generating plants at different locations on the Trent Valley Canal System to respond to a single operator. These installations pioneered techniques which later made possible complete automation.

Starting in 1917, *only three years after it first became a producer of power*, Hydro began construction of the largest hydro-electric plant in the world, "based on the most intricate calculations known in the theory of hydraulics," according to a royal commission report. There was much criticism that Hydro had not hired outside consultants. But once completed, the design proved even more efficient than the engineers had expected. It was, in short, as the royal commission pointed out, "a magnificent piece of engineering."

This famous Queenston-Chippawa project wasn't undertaken until an enabling bylaw had been approved by the ratepayers of the co-operating municipalities who were Hydro's customers. It involved several months of impassioned ideological debate. With the exception of two municipalities, the bylaw won overwhelming approval, from the same population that was described before, and has been described since, as being incorrigibly conservative, or counterrevolutionary. How was that possible?

The vote on "the largest hydro-electric plant in the world," of course, was only a single incident. The milieu in which technical departures by native-educated engineers came to be seen as the most natural thing in the world was the product of the whole populist movement for people's power. Canadian public enterprise in full social amplification, and technological creativity, went together.

Ontario Hydro's spirit of innovation didn't stop there. But the early years have a particular importance. They show a Canadian public enterprise starting out without a legacy, at the beginning of a technological age where the genius for innovation and imaginative response has lots of room to show itself. Atomic Energy of Canada and Polymer Corporation (now Polysar) are the other two notable cases in Canada.

* * *

AECL's Commercial Products Division is responsible for the cobalt therapy unit, among other technical developments. AECL builds and distributes these units, supplying more than half the world's demand. AECL's main achievement is the CANDU nuclear reactor. By concentrating on one type of reactor (heavy water, natural uranium) when other leading nations had opted for the other type (light water, enriched uranium), AECL appeared to have launched the whole country on a hair-raising entrepreneurial gamble. In retrospect we can see that no gambling was involved in the ordinary sense of the word. Sound nuclear theory and the progressive and in-depth development of technology in increasingly large and costly installations were the factors at work.

As of January 1972, only three nations are building nuclear stations based on their own original designs proved in practice — the U.S., the U.S.S.R. and Canada. These are the first-generation reactors. It appears now that the CANDU's unique modular form has distinctive advantages over the other first-generation systems, and may even be able to match, in engineering and economics, the second-generation breeder system being developed in the U.S., the U.S.S.R., Great Britain and France.

AECL's nuclear reactor program is the innovative technological spirit in a classic team form — the culmination of years of work on the technological frontier, involving highly trained personnel and large capital outlays, on a development about which most of the rest of the world had grave doubts.

Polymer was (and, as Polysar, remains) a producer of synthetic rubber, thermoplastics and petrochemicals, located in Sarnia. It recently diversified into chemically stressed concrete housing modules and computer time-sharing. It was a crown corporation until its forced sale to the Canada Development Corporation in 1972, after which its name was changed to Polysar, the corporate trademark since 1947. (See Part III, Chapter 10, subsection "e".)

Although Polymer, as a crown company, was not an exceptionally large corporation (its assets in 1971 were $220,849,000 compared to $1,648,000,000 for Imperial Oil Canada and $3,554,668,000 U.S. for Union Carbide and $3,998,500,000 U.S. for E. I. Dupont de Nemours), it was often referred to as a petrochemical giant, because its ingenuity and technical brilliance made it appear so. Polymer built up one of the largest industrial research facilities in Canada. By the time its laboratory was completed, in 1953, only 10 years after production began on an emergency basis during the war, it already had a proven reputation in both creative and control chemistry, and an impressive list of firsts to its name.

But it is for another reason that Polymer's research is important to the culture of crown corporations. The knowledge of polymer chemistry and the technical expertise gained in one field (synthetic rubber) was used to create a separate division in another field (plastics) — making new work out of old, to borrow Jane Jacobs' phrase — and for the first time, simply by doing it, breaking out of the narrowing bounds which a negative view of public enterprise in the country had imposed on the entrepreneurial form, although that lesson may now be obscured as well by the subsequent change in Polymer's status.

Not untypically, J. J. Brown, in his search for ways of making risk capital available to new technology, overlooked crown corporations, except to speculate on a crown-owned Canada Development Corporation by way of dismissing it. Brown contended that such a corporation wouldn't be suitable for the task because it would be "inevitably staffed by civil servants" who are "precisely the cadre of our society in which conservatism is most deeply ingrained." Didn't we come to that problem 50 and 60 years ago, and solve it (because we knew from previous experience we had to) precisely by creating crown corporations?

The problem was cast in the wrong terms anyway. Are federal or provincial government bureaucrats any more conservative than bureaucrats from private governments like General Motors, who nevertheless have large profits and little responsibility to shareholders, which allow them great leeway for being non-conservative? Brown was outspokenly critical of General Motors. And is the civil service necessarily conservative, or has it been made conservative by the roles it has been forced to play? As Brown himself seemed to recognize, the problem is not one of devices but of cultures. A dynamic culture creates appropriate devices as a matter of course, as the public enterprise culture in Canada has done. Nowhere in his 350 page discussion of invention and technology in Canada did Brown mention Polymer.

*   *   *

A different kind of example is the National Research Council, established in 1916 under the impetus of World War I. Permanent laboratories date back to 1932. Here the commitment came mostly from scientists, for whom private enterprise in Canada offered too little in the way of science, and bit by bit from Parliament, for whom private research in Canada offered too little in the way of creating new technology. It appears that even elements of the private business community recognized the need for government involvement; research in private industry was abysmally weak.

During World War II, defence research in the U.S. was contracted out to private industry and universities. In Canada, assigning defence research to private industry would have been assigning it to oblivion. The NRC blossomed. Again, an aspiring culture had created its own devices.

Quebec, shaking off its economic passiveness, also turned to public enterprise. A centre of industrial research (CRIQ) was established. The call went up for a government scientific complex (". . . the only way of giving us the infrastructure of a technological society; without it, how will we make it to the year 2010?"). A "national" scientific research institute (INRS), oriented to economic development, was set up at the University of Quebec, combining advanced university programs with larger practical goals. *Le Magazine Maclean* proudly noted the registration of the first two patents by the research institute of Hydro-Québec (IREQ). A passionate, direct appeal for direct Quebec government involvement in setting up an "industrial research laboratory" and other scientific facilities to aid industrial innovation had in fact been made back in 1901 by Errol Bouchette, a pioneering commentator on French Canadian political economy (Bouchette cited government expenditures on railways as a precedent!).

When the controversy about Canada's nuclear reactor program came out into the open, an engineering executive (not with AECL but with Canadian General Electric) told *Maclean's* (September, 1970) that "Canada must do some of these things, even if we fail. We must do them, or we'll never do anything."

"How do you jettison [the heavy-water reactor system] before you've proved it, before you've found out if Canadian engineering and Canadian talent can produce?" exclaimed George Gathercole, chairman of Ontario Hydro. ". . . No! We have a hell of a lot at stake, and we're backing our faith with our money."

We do these things because we must, and we must do

them because we're Canadian. Could there ever be a stronger reinforcement to act on an idea?

(2)   Where a public enterprise touches on the identity of an individual himself, as it often does in Canada, and takes on the force of community, profit motivation, as an incentive to efficiency, is eclipsed. This same motor in public enterprise can also work as an antidote to bureaucracy and red tape. What is, in entrepreneurship in Canada, is often the opposite of what is seen to be by Canadians.

Sometimes this cultural strength shows itself in small ways. When the CNR's and CPR's passenger trains were both blocked by a snow slide in the Fraser Canyon several years ago, the CPR's dining car charged regular prices for additional meals and many passengers, caught short of money, went hungry. The CNR across the river fed everybody for nothing. "No one on the train had any authority to give away meals," explained a CPR official. "The only person who can do that is the superintendent, and communications had broken down." Ron Haggart, who recounted this incident in *Saturday Night* (April, 1969), concluded that "more than anything else, [it] eloquently demonstrated which railroad was the rigid bureaucracy, and which was the responsive and flexible enterprise."

At the time, the CNR was in the middle of an imaginative effort to revitalize transcontinental passenger travel — a national service with social and historical roots in the railway and the country at large. But one could cite counter-examples. What happened in the Fraser Canyon was only an incidental illustration of a larger phenomenon.

The incentive for Hydro-Québec to perform efficiently and imaginatively, for example, and the cultural pressure on it to succeed, is a constant, and touches indirectly on all employees, because Hydro-Québec has become an economic symbol of French-Canadian self-respect. ("All those who visited the construction sites of the various dams of this complex, and the larger public who were able to admire, during Expo 67, by television, the work on Manic 5 [renamed the Daniel Johnson Dam] experienced a legitimate feeling of pride in the fact that these gigantic installations were the work of a Quebec enterprise and of French-Canadian specialists," in the words of *Le Devoir.*)

Merrill Denison, in his history of Ontario Hydro, concluded that Ontario Hydro had a decisive advantage in motivation and efficiency over private corporations, stemming directly from its public enterprise ethic — *Dona Naturae Pro Populo Sunt* (the Gifts of Nature are for the People). ("My business . . . suffers," admitted Adam Beck, "but it is my own. The Hydro's is the people's. It is too big to be neglected." The young engineering cadres, for their part, worked interminable hours meeting and solving the novel problems of the new technology, to keep Hydro moving forward.) Also, as Denison points out, public participation (in Hydro's history, mostly through the municipal hydro commissions) — "those very principles of public ownership that were so virulently attacked as being inimical to efficient and honest administration" — proved to be a contributing factor to success.

Both cases are reminiscent of the climate surrounding the CNR in its early days, and surrounding crown corporations (the CNR, Trans-Canada Air Lines, the National Research Council, Research Enterprises Limited and Polymer) during the war, the same phenomenon D'Arcy Marsh sensed, but did not altogether grasp, when he wrote of the CNR in the 1920's that "the people as a whole . . . exerted a shadowy but insistent pressure" upon the railroad's operations.

Similarly, a British air transport economist who did a study of TCA in 1958, cited at the head of a list of reasons for the airline's efficiency, the establishment of "an internal tradition that it has a special responsibility as the national airline." (See Chapter 8 for a more detailed analysis.)

In the case of Northern Transportation, which moves cargo to the western Arctic, the crown corporation had to overcome its private competitors *and the politics and culture of private enterprise* in order to follow its own public enterprise ethic and reduce prices, whereas private enterprise overcomes or comes to a working arrangement with its competitors, in order to follow its own ethic of raising profits, which may mean raising prices.

The strange debate surrounding Northern Transportation contains its own upside-down clues to our aptitude for public enterprise, and to our ingenious habit of denying it with absurdities. Although Northern Transportation had always operated at a profit, a proponent of private enterprise declared in the House of Commons in 1953 that it had outlived its usefulness and that it should no longer compete, with the aid of subsidies (which it wasn't receiving), with privately owned transport. Later, Northern Transportation was accused in the House of overcharging, and thereby slowing development of the North. Called before a parliamentary committee, the president explained that Northern Transportation had reduced its rates, but had then been accused of putting its competitors out of business. It was disclosed that one of the competitors who could not compete had asked the government for permission to submit a program to purchase it (presumably with profits accruing from the elimination of competition). Eventually, the privately owned competitors threw in the towel, and by 1966 Northern Transportation had reduced its rates to 40 per cent below maximum permissible levels for the Mackenzie basin, and 25 per cent below for the Arctic coast — these maximum levels set by the Board of Transport Commissioners between 1948 and 1951.

The efficiency is in the culture, not in the counting house.

(3) The third indicator of a lively practical culture is entrepreneurial zest — the enthusiasm which the culture generates for imaginative practical activity. This is the heart and soul of entrepreneurship, in both the narrow sense of the word and as it exists in the "mature corporation." It is what distinguishes a modern, change-oriented society from a

traditional one. Without it, even the basic problems of providing adequate food and shelter can be overwhelming, and all of society languishes. But with it, even the saddest cases of poverty of body, and poverty of mind, have been overcome.

We know that this kind of entrepreneurial motivation is culturally induced. Raw lust for gain or luxury doesn't make for entrepreneurial vigour, only for greed. Karl Weber's classic prototype of rational free enterprise man was the psychic inheritor of a rare cultural evolution which made him work hard not for the pleasures of wealth, which he couldn't allow himself to enjoy, and which he didn't know how to enjoy, but for the sake of the acquisitive activity itself − a conditioned and most unnatural habit. The lust for personal wealth and luxury does not explain, either, the entrepreneurial thrust of some change-oriented societies outside the western tradition, like China.

The mightily rich man who buys pleasure with the increment on his wealth − a commonplace in history − is the antithesis of entrepreneurial man in any system who reinvests the increment on wealth. Wealth as the guarantee of personal economic security − one of man's most natural pursuits − is also the antithesis of sustained entrepreneurship. Once a certain level of security is arrived at, entrepreneurial creativity stops. The businessman or the shareholders sell their interest. Or they don't bother to expand, or to innovate, because the effort and risk required add so little to the security already achieved, and might even put that security in jeopardy. But entrepreneurs, like artists, go on and on, and what makes them go on is something else again.

With few exceptions, the private enterprise culture in Canada has been a feeble generator of the kind of entrepreneurial zest that marks a dynamic, modern society off from a stagnant one. The sale, by indigenous private enterprise, of a large part of the country's manufacturing and mining, and above all the innovative capacity that might have gone with it, is demonstration enough. Even model private Canadian organizations have shown this unimaginative passiveness. Power Corporation, for example, the much discussed holding company, was either unable or unwilling to hold off the sale of Canadian Oil Companies (White Rose) in which it had a leading interest. And if Power Corporation had been an entrepreneurially creative organization, would Maurice Strong, the young wonder of private enterprise, have left it in his mid-thirties for public service, notwithstanding the fact that Strong always had his heart in public service, which is a revealing clue in itself? (Strong, while still president of Power Corporation, argued for a Canada Development Corporation to prop up an inadequate private enterprise for world competition, but did not stay at Power Corporation long enough for anybody to notice the irony. At the time, 1965, the argument was put to a small group of private enterprise participants calling themselves the Ticker Club, on whom, I suspect, all irony would be lost.)

Checking on Peter Newman's entrepreneurial prototypes, who "viewed the free enterprise system as a beneficial discipline, foreordained to reward the most able," and investigating their various works, we discover that in Canada the discipline may be weak and not necessarily beneficial.

E. P. Taylor's Canadian Breweries, the model of acquisitive manipulation, had no entrepreneurial issue and was sold out to foreign interests (although E. P. Taylor, not having applied new technology or brought new industry into being, was not a creative entrepreneur in the first place). Gunnar Mining Ltd., Gilbert Labine's corporate vehicle, and one of the magic names on the stock market during the 1950's, got bogged down with a construction subsidiary, and was sold out to foreign interests, without issue. Lionel Forsyth's Dosco (the product of Herbert Holt's merger skills) was sold out to foreign interests and then disintegrated, except for what was recovered and regenerated by Sydney Steel (Sysco) and Sidbec, both public enterprises. Harry Oakes' Lake Shore Mines was mined out without further issue. The remains are apparently controlled by a man living in Red Bank, New

Jersey. ("Oakes could easily have fathered a Canadian mining complex of unprecedented scope," wrote Newman. "But he allowed instead his tremendous wealth and influence to follow in the blunt pursuit of his pleasures. . . . His fortune established, he lost all interest in mining.")

Of Herbert Holt's corporate empire, Montreal Light, Heat and Power was taken over by the Quebec government in 1944. Dosco was sold out and went under, as we have seen. Control of Famous Players and Holt, Renfrew Ltd. was sold out. Control of Canada Cement also eventually was sold out. The Royal Bank of Canada flourished, among other things by financing the selling out of Canadian enterprise and withholding on Canadian innovation. Dominion Textile and Consolidated Bathurst (after Consolidated Paper) remain under Canadian control.

Holt, however, like E. P. Taylor, never was an entrepreneur in the innovative sense. It is this weak cultural legacy which is of interest to us here. Holt's corporate masterpiece, Montreal Light, Heat and Power, was a model of passivity — technologically backward, parasitical, displaying an appalling engineering weakness, and most serious of all, maintaining high rates and a rigid market to protect overreaching profits instead of lowering rates and creating new uses and demand, as did Ontario Hydro. The development of the huge water powers of the St. Lawrence and lower Ottawa Rivers was retarded. So was the industrial development of Quebec.

Holt was on the other side from men like Adam Beck or Henry Ford. .

It's not surprising that Newman, who mistook Holt's financial cleverness for a "phenomenal mastery of the entrepreneurial art," should, in the same book, have described Canada as "one of the world's economically most animated nations" in a period, 1959, when the country was sinking into perhaps the most passive and colonial stage in its economic history — culturally imitative and dependent as regards entrepreneurship, selling out enterprises, losing control of large reserves of natural resources — what is now seen clearly as "incipient stagnation," to borrow a phrase from the Senate Committee on Science Policy.

That's the legacy.

The indigenous public enterprise culture, in the colony, persists, however, in keeping its own, submerged momentum going.

Pierre Elliott Trudeau's father sold out to Imperial Oil, but Hydro-Québec remained intact to profit by the entrepreneurial energy of a new generation. Sidbec and other Quebec companies were launched in this post-war period. The St. Lawrence Seaway was built despite generations of U.S. stalling; Canada forced the issue by starting out alone. W. A. C. Bennett's public enterprise undertakings also occurred in this period.

The Manitoba government rejected a U.S. offer to buy the small crown-owned A. E. Mackenzie Co. Ltd. (125 employees), which nevertheless was the second-largest seed firm in Canada, because they "have enough confidence in Manitoba to believe we are capable of promoting and developing a few industries of our own"; a whole series of public enterprise initiatives got underway. The cultural attitude revealed in that particular declaration, however, is the important factor. The recent B.C. initiative in Canadian Cellulose had behind it some of the same entrepreneurial quickening and native defiance: the notion that British Columbians didn't have to leave themselves to the mercy of an ineffective absentee multinational corporation in New York. The public enterprise innovation in automobile insurance was also of particular cultural importance, and also involved a certain amount of repatriation. So, for that matter, did the rescues of Sysco and Ocean Falls, by default.

Similarly, in the wake of inroads into Canada's natural resources by foreign corporations, and large-scale alienation, public enterprise devices are now being seized upon. The Alberta government has committed itself to a natural gas exploration program in the Suffield block. As of this writing, the Ontario government has put forward for consideration new investments in energy, energy technology and exploration, not just in Ontario but also outside the province. The provincial minister (Darcy McKeough) discussing these possibilities, including the idea of a publicly owned petroleum company, was, until this juncture, a private enterprise dogmatist. Manitoba and Quebec already have small exploration companies in the field, and Saskatchewan is planning a crown corporation to participate in oil and gas exploration. "Private enterprise" nationalists, like Eric Kierans and Walter Gordon, can call for crown corporations on a massive scale (for all exploration and mining in Manitoba; to control all oil and gas development in the North) knowing that the entrepreneurial fibre is there to do the job that Canadian private enterprise can't do or won't do or shouldn't do.

The contrast at times runs even deeper. In a country which has come to accept, as a sorry fact of life, that it does not have the entrepreneurial cadres to develop its economy itself, mature crown corporations often have an entrepreneurial surplus, and are exporting entrepreneurial services.

*   *   *

In 1968 the CNR established an International Consulting Division to meet requests for help from foreign governments, international organizations and other railways. By 1970 the division was involved in work on four continents, from technical and management aid to complete railway reorganization, and had become a "profit centre" for the company. In 1971 the division was reorganized as part of Canac Consultants Limited, a joint venture with Air Canada to sell management and advisory services covering all aspects of air and surface transportation, hotel and telecommunications systems on a world-wide basis.

Polymer, finding itself with an excess of entrepreneurial talent in the late 1960's, applied it not only to diversification but also to increasing export sales of technical and administrative synthetic rubber expertise, often as part of licensing agreements, and in competition with other world leaders. Its 40 per cent interest in Hules Mexicanos S.A. was the result of an earlier licensing and design contract. (At one point, with a partner, Polymer did a feasibility study for improved production in Malaysia, the natural rubber heartland; they decided against the proposed facility, however, primarily because of the price at which latex was sold by the small rubber holders.)

Atomic Energy of Canada, as an integral part of its development, has been involved in collaborative programs with foreign agencies, also in international projects and in technical training arrangements for foreign scientists (aside from its development and collaborative projects with Canadian companies and scientists). The building of nuclear reactors abroad, as in the recent sale to Argentina, represents the export of a highly advanced entrepreneurial package, on a turnkey basis.

*   *   *

Usually the sale of private Canadian corporations to foreign interests is explained in quantifiable money terms, or in terms of brute mercantile power. The sale is made because the offer is so high as to be irresistible; because the buyer can write off some of the costs of acquisition against taxes; because a U.S. giant can provide ready access to the American and other foreign markets, or because it can provide certain technical expertise unavailable otherwise; because the Canadian company, after a strenuous entrepreneurial effort, finds itself having to expand to fill the market it has created, but can't raise the capital to follow through, whereas the U.S. company, even in the Canadian money market, has no trouble financing both the acquisition and the expansion. All these factors push forward the Canadian dialectic and create a greater commitment to public enterprise by Canadians in return.

But if, as I have argued, this dialectic has been at work continuously for 150 years, and if we never had an ideologically lively liberal capitalist society in the first place, and these two broad forces combined to weaken the private enterprise culture and strengthen the public enterprise culture, in the myriad, uneven, many-splendoured ways in which cultures develop over time — if that's the case, then there is another factor involved, a cultural factor, already long internalized in our temperament and inclination and social milieu, which, in the private enterprise context, manifests itself in a *non-quantifiable lack of entrepreneurial will.*

So a supposedly rational decision to continue or to sell out may be infected with human ambiguity.

Take the case of W. Freeman & Son Ltd., the largest manufacturer of lighting fixtures in western Canada, when it was sold to Sylvania Electric in 1966.

The history of W. Freeman & Son, Vancouver, British Columbia, is a classic private enterprise story. It was begun in 1931 by William Freeman, a Russian-born firescreen maker. Over the years, five competitors had packed up and left. By 1966 the company found itself with a semi-closed territory in western Canada, and was strong enough to fight off any challengers from the East. The biggest of these was Sylvania Electric, which had just acquired the largest lighting firm in Canada, in Montreal. Freeman & Co., besides doing its own designing, had many technical innovations to its name, including a unique machine for weaving fire-screen mesh. It was able to place orders as far away as Venezuela and was capable of handling the largest industrial contracts. In its last eight years, sales volume had expanded tenfold. It had never had a money-losing year.

Yet in 1966, the head office of the company's bank refused to increase credit to cover expansion. The president and owner, Arthur S. Freeman, believing "that you must fill the market available to you, or you are asking for someone to take away your leadership," decided to sell. The prospect of having to retrench while his market was expanding was intolerable to him. Sylvania, although it could not compete against W. Freeman & Son in the West, nevertheless had a hurtling mercantile power, and had no trouble raising the money.

On one level, then, we have another ironic instance of a backward, self-centred eastern bank sabotaging a western enterprise; of mercantile power again reaping the ultimate benefits of genuine enterprise; and of tight money stemming from pressures in the American economy, and the American war in Vietnam, causing the demise of a Canadian company to the benefit of an American one. This is the level on which the sale was reported.

But since all economic activity is infused with humanity, there is another level, the psychological level, where ambiguity creeps in, and where the culture in which the activity takes place becomes important.

There were choices.

First, the Canadian owner, instead of quietly accepting conservative central Canadian banking power, could have challenged it publicly, in a country, and in a province, where a challenge might have had an effect. The refusal of credit occurred in the middle of W. A. C. Bennett's campaign for a Bank of British Columbia. In fact, the establishment of the bank wasn't too far off. Bennett had always been against that kind of eastern financial power. An open challenge would not have found the owner without allies.

There was another more practical and obvious alternative — organizing W. Freeman & Son into a "public" company, and selling shares to the public at large to raise the necessary capital. The corporation whose shares are listed on the stock market is a paradigm of modern private enterprise. The merits of "going public" were great enough in this particular case that even after the Canadian entrepreneur had sold his company to Sylvania, he wasn't sure he had made the right decision. But in the end, the sale was made, and like a lot of other exceptional Canadians, the entrepreneur gave up the ascendant entrepreneurial function.

Why did he shy away from private enterprise's most

advanced and accomplished corporate form? Considering the liveliness and imagination of the company until then, this raises all kinds of questions about the culture in which it happened.

Compare this, and other cases where Canadian entrepreneurship has withdrawn from the game, to the history of Polymer Corporation as a crown company. According to the objective criteria of culture-free economics, Polymer should have collapsed in its early years and after. But it survived and flourished nevertheless, because of the subjective strength of the public enterprise culture surrounding it.

Polymer is an interesting case for another reason. Unlike most crown corporations, and unlike many large multinational corporations, it functioned in a highly competitive international market, generally kept out of bounds to Canadian public enterprise by prejudice. Polymer itself was an historical accident. If World War II had not occurred, creating an emergency need for synthetic rubber, and if it had not occurred to C. D. Howe that crown corporations were a dynamic entrepreneurial form, Polymer would not have occurred either.

If, also, Polymer's sale to the Canada Development Corporation — destined for private ownership — adds a touch of irony to its public enterprise past, so much the more instructive our appreciation of what that past involved.

There were three different stages in Polymer's history where, with not too much imagination, one can visualize its closing its doors or selling out, had it been a privately owned Canadian company.

The first took place at the end of the war when Polymer found itself with a plant that had to sell 40,000 tons annually just to break even, with a maximum domestic market of only 20,000 tons. The United States had 50 plants of its own. Natural rubber was still superior in quality to synthetic rubber, and was again available. Most expert opinion wrote off Polymer's peacetime prospects as non-existent.

Instead of giving up, however, the men in charge of

Polymer launched the company on an adventurous export program in Europe, to create a market for its surplus, and on a bold technical program at home, to improve its product. That seems ordinary enough now, looking back on it, but at the time, it was an unconventional longshot. In 1947, Polymer barely managed to sell the necessary 40,000 tons, and earned a negligible pre-tax profit of only $25,000. Earlier, when the war ended, the government would have welcomed a buyer, but there were no bids.

The second crucial stage came in 1960. U.S. plants had been turned over to private companies in 1955 and had moved heavily into the world market. Polymer, with export sales of 108,000 tons (compared to U.S. exports of 342,000 tons) was stretching its capacity. It had to expand, or lose its momentum. This is the point at which we have come to expect Canadian entrepreneurship to surrender, and where, in those years, surrender was almost automatic.

All the arguments for selling out applied to Polymer as well, and were made. Private business leaders declared that Ottawa should have divested itself of Polymer long ago. They argued that American producers had created excess capacity and were pushing world prices down, and that Polymer on its own would be forced to the wall. Prices had already been cut and profits were falling. The creation of the Common Market threatened Polymer's sales in Europe to which it was heavily committed. The chairman and president of Goodyear Tire & Rubber Co. of Canada (Polymer's wartime president, as it happened) declared that "it's late, but not too late for private owners to control the situation," and allowed that Goodyear "might be interested in participating in ownership." The *Financial Post* reported much bitterness among "officials close to the industry" over Ottawa's failure to follow the American lead and turn over synthetic rubber plants to private interests. An oil company official remarked that it was "typical that the government, unable from Ottawa to understand the complexities of this business, is only now considering the future of Polymer when the future looks pretty gloomy" (although the government, from the same Ottawa, was able to understand "the complexities of this business" pretty well in 1942).

The clincher seemed to be that despite Polymer's "world-wide reputation for leadership in rubber research" and its remarkable sales organization and profit record, there was, as the *Financial Post* was told, "a great deal of complex technological know-how involved in keeping Polymer success-ful and growing," and "only companies in the petrochemical industry can handle this large proposition — and it may be too big for any one company." Under Polymer, "the good management and research team built up over the years" would be stifled. More scope was necessary to expand its range of products. Unlike most of the American synthetic rubber plants, which were tied to other oil, chemical or rubber interests which bought their production, and which could fund their expansion, Polymer, like an orphan, was all alone in the world. Like other sensible Canadian orphans, it should have been looking for an American family.

For all of the outside interest, and record profits, as it happened, Polymer in 1960 was a questionable private enter-prise buy, whose market value was already being discounted. It is doubtful that anybody would have paid the high replacement price, knowing that a considerable expenditure had still to follow for expansion, when the world sales picture for rubber was cloudy and growing cloudier.

That makes Polymer's entrepreneurial leap of 1960 all the more astounding to the Canadian mind. The government in Ottawa, which was "unable" to understand, and which, at the time (the Diefenbaker years), was full of suspicion of public ownership and belligerent memories of C. D. Howe, nevertheless backed Polymer's plans for production abroad (contradicting previous assumptions about what "top-level opinion" had been). Roughly $50 million was spent on an additional unit in Sarnia and two units in Common Market countries, equalling the total original investment for the company. A new international marketing organization was established in Fribourg, Switzerland. Joint ventures were entered into in Mexico and South Africa (the latter interest since disposed of). Sales continued to rise. Net income held at high levels. Polymer not only survived the "jungle war" competition, which so alarmed the *Financial Post*'s informants, but was strong enough to repudiate the jungle war itself (see below).

Polymer showed its entrepreneurial independence in another way. One of the arguments in 1960 for selling the company to a large multinational firm was its alleged inability to expand the range of its products. Polymer, in fact, had been offering a wider range of synthetic rubbers than any other plant in the world. It was simultaneously argued that Polymer had to specialize more in order to keep its prices competitive, because in the U.S. most of the variant rubbers were being turned out from specially constructed units. Polymer, being the master of its own technology, rather than the servant of a parent company's technology, was able to maintain its product range and keep prices down at one and the same time. Not long after, Polymer branched out into plastics, using a polymerization process developed by itself at home.

The third important development came in the late 1960's, when Polymer, with 10 per cent of the world's synthetic rubber market — a maximum figure since most industrialized countries were now also producing synthetic rubber — found itself unable to expand any faster than the market itself. In such situations, several possibilities are open. The company can sell out to a giant mercantile power, where its potential for expansion might be better utilized. Or the company can gain more of the market by itself acquiring complementary subsidiaries at the going rate, which Polymer did to a limited extent. The other possibility is to open up new fields, and to finance the diversification not by merging with a larger company and using its resources and credit, but on the strength of administrative and technical vigour.

Polymer chose this last alternative. It reorganized its

administration, creating a new corporate development branch, and in 1970 announced its entry into industrialized housing (based on chemically stressed concrete modules) and into computer time-sharing, in both cases under licensing arrangements with U.S. companies, by which Polymer retained corporate independence. While profits the previous year had gone up $6.8 million (to $13.8 million), the new development program pushed capital spending from $9.1 million to $29.3 million. There was no problem with money.

Shortly after, however, Polymer found itself in a situation similar to the one in 1960, except this time the new competition came from countries like Japan. A reduction in work force was necessary. Citing competitive export selling, rising costs of energy and feedstocks, pressures of inflation, the increase in the value of the Canadian dollar, and a ten-year downtrend in prices (all the plagues of their world), the company reported only a nominal profit for 1971. By the fixed considerations of prices, markets and profits in synthetic rubber, Polymer's future did not look promising. By the different, cultural considerations of entrepreneurship and adaptability, and the development of new fields and new technology, on the other hand, Polymer was just beginning to explore its full potential.

By mid-1972, when Polymer was sold to the CDC, its profit position was already showing recovery.

*   *   *

The most notable offer for purchasing Polymer in those years was made in 1959 by Ventures Ltd., a subsidiary of McIntyre Porcupine, and largely a holding company drawing its main dividend income from stock in its own subsidiary, Falconbridge Nickel. Ventures' president was once also president of Polymer.

We know, of course, what happened to Polymer. But what happened to the prospective buyer, which considered itself a proper, viz. a private enterprise, vehicle for Polymer's potential?

In 1961-62, Ventures merged with Falconbridge amid public and newspaper cynicism, in which the Toronto Stock Exchange temporarily suspended trading in Ventures stock, claiming misleading statements by a Ventures executive. Falconbridge is now controlled by McIntyre Porcupine (37.1 per cent interest, Dec. 31, 1972). McIntyre Porcupine is controlled by the Superior Oil Company and its subsidiary Canadian Superior Oil Ltd. (39.4 per cent, Feb. 28, 1973). Superior Oil Company's general office is in the First City National Bank Building, Houston, Texas.

*   *   *

What lay behind Polymer's exceptional vigour in those challenging and unusual days?

When I first took an interest in crown corporations, what now seems crashingly obvious had not occurred to me: that in Canada there was a public enterprise culture equivalent in role to, and stronger in historical force than, the private enterprise culture of puritan, acquisitive individualism in the style of K. C. Irving and Roy Thomson, and of financial cliques like Power Corporation and Argus Corporation. I knew that in large privately owned corporations with widespread ownership there was little upward pressure from shareholders. I knew also that crown corporations had performed generally well, and that in the case of Polymer, which by accident was in the profit-making sector, public ownership was financing its own expansion. And I knew that there was virtually no interference in Polymer's operation from the company's owners — the people of Canada through their federal government.

It seemed to me that in the same market, subject to the same economic forces, and dependent on the same profits, a crown corporation would perform in exactly the same way as a privately owned management-controlled corporation. If this were the case, then our prejudice against public ownership, and particularly against letting it participate in the profit-making manufacturing sector, would be totally irrational, all the more so considering the poor record of Canadian private capital in funding new, technologically advanced enterprises. It was just this prejudice against public ownership that I was interested in debunking.

I expected, then, to find Polymer in what I conceived of as a world of "bureaucratic anarchy," populated by many other corporations as well, responsible not at all to their passive shareholders, and motivated to passionate effort and creativity by the objective considerations of the game alone. In that case, it didn't make any difference to performance who owned the corporation. It might as well be the crown as anybody else, and theoretically, it could be nobody at all.

I wasn't the only one in that frame of mind. In a free-wheeling article on Polymer in 1966, Otto Scott, the editor of *Rubber World*, a U.S. trade 'magazine, suggested that Polymer could retire or purchase the government shares "if the atmosphere permitted," which, taken literally, would leave Polymer owned by itself — an entrepreneurial flying machine hurtling through corporate space, beyond the gravitational pull of any ownership. Scott quoted a Canadian official describing proprietary crown corporations as "private enterprise with public accountability." The accent, in Scott's appreciation, was on the "private." The real value of Polymer's "public accountability" was that it demonstrated, to him, that it was possible for the U.S. government to assist a private enterprise without stifling it to death with controls.

In addition, most of the members of the board of directors were from private corporations. Polymer also was a "multinational" corporation, with subsidiaries, joint projects and sales offices abroad. Its original technology had come from U.S. companies during the war. Not only did Polymer appear no different from a privately owned corporation, it appeared no different from a non-Canadian one.

But Polymer was different, as the editor of *Rubber World* realized, and as the *Financial Post* and Polymer's neighbours in Chemical Valley probably always knew. Reading the old newspaper clippings and the articles about the company, one quickly senses from the details that Polymer evolved in exceptional ways — ways that can't be explained in terms of Canadian private enterprise (which turned its back on Polymer after the war), nor in terms of the world of the multinational firm (which was blind to, or chose not to see, Polymer's creative momentum in the uncertain days of 1960), but only in terms of the subjective impulse of Canadian public enterprise, if that evolution can be explained properly at all. Even in the relatively remote world of the international synthetic rubber market, the Canadian dialectic inside Polymer showed itself (which also suggests that the "neutral" multinational firm is a scholastic hoax; can any organization of men be without culture and prejudice; and if it were, would it still be alive?).

One of Polymer's U.S. competitors is reputed to have fed the salient facts about the company into a computer in order to project its future and the computer predicted bankruptcy. The men who programmed the computer, of course, weren't Canadians, and weren't in public enterprise. They were bureaucrats from another culture, and missed the point.

Otto Scott, in his *Rubber World* article, in recounting the story, remarked that they failed to program on the men. But that's only begging the question. It's true that Polymer had an unusual stability at the top. The handful of men who led the enterprise out of the war, including E. R. Rowzee who designed the original plant and was president until 1971, stuck with the company through thick and thin. Polymer was their creation, from the beginning. But the man who sold out W. Freeman & Son was also there at the beginning of his company, and had also seen it through the embryonic stage into a technically capable, commercially tough organization. The same can be said for many other cases where Canadian companies have sold out to American ones. The question still remains: What was there in the culture of Polymer that engendered such loyalty and maintained it?

Polymer, unlike the others, was created in a context of

high national purpose – World War II. "Born in war, matured in emergency, managed by men who have cast their own destinies into the survival of the company . . ." was how *Rubber World* described it, using the language of melodrama. Wars end, of course, and the high collective purpose of war falls off. But World War II was also a great age of Canadian public enterprise – of wartime economic administration, of defence production, of long CNR trains trundling towards Halifax, of the quick coming of age of Trans-Canada Air Lines, of radar and nuclear technology, of C. D. Howe pulling crown companies out of a hat – an age when Canadians came to sense that they had an economic genius of their own, over and above growing wheat and cutting down trees. This was the legacy which seems to have inhered in Polymer's culture.

Rowzee, an American on loan from Goodyear Tire & Rubber, resigned from his company and his country, and took out Canadian citizenship, because he felt, even at that stage, there were better opportunities in Canada to develop synthetic rubber. The man who was to become vice-president, finance, left the U.S. Petroleum Administration for War. The future research and development vice-president left Imperial Oil. Rowzee, a graduate of the Massachusetts Institute of Technology, had headed Goodyear's own synthetic program, begun in 1935. Has Canada's economic culture ever had that kind of drawing force before or since, except in another period of ascendant public enterprise, the building of the CPR? When Rowzee joined a group of technical people from the United States and Britain investigating German synthetic rubber plants as they were taken over, he went as a member of the Canadian, not the U.S., army.

As with Macdonald and the CPR, Howe saw Polymer not simply as a viable enterprise, or a wartime exigency, but in terms of economic nationalism – as the possible basis of a petrochemical industry in Canada. Debating the status of Polymer, in the House of Commons, in 1943, Howe announced that it was "the intention of the Government to continue to operate the plant at Sarnia to make rubber for the country at war and the country at peace." Later, American inroads into the Canadian economy became a factor. The sale of a non-strategic privately owned Canadian company to American interests was considered neither here nor there, but in 1960, when the possibility of Polymer's disposal was again raised, the economic nationalism in the commitment to Polymer became visible again. Many of the potential buyers, as the *Financial Post* acknowledged, were large foreign-controlled firms which might terminate both Polymer's independence in marketing and its Canadian character. Hence the federal government's reluctance to sell, in the past, and its decision not to sell, again in 1960.

Rubber World intuitively made this connection between U.S. control of Canadian industry and the crown corporation as a means of offsetting it, and between "Polymer of Canada" and the indigenous Canadian spirit, seen most particularly in the uniqueness (taken in its unique context) and the aptness of the entrepreneurial form. There was, in Polymer, a quiet psychological link between its performance and public ownership . . . always a shadow of combativeness in defence of its indigenous mystique. With just a hint of pride, Rowzee told the *Globe and Mail* in 1969 that while many North Americans attach a certain stigma to government-owned companies, in Europe such companies are viewed as assets, and this has been helpful to the company there. Rowzee and the others at Polymer were quick to point out that the company received no overt subsidies, and no hidden subsidies either, that in its capital borrowing, there was no co-signer, and that it paid the same taxes other companies paid. "It has a dedicated and highly motivated group of people," Rowzee told the *Globe and Mail* (a "stubborn determination" was how *Rubber World* put it), "and some of their motivation derives in part in demonstrating that a government-owned company can be successful."

Created by public enterprise, Polymer also endured and excelled in public enterprise. Over and above that, it manifested, in its operations, a recognizably Canadian public enterprise style (and demonstrated, incidentally, that it might be possible to create a community of interest among the supplier of raw materials, the producer of goods, and con- sumers, without rapacious vertical integration). The best single adjective for it is "civilized" — a civilized style which, in Polymer's case, stemmed in part from the ambiguous character of Canadian nationalism itself.

Clues are found in Polymer's export and subsidiary policy in Europe. Instead of greedily exploiting Europe's shortage of materials after the war, Polymer decided, first of all, to sell in Europe only through Europeans, and secondly, to educate Europe to the uses and applications of synthetic rubber, no matter what the commercial advantage in making quick sales (which is reminiscent of Ontario Hydro's campaign to educate the public in the uses, and safe use, of electricity). Polymer also left its European agents free to handle products from other companies so they would never have to choose between Polymer and fellow nationals. At one point, when some U.S. producers were dumping synthetic rubber in Europe, and arousing bitter resentment in European rubber circles, Polymer actually raised its price in defiance, and most of its customers stayed with it. Overseas customers were also loyal during a 97-day strike in 1959. Rowzee, the naturalized Canadian, told *Rubber World* there was a cultural link — a closeness between Canadians and Europeans, in counter- distinction to the "great gulf" Americans feel between themselves and Europeans (presumably a gulf stemming from mutual ethnocentrism, and unbridgeable by the bureaucratic devices of trade and subsidiaries alone).

It is of the paradoxical quality of the Canadian contradictions that Canadian nationalism, in its sensitivity to economic imperialism, should have made Polymer more international in bearing; and that public enterprise, which the American-ideology-in-Canada stigmatizes as bureaucratic, should have been a subterranean but nonetheless continuous (because cultural) force keeping bureaucracy at bay, even in that most "private" of public enterprises, and when its privately owned American counterparts were and are giving way to bureaucratic habits.

The compelling force of our public enterprise culture manifests itself in other ways. Rowzee, like Van Horne, becomes the compleat Canadian. Henry Thornton, also an American private businessman by background, becomes such an outspoken advocate of the spirit of public enterprise, after his tumultuous, heartbreaking stint with the CNR, that his biographer feels obliged to apologize for him. Although also a private businessman before and after, R. B. Cameron, while chairman of Sydney Steel, attacks private companies which shirk responsibilities to society, and declares that government must take them over. In another era, Adam Beck, a conservative cigar box manufacturer, becomes so committed to the public ownership principles of Ontario Hydro, that he calls for public ownership of the telephones and the railways, and wonders out loud "why the people do not awaken to their rights."

The same mechanism touches on politicians, often despite their politics. In a speech in the House of Commons on uranium and the virtues of free enterprise, John Diefenbaker finds himself headlong in a romantic appreciation of the work of Atomic Energy of Canada and, indirectly, of Eldorado Mining. C. D. Howe instinctively interrupts to claim "a victory for public enterprise." Diefenbaker replies that he knows of "no one who, in his own life, represents more the activities of private enterprise and all it means and the benefits that it extends" than does Howe. Then, in making his case for private enterprise, Diefenbaker goes on to analyze and to praise the public enterprise initiatives during the war, and to call for greater state participation.

W. A. C. Bennett, in putting down a rumour that the PGE (B.C. Railway) was for sale to the federal government, describes the railroad as "one of our main enterprises for developing our province," and declaims that the PGE "is part of the great public ownership" of British Columbia.

The culture becomes part of the men, as the men become part of the culture.

CHAPTER 6

Public Enterprise and Identity

There is the Canadian continuity, in its economic dimension, going back at least to 1820, and in its lack of a free enterprise system, going back to the first days of French settlement. The dialectic which gave it form — from out of the contradiction between the small Canadian market and the North American continent — is still operative, acting as ever as a forcing instrument of new public enterprise (of new forms of practical self-expression) and, as ever, fed by the nationalist impulse. There are other dialectics at work, stemming from the contradictions between French and English Canadas, and between the regions and the federal centre. These dialectics are also forcing instruments of new public enterprise (and in Quebec's case in particular, also of co-operative enterprise, which is a vigorous culture in itself and which, in the *caisse populaire* movement, has deep roots of self-assertion and definition).

These enterprises are not simply separate economic devices financed with public money. They are part of a dense, continuous economic culture, full of precedents and political history, and of accumulated knowledge about the proper relationship of economic organizations to the community.

This culture has within it the symbols of our practical life. These symbols are necessarily nationalist symbols, as well as symbols of technique; the public enterprise culture is the practical expression of Canadian nationalism, and of Canadian nationalisms. The culture is also, after all these years, and under great historical pressure, internalized in our collective temperament. There is a unique public enterprise style, or aspect, to Canadian life. This shows up in the economic culture, if we look for it, and in communications, which are linked to the economic culture. But beyond that, it inheres in our psyche in ways yet to be elaborated on, just as a growing sensitivity to cultural differences, arising out of the French-English contradiction, but going beyond it, also inheres in our psyche to a greater or lesser degree.

Now, there are two basic ways of describing Canada as an economic culture. If we describe it in terms of the inappropriate colonial ideology – the American-ideology-in-Canada – we see it as some kind of free enterprise country. We judge it whether consciously or not in terms of that American mystique. And no matter all the exhortations and all the drum-beating about the free enterprise Canadian way of life, and all the assurances of scholars and chambers of commerce and all the rhetoric of politicians; no matter, also, our own immediate experience, in which Canadians seem to be capable, and even imaginative – no matter all that, and our own self-esteem, we can't escape the feeling that Canadians are an imitative, second-rate people.

So that if, like the newspaper columnist, we write that "private enterprise . . . provides the muscle of our economic system" and that "Canadian progress and prosperity have been built and still thrive [on] the private enterprise system," we will inevitably also write, as he did, in fact, "Let the Americans show us the way. Like it or not, that's what our national prosperity was built on." Or, like another columnist, an admirer of the late Robert Winters, we will come to describe Canada as "lazy, ill-educated and unenterprising . . . trading its resources for the beads and baubles of superior peoples." Or we will see Canadians as "a timid people, afraid of ourselves and terrified by the demands of the real world," and inflicted with "a conservatism carried to the extreme of idiocy" (J. J. Brown in *Ideas in Exile*). And in terms of the prevailing American-ideology-in-Canada, we will be right.

Similarly, when an investment banker from Chicago, who manages high-risk venture capital, says that Canada is thin in "entrepreneruial background" and has "too many gaps in technological know-how" to create new industry on a sufficient scale, or when J. V. Clyne, the former chairman of MacMillan Bloedel, says that Canada is weak in first class corporate executives, we have to agree. For to see Canada across the colonial ideology (or, if you like, the imperial ideology) is to exclude the indigenous culture, where entrepreneurial strength is likely to be found, as the investment banker from Chicago did exclude it, or, when it can't be overlooked, dogmatically, masochistically to discount its significance and to denigrate its performance, as J. V. Clyne and most other Canadian spokesmen have discounted and denigrated it. This is an ideological matter, deeply rooted in colonial psychology: the American-ideology-in-Canada is so much with us that it becomes impossible to imagine, or to countenance, a most natural possibility — that a native economic culture should be more appropriate than a borrowed, imperial one.

Again, when René Lévesque reminds us that "apart from U.S. enterprise, it's been said unkindly that Canada is kept going mostly by the Communist world's temporary inability to grow enough wheat," the implication being that Canada has no practical dynamic of its own, reflecting an absence of real identity, and should therefore be dissolved, we will sense that he is wrong, and is not doing justice to the Canadian experience — but we will not have an answer.

The end effect of this familiar, deep-seated inferiority complex and habit of self-disparagement is to submerge the practical expression of our identity — to ashamedly lock it away in a subconscious closet — leaving us with local folklore and romantic dreams about the land, so that it really isn't out of line to claim that "we are almost carbon copies of the Americans now," or that there is "no major difference" between Americans and Canadians. We become nuanced, sometimes bicultural Americans, with occasionally eccentric habits, an "American alternative to what has happened in the United States," to repeat William Kilbourn's phrase.

The American-ideology-in-Canada downgrades the symbolism of Canada's practical life, along with the rich, suggestive culture behind it, which amounts to pushing into the background one of the most important ways – in English Canada's case, perhaps the most important way – the ordinary Canadian has of sensing his community's history and identity. "The role of the state in the economic life of Canada is really the modern history of Canada," wrote Alexander Brady, a Toronto political scientist, many years ago. Wipe out a nation's modern history, and you deny that nation its character.

But there is another way of looking at this same economic culture, the native way, in which the Canadian public enterprise tradition is seen in its own indigenous terms. And then Canadians appear altogether different – not as lazy, mediocre oafs, dependent on the efforts of others, and particularly incapable of starting new enterprises, but as a highly motivated, enterprising, imaginative, unusually determined community. The editor of *Rubber World*, for example, focusing on Canada across the crown corporation Polymer, and the projected Canada Development Corporation, and government economic initiative during World War II, just as inevitably comes to describe us as "the energetic Canadians, who seem nationally addicted to creating new corporate and governmental forms almost as a pastime."

Far from having no depth of entrepreneurial background, the public enterprise culture, in many cases, is rich in entrepreneurial cadres, as one should expect in this country. We discover that other nations industrializing late have leaned on us in their efforts to meet "the demands of the real world." Crown corporations like the CNR, Polymer (circa 1942-1972) and Atomic Energy of Canada are seen to be exporting entrepreneurial services.

Not only has Canada's economic culture a robust dynamic of its own, contrary to the impression René Lévesque has passed on – and it's an impression of all our making, not of his alone – but also, paradoxically, this very same public enterprise culture informs the practical dimension of the separatist impulse of René Lévesque and has, in turn, been enriched by it. In a sense, the province of Quebec, by partaking of and contributing to this economic culture, joined a Canadian mainstream that nobody suspected was there. But such cultural contributions defy measurement.

Once having cast aside the American-ideology-in-Canada, we become aware of this economic culture, and sense the continuity and community behind it. The symbolism comes alive. The unique spirit and mentality which it engenders is occasionally noticed in men, and in the historical records of men. And economic cultures being dense and rich by nature, identification with this Canadian experience takes on the sure "sense of being" characteristic of community.

Canada, in its essentials, is a public enterprise country, always has been, and probably always will be. Americans have, or at least had, a genius for private enterprise; Canadians have a genius for public enterprise. As long as we describe Canada in terms of the American model, we will continue to see ourselves as second-rate Americans, because we *are* second-rate Americans, not being Americans at all.

Conversely, once the powerful impulse of Canadian nationalism combines with a liberated public enterprise culture, Canada will experience a golden age of entrepreneurship, because nothing in modern times is quite so creative as practical self-discovery.

PART III

Colonial Ideology
Begets
Economic Masochism

CHAPTER 7

Mining Promotions as an *Exotic Example of the Colonial Economic Culture at Work (with Particular Reference to the Financial Hinterland)*

The American-ideology-in-Canada is neither American nor Canadian. It is a weird, inappropriate colonial graft. It is weird because it comes from another people's experience, or more precisely, from another people's experience that never really was, except in mythology, which makes the colonial graft doubly strange. It is inappropriate because it hides or discounts the Canadian identity, most of all its economic dimension.

Since problems of ideology touch the life of the people, there are practical consequences. The inappropriate ideology makes Canadians do foolish things in large ways, which costs them money — much money — and makes them look ridiculous in other people's eyes, and sometimes in their own.

Take the case of mining promotions, and their ideological background.

Canadians are berated for not financing their own economic development. In natural resource development, the pioneering vehicle traditionally open to them has been participation in mining promotions, and still is in the financial hinterland (Vancouver, Montreal) of the financial hinterland (Toronto). But mining promotions are illogical (as well as disreputable). They do not make sense, even as gambling. They have declined into a marginal economic phenomenon, which indeed they always were in the real world of exploration and development. They are, however, sustained on the edges of economic activity by an exotic strain of the colonial ideology. And mining promotions are only the most anachronistic and illuminating branch of the larger, backward colonial culture — the American-stock-exchange-culture-in-Canada. On the other hand, native public enterprise as a vehicle for exploration and development is put down by the colonial culture. Canadians continue to be berated for not financing their own economic development.

The illogicality of mining promotions is embedded in the promotional machinery itself.

According to pilot figures compiled for the Royal Commission on Banking and Finance (the Porter Commission) in 1964, only 18 per cent of the money invested in speculative mining stock, from 1953 to 1960, actually went into exploration and mining (including oil and gas) development. Also, since the companies involved did not, by and large, have the cost control apparatus of large corporations, that 18 per cent was probably not too well spent either. Indications are that in the interim, despite new regulations, the percentage has not become much more respectable. Perhaps as much as $2 billion or more has gone down the drain in Canada since the end of the war in this ancient form of mammonic worship.

There must be an explanation for such waste, over and above the larcenous spirit and uneven morality of the promotional world. And there is. The system is built on inefficiency. To get an ordinary promotion off the ground, a staggeringly high allocation of receipts goes into the sales structure, of proportions that most other businesses could not afford. What doesn't go into the sales structure may go into the pockets of promoters; the culture of speculative promotions puts a premium on unproductive manipulation. (A good description of how a promoter plans for, and takes a profit on, the eventual collapse of the stock, and how he often contributes to the collapse by doing as little as possible in the field, is found in *The Stock Promotion Business*, by Ivan Shaffer, 1967).

This grossly wasteful nature of the promotional structure is now a matter of wide knowledge, and is openly admitted, inside and outside the industry. Mining promotions, for the most part, develop only mining promoters. The mining is mostly the mining of the pockets of the public.

The promotional ritual itself is an irrationality. To finance the initial stages of exploration, the promoter must provide capital. To cover this outlay, he must sell hundreds of thousands of shares, at steadily increasing prices. To sell these shares, he must have some facts about the property which mark it off from others. But to get these facts, he must finance, in most cases, the initial stages of exploration. By the rules of logic, his job is impossible.

The promoter takes that as a given. His craft consists of circumventing logical impossibility by manipulating the irrational in the cultural make-up of his clientele. Technically speaking, he must not lie about the prospects. That would be fraud. But due to the shortage of meaningful news, cleverly concocted propaganda or rumour is considered fair practice (not to mention priming the market with clients or otherwise, to get some action going and draw in the "bigger suckers"). Such tolerance amounts to an institutionalized cheat allowance. By applying his art inside this cheat allowance, the promoter of a speculative, unproven property can function.

(Of course the ritual could be rationalized to eliminate first the waste, and secondly the deception. But there would be one side effect — nobody would buy any stock because, on the whole, it is impossible to differentiate the prospects of one unexplored claim from another. Without the manipulation of the investor's emotions, or the market, there is nothing. Except for a few softheaded addicts, the level of expectation would be low. The man interested in capital returns from mineral development would invest not in Dry Hole Oils but in Standard Oil of New Jersey, and the man with a weakness for gambling would go to the races, where, at least, he has a fighting chance and can get some fresh air. You cannot rationalize irrationality without rationalizing it out of existence.

(Restrictions by the Toronto Stock Exchange following the Windfall affair in 1964, and by the Ontario Securities

Commission, in an attempt to put at least some sense into the financing of mines, have had somewhat that effect. According to the *Toronto Star* (February 7, 1972) public interest in Toronto in mining promotions has become virtually non-existent.)

That is a description of legal promotions. Semi-legal and illegal promotions are something else again and, at the same time, intrinsically similar. Mining promotions in Canada have a long history of scandal and of underworld connections. Some of the dominant figures of the mining promotion boom after the war, like A. E. DePalma, were criminals on the run. Novel precedents in extradition law were established during this period. The most evocative, and accurate, descriptions of incident and character of this era are not found in back copies of the *Financial Post* but in court records, particularly in records of direct testimony. There were also some connections to the Mafia, and still are. Yet the craft being what it is, the line between legality and illegality is so thin as to be invisible. Promotions exist in the wrinkles of the law. Generally speaking, the whole of the promotional culture is a low culture.

And everybody knows it.

The riddle begins here. Given the systematized waste and illogicality of speculative mining promotions, why haven't we eliminated them? Imagine the uproar if, for example, four-fifths − or even one-fifth − of Canadians' tax money was spent on collecting the taxes, while the employees of the Department of National Revenue and the provinces were, as a group, badly trained, not very respectable, in some cases unsavoury, but nevertheless in a high income bracket, and if they justified all this by claiming that *they* were keeping Canada moving by making defence, justice, transportation, social welfare, etc. possible. Or imagine a situation where the costs of collecting health service payments, or United Community Services payments, were up to 80 per cent or 60 per cent or 40 per cent of gross receipts, not including the possible waste in distributing the remainder to various agencies, with not too scrupulous officers of their own to pay, and if the whole procedure functioned by an irrational mechanism that could not be reformed without destroying it; or if the pari mutuels at the race track — an honest-to-goodness gambling form — returned to winners only a half or a quarter of money wagered.

Daniel Defoe's angry declaration about promotions, in 1719, holds true to the letter here, ". . . that the government, looking upon them [the promoters] as they really are, rather enemies than friends to the general interest, should rather incline to root them out than preserve them." A rationalist, modern people would simply abolish the practice.

Let us envisage how an anthropologist from a contrary culture, like China or the ancient Canadian Arctic, or even from a proximate culture, like Israel or Sweden, would react to the situation.

First of all, he would be intrigued and delighted by such aberrant behaviour.

He would discover quite soon in his investigation that full knowledge of the impracticality and gross waste of the institution was not always a determining factor in attitudes towards that institution, even among the native people who put forward practicality as the leading principle of their society. He would also come across cases of inverse relationship between practicality and evaluation, in which natives pair a lucid appreciation of the sordid immorality of the institution with righteous "moral" approval of the institution.

He would, for example, record the case of the deposed provincial chieftain (W. A. C. Bennett) who, when political leader, prided himself above all on his acumen for public finance; who was and always had been personally scrupulous in economic transactions; who in his early career as hardware merchant had been as good a model as any of puritan, rational, capitalist man; who had reportedly scorned the practicality of mining promotions (telling the stock exchange in Vancouver that if 10 per cent of the money that went through Howe Street ever found its way into the ground,

B.C. would have a mining industry that would stun the world) — and under whose administration, mining promotions had been encouraged to proliferate in all their inefficient and manipulative wonder.

He would also record the case of the public relations man (Ivan Shaffer) who wrote an uninhibited, irrefutably damning exposé of the promotional culture; who came to the inevitable conclusion, in his own words, "that mining has little to do with mining stock" and, conversely, that mining promotions have little or nothing to do with mining, except for the mining of the small investor — and who ended by denying that his exposé was an exposé, and by righteously denouncing suggestions of eliminating, or even effectively reforming, the ritualized waste he had so conscientiously described.

Even in the patriarchal heartland (Ontario), where mining promotions were now publicly condemned, he would find that while they were persecuted in the principal market-place (the Toronto Stock Exchange), they were still legal and still philosophically upheld, and that, in fact, the primitive force at work was strong enough that new arrangements had been made by the authorities and the exchange to revive the speculative mining market.

The anthropologist would then come to his own inevitable conclusion that since his subjects in the field were aware themselves that mining promotions had little or no practical function, and since they nevertheless still kept promotions in their culture against their own most forceful reasoning, then the promotional subculture must have some totemic, spiritualist function. But by this time, he would also likely suspect that the natives were collectively pulling his leg, and he would pack up his dictionaries and go home.

But he would have been right; the main role of mining promotions in Canada is a spiritualist one.

One of the central symbols of the American-ideology-in-Canada is the stock market. Two of the venerable totemic figures who inhabit this symbolic stage are the bold, acquisitive promoter and the equally risk-taking and acquisitive investor — together bringing new enterprises into being — both idealized archetypes of what is imagined to be the American free enterprise spirit. Mining promotions are atavistic enough to give this totemism reasonable play, and are particularly important in hinterland areas like Vancouver, and to a lesser extent Montreal, where that mythic side of the stock exchange ritual would otherwise be weak or non-existent.

In this dying, back alley totemism — not in the performers (who are just cynical operators) but in the shadowy ideological backdrop which allows them to function — we discover also the roots of some of our own, larger economic superstitions.

Shaffer, for example, who is a worshipper, declares that "promoters are the quintessence of our capitalist society" and imputes to them a magical life force, without which, from what we can infer, the community would sink into an unrelieved lethargy. The more fanciful the procedure, the less its financial effectiveness, which is why the procedure should be eliminated, but also the more its spiritual effectiveness, which is why the procedure has not been eliminated. Shaffer's detailed, muckraking exposé might at the same time be a celebration, could even be principally a celebration, of the promotional culture, and on reading it, there is no mistaking, from the tone and the conclusions, that's exactly what it is.

The cultural implications go further. If we accept the ideological underpinning of mining promotions, no matter how much we dismiss the actual practice, we also accept a certain image of ourselves. Shaffer writes:

> [Promoters] are no more dishonest than anyone else. They just make money on a staggering scale. They may cheat more, but it's only because the stakes are bigger. And after all, how big a lie do you tell when you pad your expense account? Or if you are a secretary, and you take pencils and paper home? Or if you steal a

pound of butter from the supermarket? It is an everyday posture for people to lie and steal and cheat, even
themselves.

And also:

There is chicanery in the stock market. The politicians
have been able to convince the public that it was Wall
Street chicanery that caused the crash in 1929 and the
Great Depression. Since then they have been trying to
legislate what Wall Street represents out of existence.
The Communists for years have been trying to convince
us that the profit motive is bad. Their propaganda and
our own — pick up any newspaper and see if I'm not
right — seem designed to destroy the basic drive that
has given us whatever prosperity we have. That drive
is greed, self-gain, which in its fruition creates wealth
for everyone.

. . . from which we can infer that if greed is what animates
our practical life, and if the maximum of cheating and
chicanery is a sure indicator that the impulse is at work, then
those of us who cheat only occasionally, or in extreme
circumstances, can rightly be suspected of holding the country back, while those of us whose greed is only moderate
are doomed to do no better than moderate failure.

In a review in *Saturday Night* of a novel by Shaffer
dealing with the same subject, the reviewer more or less
concedes, and without any argument, that "subterfuge,
brazen lies and manipulation" are "at the very core of the
democratic capitalist method."

"This is the nitty gritty of the economic world in which
we live," she writes, "the sort of apparatus that makes our
society work." She points out she has no expertise in financial
matters. Her appreciation is that of an ordinary citizen, or so
it appears.

Such is the astonishing grip of dogma. For given the
faintest winds of empiricism — I mean by that, simple
observation — this whole superstructure of totemic beliefs
comes tumbling down.

Of all of the people in Canada, how many lie and steal and cheat every day, as part of their work function, and for the sole purpose of increasing their personal wealth? Mining promoters are, simply, unusually dishonest. The promoters Shaffer describes are so compulsively dishonest that they fit into a psychological category almost unto themselves.

More than that, "subterfuge, brazen lies and manipulation," far from being "at the very core of the democratic capitalist method," are subversive of it. Economies are cultures binding men to each other with common ties. Unscrupulousness tears them apart and weakens the culture. Over time, the unscrupulousness has to be subdued. The predatory pursuit of selfish interests leads most often only to chaos, as it did in 19th century America and in post-imperial China, and anywhere else and in any other time.

No complex culture of production and distribution can survive everyday lying and cheating and predatory gouging by the mass of the people. The attempt by U.S. governments "to legislate what Wall Street represents out of existence" is really an attempt to protect whatever capitalist value Wall Street has by legislating subversive cannibalism out of existence. Or to quote Max Weber: "The universal reign of absolute unscrupulousness in the pursuit of selfish interests by the making of money has been a specific characteristic of precisely those countries whose bourgeois-capitalistic development . . . has remained backward."

Where does that leave the quintessential spirit of capitalist society? Weber, who made a systematic search for the theoretical quintessence of capitalism, found its most lucid expression in the bourgeois maxims of Benjamin Franklin, for whom honesty, thrift, industry and respectability were the best policies. The essential capitalist man was "above all temperate and reliable," Weber discovered. Honesty and discipline in the lower ranks were perhaps the most important elements of all in capitalist society. The commitment to work was "the product of a long and arduous process of education," because the precapitalist worker, instead of being impelled to labour by greed, might stop working or slow down his rate of work as soon as he could possibly do so, according to what earnings he was accustomed to and what took care of his traditional needs.

But Weber took capitalism to mean the rational application of capital after profits, supported by a culture of rational economic conduct, and tied together by rational structures of law and administration — the whole overriding whatever magical and atavistic forces were left from traditional society. All modern economies which bring prosperity to the mass of the people strive after this rationalism. That is exactly capitalism's historical contribution to other cultures and new ideologies. Mining promotions, on the other hand, live in a debased strain of the magical and the irrational. Between the one style and the other, there is an unbridgeable cultural divide.

Honesty and conscientiousness are "the nitty gritty of the economic world in which we live." Mining promoters, as evoked by Shaffer, are just what they seem to be — unrepresentative of others, in various states of maladjustment, the quintessence only of lying and cheating and other predatory forms of behaviour. The "greed and lies" description of economic behaviour, and of human behaviour, which is meant to be, and which is often taken to be, hard-headed and realistic, turns out, after some ordinary observation, to be just the opposite. Once it generalizes from an aberrant remnant of society to society as a whole, it loses itself in woeful romanticism.

The inhabitants of the promotional culture like to recount its outrageous folklore and to project it outside themselves. They like to dwell on what they consider the irremediable greed of man. The illicit colour of mining promotions helps them to feel they are living in the real world of unprincipled opportunism as against the phoney world of idealism, which is how they interpret other behaviour. This is their only possible rationalization. They have to believe that we are all sons-of-bitches all of the time. And since they deal every day in other people's greed, and practise opportunism almost exclusively, they are able to go to their graves without having to admit otherwise.

The observations of life, and the emotional range, of the inhabitants of the promotional culture are circumscribed by their narrow routine. They live in a ghetto of cramped psychology. But why the same escapist sentimentality by people outside the promotional culture, particularly in Canada, whose essential practical expression is public enterprise, where greed and chicanery have always been taken as altogether negative factors?

Of all the various mythological strains that might be feeding this inverted romanticism, the most promising possibility seems to be the old-fashioned, nostalgic romanticism left over from the days of the American frontier and the settling of the continental United States, when there was, briefly, a no-holds-barred pursuit of gain, with economically profligate and humanly bloody results.

However, the practical life of the United States was not like that, and has not been like that since, and was not altogether like that at the time. As for the role of stock promotions in that legendary era, reports of their contribution have been greatly exaggerated.

But let's take a closer look, by going back to the beginnings of American private enterprise and retracing its development, parallel to the origins and development of Canadian public enterpise, already explored.

The mother-lode of the American entrepreneurial spirit was the "pleasing uniformity of decent competence" of the 18th century yeoman and his commercial counterpart, which so impressed sympathetic European observers (just as the pleasing uniformity of decent competence now impresses sympathetic outside observers of the new entrepreneurship in China). Honesty and conscientiousness were part of that American spirit. And ambition. So, however, was an uncanny aptitude and zest for the practical arts. Benjamin Franklin, publisher, inventor, middle-class philosopher, and Thomas Jefferson, lawyer, botanist, also an inventor and improviser (from mouldboard ploughs to decimal coinage), were models and symbols of the age.

The liberal capitalism of the Jacksonian era that followed did not subvert the practicality of America; it amplified it by making capital and opportunity available to the small capitalist, and by holding out the same possibility to the expectant capitalist, who was the rest of the country. In the Congressional session of 1823-24, at the beginning of the Jacksonian era, Daniel Webster observed: "Society is full of excitement: competition comes in place of monopoly; and *intelligence and industry* ask only for fair play and an open field" (my italics). In the midst of the era, in 1836, an immigrant saw America as "one gigantic workshop." "Business is the very soul of an American," he wrote. "He pursues it, not as a means of procuring for himself and his family the necessary comforts of life, but as the fountain of all human felicity."

At the same time, speculation in land and in banks flourished as the acquisitive ethic broke out from the old mercantile bonds. Franklin himself, in an earlier period, had apparently speculated in land in the Washington area. But this was an extension of the American spirit, not the basis of it. The great speculative promotions until then had come from other cultures, like mercantile England and royalist France. What did the spoiled, landed gentleman who threw away part of his inherited wealth in the South Sea Bubble have in common with the cunning and ambitious self-made farmer or merchant or banker of the Republic? Tocqueville and his contemporaries knew they were witnessing a new phenomenon, in America. Stock promotions were an old one.

As it turned out, the early American, looking out towards the frontier, showed himself to be the shrewd man the Republic had made him. He either embarked westward himself, or held back with his money until governments paved the way with subsidized railroads and other public works. Before 1840, no corporation was well enough known to establish credit with investors. Many ventures that had preceded government into "uncharted" territory — the approximate equivalents of our promotions — failed. Not until such crushing diseconomies of risk (including Indian wars) were taken care of by the state, and the psychological climate improved by government initiative, did the headlong expansion take place. Or, as in the case of the buffalo robe trade in the upper reaches of the Missouri, the frontier development, when it required eastern capital, drew on traditional sources, with the man in the field (the "free trader") linked to the merchant in the territory, and the merchant linked to the bankers of St. Louis and Chicago and beyond. Or as in the much earlier case of the legendary John Jacob Astor and the American Fur Company, an empire was founded on the primary capital accumulation of one man alone, acquired, in Astor's case, by alternate boldness and parsimony, and most of all by the hard work of himself and his wife.

This same combination of practical vitality and government largesse also underlay the explosive industrial growth of the latter half of the 19th century. Western wheat, mines, and iron and steel production — in fact the creation of a national market — were tied into the extension of the railroads which government had made possible. Not stock speculation, but the Civil War, and the publicly financed plunder it offered up, provided the basis of the new industrial capitalism, when government again — through lucrative contracts and lavish expenditures, and the floating of bonds and paper money ("greenbacks"), and subsidies, and protective tariffs — underwrote northern business and created a class of profiteers who were to become the new masters of the nation.

As always there was that characteristic inventiveness and technical aptitude — an acute, even irrational joy in technical progress as such. The production of a practical reaper by Cyrus McCormick was a revolution in itself. Then, later, came the telephone, typewriter, linotype, phonograph, electric light, cash register, air brake, refrigerator car and the automobile, and others, and their applications. Just as Franklin had owed his success as a printer to his close study of new machinery in London, Carnegie owed his empire in iron and steel to the master craftsmen at the original works of Kloman & Co. and the Keystone Bridge Company.

Also in the latter half of the 19th century, the classic, ordered, rational entrepreneurial spirit surfaced again, in its most dramatic form in John D. Rockefeller. Rockefeller, the archetypal embodiment of puritan acquisitiveness, once stated, "I believe the power to make money is a gift of God . . . to be developed and used to the best of our ability for the good of mankind; having been endowed with the gift I possess, I believe it is my duty to make money and still more money, and to use the money I make for the good of my fellow man according to the dictates of my conscience." Actually Rockefeller's "protestant ethic" had been present in most of the others all along, even in the most predatory of buccaneers, like Jay Gould, and even in the wildest days of coarseness, lawlessness and profiteering.

In outline, the Jacksonian period, which destroyed the "monopolistic" Bank of the United States and other corporate privileges of the ordered "American system," opened up the way in the market place for disorder and an unbridled lust for gain. With the California gold rush (1849), the Civil War (1861-65) and the settling of the West, the lid blew off. Frederick J. Turner's classic description of the frontier American, "strong in selfishness and individualism . . . pressing individual liberty beyond its proper bounds," applied back of the frontier as well. The frontier worked on, and shaped, the whole national character.

But as early as 1868 — only 20 years after the gold rush, which ushered in the "heroic period" of the first of the giant buccaneers, Cornelius Vanderbilt — the new economic rulers, in this case, the salt producers of Saginaw Bay, Michigan, were trying to force the lid down again and lock it and throw the key away, by forming a pool and controlling the market. John D. Rockefeller's first attempt to rationalize oil refining in the same way began in 1869. The frontier-like anarchy of the industry, from the guerilla fighting of drillers in Pennsylvania to the fluctuating charges of rail transport, intriguing as a romantic example of individualist grasping, struck Rockefeller as unnatural in the predestined capitalist order of things. "I had our [pooling] plan clearly in mind," he was reported to have said. "It was right. I knew it as a matter of conscience. It was right between me and my God."

Throughout, the work habit and inventiveness, characteristic of America from the beginning, persisted.

What about stock promotions, and greed and chicanery in such stock promotions, during this period which ended roughly around 1890? It appears that at best they only facilitated the working out of this momentous energy and acquisitiveness, and then only in a minor, often aberrant way, and involving a limited number of people, while at worst they hardly contributed at all (as in their inability to open up the West), or they held back development by their waste and corruption and instability, which hindered the raising of capital.

A cursory look at what actually happened shows that *the real development (venture) capital came from elsewhere.* John Jacob Astor's original grubstake was underwritten by a loan from his brother Heinrich, a New York butcher. Cornelius Vanderbilt's early capital began with $100 borrowed from his mother for a two-masted barge, and expanded from there. The Union Pacific — the transcontinental line which opened up the country, and the kind of momentous development on which so much else follows — was sponsored and financed by the U.S. government. But as mentioned before, the railroad era in general was underwritten or otherwise assisted by governments — state, federal and local — in the form of massive land grants and other subsidies, grants and privileges, as had canals and other public works in the earlier period. Private action was believed to be too uncertain and too slow; in any case, private companies could not hope to raise the large sums needed. The most important of canals, the Erie, whose financing enabled New York for the first time to threaten the older financial centres (Philadelphia, Boston), was constructed at public expense and owned by New York State.

To return to private financing, the crucial first investments in iron and steel made by Andrew Carnegie, the King of the Vulcans, came from his own savings and a loan, with additional participation by his brother and two friends. John D. Rockerfeller's original underwriting was a $1,000 loan from his father. The capital for his first investment in oil refining, in conjunction with a partner whom he later bought out, came out of his pocket. Extra capital came from a rich whiskey brewer and salt maker who was the uncle of the wife of an associate. Henry Clay Frick, the strong man of the coke industry, got his original capital for buying up coal land and coke ovens from Judge Thomas Mellon, the Pittsburgh banking patriarch, and from cash from his family. Mellon's own wealth grew out of his law practice. Cyrus McCormick, as well as using his own capital, got his crucial backing from Chicago tycoon William B. Ogden. Marshall Field's early capital was saved by sleeping nights on a straw tick on top of a counter. Aaron Montgomery Ward opened Montgomery Ward & Company with an $800 loan from a bank. The Great Atlantic & Pacific Tea Company (A & P) was a partnership. George Pullman's primary capital came from his accomplishments as a contractor (later Marshall Field money would be added). The famous Anaconda Copper was financed by three friends of the prospector Marcus Daly. Of the other copper-plated kings, William Clark got his initial fortune from a spectacular tobacco sale and other trading ventures, and Fredrick Heinze from selling a nuisance railroad and smelter at Trail, B.C. to the Canadian Pacific. James J. Hill, of the Great Northern, built the road on the back of the notorious St. Paul & Pacific purchase, financed through Donald Smith and George Stephen of the Hudson's Bay Company and the Bank of Montreal, as well as with his own resources.

The great Du Pont dynasty grew out of a powder mill along Brandywine Creek near Wilmington, Delaware, two thirds of which was financed by a colonization company organized by Pierre du Pont for an altogether different purpose — creating a utopia for distinguished Frenchmen fleeing the anarchy of revolutionary France — and among whose shareholders were La Fayette, Beaumarchais, Talleyrand and Jean-Jacques Rousseau. The French investment served in effect as long-term bonds, which the Du Ponts eventually retired. The backing for a new method of smelting aluminum, which evolved into the Aluminum Company of America monopoly, was financed by Andrew Mellon, son of Thomas Mellon (which set off the organization of a whole series of stockjobbing aluminum concerns manned by fast promoters, all of which quickly folded). The Mellons and their associates would also finance the J.M. Guffey Petroleum Company (1901) — later to become Gulf Oil — and otherwise finance or acquire a gigantic industrial empire. Every cent that went into the Philadelphia Smelting & Refining Company ($1,500,000 capitalization) belonged to Meyer Guggenheim himself. William Randolph Hearst's newspaper empire was financed by money made by his father, a miner-prospector who struck it lucky on the silver-rich Comstock Lode in what is now Nevada. The venture capital for the development of the telephone came from the fathers of two of the young Alexander Graham Bell's deaf mute students, one of whom was to become his father-in-law. When commercial exploitation began, the Boston banking community supplied the money. Wide stock distribution occurred only subsequently.

Later, in 1903, the Ford Motor Company was begun by Henry Ford and 12 partners, whom he eventually bought out. William Durant, who put together General Motors, started out by buying into a carriage factory with $2,000 scraped together from friends. Capital to cover General Motors expansion in 1910 came in a high-priced mortgage-secured loan from two banking houses after Durant had run out of resources. In a subsequent crisis, following World War I, when Wall Street refused to underwrite a common stock issue, Durant had to turn to an English-Canadian banking group, and then to the Du Pont Company, which took control. Meanwhile, countless automobile companies projected by stock promoters had come and gone, few of them producing many cars and some no cars at all, "leaving stock certificates to go into attic trunks," as a U.S. business historian described it, "along with yellowing certificates of shares in canals that were never dug and railroads that were never built."

And so on, with a few exceptions to prove the rule. "In the fields of manufacturing, distribution and marketing (not to mention agriculture)," summarizes an historian of capital formation in the United States, "the family-owned or closely held company was predominant throughout the greater part of our history." Beyond the original venture stage, the great majority of these organizations met their capital requirements out of earnings.

In the same way, in England in an earlier era and a different situation, a revolution in manufacturing (the great Industrial Revolution) was financed almost exclusively by primary accumulation, partnerships limited to six members fully liable, mortgages, bonds and loans. The joint-stock company, except in specially legislated areas like banking and transport, was virtually precluded until the last quarter of the nineteenth century, as a result of an act passed in 1720 following the shock of the South Sea Bubble collapse.

A look at this same American phenomenon from the other side — the New York financial district — corroborates just how feeble and incidental the stock exchange culture was next to this profound and massive burgeoning of a people and a continent.

Until the Civil War, for example, despite the financial boom of the Jacksonian period, business was so comparatively scarce that brokerage remained a part-time pursuit. A panic, like the one in 1837, could bring trading to a near halt, as it did. No continuous market was made (on one day, in 1830, only 31 shares in two companies were traded); brokers arrived at periodic call times, did their business quickly, and departed. What there was of trading, moreover, was carefully sheltered. The Exchange Board kept its proceedings secret from the public. No one but the members had access to information on transactions.

Speculation began, in the early years of the Republic, with Continental Congress printed money and scrip. Following the turn of the century, trading was mostly in government securities, banks, and insurance companies, in that order of importance, with federal debt obligations alone exceeding the combined volume of the other two. The market staples for the rest of the century, when the industrial pioneering took place, were canals and railroads — both, except for the later railroads, largely underwritten by governments. The big action during the Civil War involved gold against greenbacks. As regards mining promotions, most were swindles, marginal speculations, or at best inflated hopes of unrealistic stock jobbers. Criminal elements were sometimes involved. The California gold rush, of course, began with greedy men rushing to California, not with greedy men rushing to Wall Street.

Three broad aspects come to the fore in all this. First. government undertakings or commitments rather than private ventures seem, ironically, to have made the New York financial district what it was. Continental Congress money, Union greenbacks, United States debt obligations, city and state bonds, railroads, and canals have already been mentioned. Government wars were particularly important in exchange history. The War of 1812 was a seminal influence. The Civil War was a decisive one (and, incidentally, put an end to the depression following the panic of 1857, just as World War I put an end to stagnation following the 1907 panic, and World War II put an end to stagnation following the 1929 panic). Jay Cooke's syndicated distribution that revolutionized the industry by spreading the influence of

Wall Street and the phenomenon of stock or bond ownership
— the first broad distribution in the country — involved the
sale of Union bonds during the Civil War, and relied heavily
on appeals to patriotism. (Cooke had developed his technique
in underwriting a Pennsylvania State issue!)

Secondly, speculation in the market by large numbers of
small investors was unknown. The ordinary American held
shy of the culture, for good reason. The *New York Times*,
close to the scene of the action, habitually described the Wall
Street community as a den of thieves. It *was* a den of thieves,
and remained one (and according to recent accounts, still is
one). Even Jay Cooke in Philadelphia, who stood one step
above the exchange culture in the eyes of the people because
of his Civil War fame, could not change that wariness. His
go-for-broke distribution of Northern Pacific bonds, although
it did bring in a considerable total of money in small amounts,
got nowhere near the response he needed, and the Northern
Pacific and Cooke's financial empire went under, closing the
Exchange and touching off the greatest international panic
ever (23,000 commercial and industrial failures were recorded
in the U.S. during the panic and subsequent depression).

Thirdly, as regards the crucial innovative entrepreneurial
function, the stock exchange culture was in good part neutral
or negative, maybe essentially so. The large investor if he were
innovating rather than plundering, involved himself, where
possible, directly with entrepreneurs and craftsmen, as did
Rockefeller, Carnegie and Mellon. The great Wall Street
battles of the century, on the other hand, like the Vanderbilt-
Daniel Drew fight over the Erie Railroad, were waged largely
among a few insiders, and had to do with control over who
would manipulate what rather than with construction. "There
are such creatures as investors," wrote the *Times* at the
end of this period, in 1887, "though a broker may pass a
busy life without falling in with one." (In a different but
related way, the main achievement of the investment banking
firms, like the House of Morgan, which rose to power at the
end of the century, was consolidation and rationalization —

railroads, steel, etc. — often accomplished by unloading watered stock on an innocent public.)

Drew, along with Jay Gould and Jim Fisk — the most notoriously smart stock market players of the developmental post-Civil War period — were also known as wreckers, or hyenas, and wreck they did. Even in acquisitive America, the entrepreneurial spirit was apart, and different from that.

It is not surprising that two of America's greatest entrepreneurial prototypes, Andrew Carnegie and Henry Ford, of the steel age and automobile age respectively, scorned the stock exchange crowd and found the culture repugnant. The proposition that a bunch of primitive, grubbing stock jobbers were "the quintessence of capitalist society," to say nothing of the dismal Canadian sub-species Shaffer had in mind, would have struck them as the ravings of a lunatic. (Ford also hated banks and bankers, and regularly denounced the profit motive. "For all his immense fortune," writes Stewart Holbrook in *The Age of the Moguls*, "one is prepared to believe that Ford really did not care for money.")

Nor is it surprising that not until 1910 did industrial stocks become favourites of investors and speculators alike, replacing the rails for the first time. By then, industrial America had already been created and was self-sustaining!

It appears that stock exchanges, in broad cultural terms, do not create economic activity but follow it, as a bureaucratic or manipulative (predatory) overlay, and at a respectful distance. At least, that has been the United States experience. When the critics of unrestrained speculation in the 1920's challenged the morality of insider manipulation, they were also able to argue that actually stock speculation had played only a minor role in the growth of American enterprise.

This brings us back to the ideological question.

In terms of the American economy, what survived the grasping and violent settling of the continent, and the parallel industrialization, were the large trusts in steel, oil and other sectors which forced order on a national scale out of chaotic overinvestment and competition, by crushing independent entrepreneurs and manipulating — in effect, robbing — the small investor, not to mention trust funds, insurance companies and the public purse. These were the ancestors of the rational modern corporation. In their own era, their remorseless methods of incubating wealth at others' expense were known as "the system." J. P. Morgan, as everybody was aware, did not believe in gambling.

In terms of mythology, what survived was quite a bit different: the legends of the buccaneers and robber barons, of course, but also the Horatio Alger myth, and closest to the frontier, the idea of the adventurous, individualist American, unrestrained by community, throwing in his all after the main chance, the whole coming together into a compelling mythology of risk and reward. The government involvement that had been indispensable to the process — and also the looting of public funds — did not interfere with this mythology. State participation had since been downgraded and its memory pushed aside.

This nostalgic mythology of risk and reward, hearkening back to a frontier past, blossomed and took on a new dimension in the speculative boom of the 1920's. Although stock promotions also have a long history in Canada, the mining promotion way, as we have known it since the war. dates from this period, and derives its ideological potency from that American milieu.

To begin with, the stock market boom in the 1920's offered to the world, for the first time, the impressive spectacle of large numbers of middle class people participating in speculation. No Canadian exchange could have mounted such an extended ritual. The backbone of the market was provided by the great American corporations, many times removed from the primary distribution of mining stocks or the stock of fledgling industrials. These major corporations had histories and made profits. Most of them were solid enough to survive the Great Crash. To invest in General Motors or American Telephone & Telegraph or Radio or United States Steel was in a sense to invest against the frontier mentality, although the mass of investors might not have appreciated such a contradictory idea.

Spiritually, however, speculation in General Motors or Montgomery Ward, in the late 1920's, was at one with mining promotions. "Money is king," wrote a chronicler of the era, "but there is something else. It is a high, wild time, a time of riotous spirits and belief in magic rather than cold calculation, a time of Dionysius rather than Apollo. People speak of 'luck' and 'the breaks' more than of earnings and dividends." The boom had lifted the stock market out of the real world, which is how mining promotions function, and which opened the gates to massive fraud.

At the same time, the techniques and the ideological style that were used later in mining promotions in Canada were devised or perfected here in New York in this period. The "tipster sheet" or "tipster report," born at the turn of the century, became a standard device. So did "sucker lists" and "double talk," of similar origin. "Pulling the plug" and other phrases of market dialect were coined or elaborated on. (The words "bucket shop" dated back to the Civil War!) The first important market letter on Wall Street, the *Jones & Baker Curb News*, with assay reports written by engineers, appeared around 1920. Imitators took the market letter one step further by slipping in advice to buy the stock they were touting inside the rest of the copy, which was rigorously true. The *Wall Street Iconoclast* attacked financial swindlers and warned its readers against them; that device for disarming suckers also found its way to Canada after the war.

Some of this milieu came across the border as cultural overflow. Shaffer appropriately finds his principal symbolism in Wall Street, to the exclusion of the Canadian past and the public enterprise reality. As regards that American culture, Bay Street and St. James Street have been, and continue to be, insignificant colonial outposts.

A more energetic cultural strain was brought over first-hand by refugees from 1934 on, fleeing from the dark glances of the Securities and Exchange Commission; some were still arriving in the 1950's. Whereas these American salesmen now touted stock from Canada, many of their customers, in some cases all of their customers, were in the United States. They brought to the country not only technique and their own cannibalistic psychology, but also an understanding of Americans' ideological weakness — their enduring free enterprise sentimentality — across which they could unload stock in enormous quantities.

Without this immigrant wave of pariah salesmen and their incorrigibly ethnocentric American variant way of life, and without the customers in the United States and their complementary American variant way of life, the mining promotion culture in Canada would be even more superficial than it is. Shaffer's book likely would not have been written. Our own promotional age, the railroad one, which was a beast all of its own particular Canadian kind, left no legacy even remotely like it.

We came to public enterprise instead.

*   *   *

But it is the American legacy which overwhelms us in the drawing up of man's image, after that other past, in magazines and fiction and films and ballyhoo. Mark Twain wrote about American frontier man, and he was read everywhere. What folk novelist has come as close to putting his finger on what happened here? America has *Fortune* magazine and others, for herself and the colonies. Where is the magazine of the public enterprise culture for innovative Canadian man?

Even the evocations of the American frontier, and of legendary American protagonists, that are apparently remote from economic life — the American western, for example — can enter perversely into the ideological mix. Jean-Paul Sartre, as a boy, was an addict of westerns because they represented, for him, the liberation of the individual from the closed spaces and encrusted procedures of Europe. Not until later did Sartre realize how genocidal and repressive that American frontier spirit could be. But while there was repression in the Canadian West, what was repressed was largely the American spirit of excessive individualism; what was repressed was the American frontier itself, and its symbolism of the new man as a gambling, anarchistic, individualist warrior.

Imagine if Canada had had a flourishing feature film industry all this century, instead of borrowing from others as if there were nothing for us to make feature films about, the Canadian experience supposedly not really counting for much in particular. And imagine if it had churned out countless spectacles of the Hudson's Bay Company (the Company of Adventurers!!!) holding off the destructively acquisitive Americans, or of the North West Mounted Police driving the grubby and greedy American liquor traders across the border and doing other legendary he-man acts. (How the West was won for monopoly charter! The Canadian bureaucracy rides again!) No child growing up with that could possibly be romantic about dubious, profligate stock promotions. Nobody who was even faintly, subconsciously aware of the supreme economic effectiveness of the Hudson's Bay Company's rationalism — an altogether brutal, unromantic rationalism — would make the mistake of associating economic effectiveness with uncontrolled greed, and systematic lying and cheating. Had John A. Macdonald been addicted to American westerns instead of to Upper Canadian whiskey, would he have bothered pushing the CPR through, or would he have been riding a horse in the Cariboo country or, more likely, running a saloon in Montana or the Oregon Territory?

So colonial passiveness in the arts comes to mean blindness in the practical life of the people after all. Should we have expected anything else?

*   *   *

The speculative spirit in America, in short, was just one of the elements of a complex historical current which belonged to the United States apart, where stock promotions in themselves made little or no contribution to development, and where the real pioneering force, as early as 1870, was the great U.S. enterprise which forced its dominance on the country in one generation by superior strength and "rationalism," and which was to become dominant in Canada as well. Canada, for its part, was on the outside, or on the edge, of that current in all the ways that counted. Trying to duplicate that spirit by propped-up stock exchange machinery was to take the American myth without the American reality, which we couldn't take anyway, Canada having an inescapably different reality of its own.

The ideology of mining promotions in Canada, then, or better still, the American-ideology-of-mining-promotions-in-Canada — the notion, for example, as expressed by the president of a hinterland stock exchange in Canada in 1973 (!) that "business needs the small investor for his speculative capital; the formation of development capital depends on smaller investors, willing to take risks" — has its roots in a dead age, in an alien situation, which never really existed. It is colonial ideology in the classic sense, removed both from the indigenous Canadian experience and from the metropolitan American one as well — *ideological double fault.*

*   *   *

A schema of ideological double fault: It not only imposes a distorting metropolitan point of view on a native situation, forcing the native population into impractical responses, which is the first fault. It also goes on doing so, freezing the colony in impracticality, long after the orientation has changed in the metropolis itself, which is the second fault. Pragmatic ideologies are rooted in experience, and change with experience. Colonial ideologies, on the other hand, exist in a rigid, idealized, make-believe world, isolated from the indigenous experience and also from the metropolitan one.

Canadian history, being largely a colonial history,

provides some broad illustrations. The Family Compact, for example, could be more British in Canada than the British themselves. What could be more artificial and colonial, and impractical, than a privileged, ruling aristocracy in the North American backwoods? The ideology which legitimized this privilege and style of the Compact did not fit the reality. It was incongruous. That was the first fault. This same reactionary, feudal ideology was expounded and defended in Canada when it had long since been bypassed by history in the home country. In the heyday of the Family Compact in Canada, Britain was undergoing the first stages of a decisive liberal revolution. That was the second fault.

Similarly, the French colony in Canada could be more royalist and more clerical than the home country from which it derived. The colonial functionaries valiantly attempted, and failed, to impose the borrowed ideology on the irascibly indigenous *coureurs de bois*. The ideology persisted, dogmatically, for a century and a half after the French revolution, until its impracticality became so overwhelming that it disintegrated in disrepute.

*   *   *

The practical effect of such double-faulted ideology, as it bears on stock promotions, is to aid and abet our economic colonization.

First, the wasteful promotional procedure does not stand up to alternative systems: the allocation of exploration capital by large "rational" organizations, which are, in Canada, predominantly foreign-controlled. That's where all the action is in terms of economic development, not on the floors of stock exchanges. The Porter Commission, for example, reported that in the case of mining "some 86 per cent of prospecting expenses each year are now in fact made by producing mines." And ". . . the independent prospectors remaining have sufficient financial resources to safeguard their bargaining power," enabling them, if their claims are any good, to deal directly with syndicates or large organizations, and to bypass as well the wasteful promotional structure.

The subservience of mining promotions goes further. Sufficient capital to rise to a competitive level through to production can only rarely be reached by a promotional procedure. More and more of the few promotions that do find something worthwhile sell control to established operations or otherwise trade an interest for outside financial help. The lucky speculator may do very well then, but the long-term profits go largely to the superior organization, which has paid well for its acquisition but has saved itself the costs of explorational trial and error. Seen in their entirety as a class, speculators are subsidizing established capital, which has the upper hand.

Mining promotions allocate capital to an inefficient, handicapped, marginal and native sector of mining as against a superior, technically advanced, dominant and predominantly foreign sector of mining.

But that's a minor cost. Canadians don't throw away great amounts of money on penny stock. The most notable buyers in the past were American. Europeans also participated, and through the recent wave of promotions in Montreal are involved once more. But note again that the main function of mining promotions is a spiritualist one. For all of the chicanery of the financial acts, what really matters are the ritualistic acts, which keep alive the old ideological atavism, sordid as actual practice may be, at the cost of more practical devices.

Shaffer, for example, argued that since Americans are the biggest customers of promotions, we might as well take their money and help out our balance of payments, even if the promotions don't do anything else. But again, they do. They finance backward ritual, which damages the economic culture.

To cite a case history, the government of Quebec decided in 1969 to countenance more liberal promotional styles, in order to take advantage of Americans' irrationality. The argument ran that since the dollars were going to come to Canada anyway, they might as well come to Quebec as to British Columbia; perhaps some economic development might actually occur in the process.

Unlike financial statements, however, economic cultures are organic and indivisible. What either province might gain in American dollars, it stood to lose many times over by distracting and corrupting the economic community — distracting it from productive commitment by dubious games, and corrupting it by condoning dubious practice in one part, which touches all the others.

As it turned out, the upshot came remarkably soon. In late 1971, scandal broke out in the Montreal exchange community, plunging it into uproar, and revealing behind the broken ritual of prospectuses and puffing of stock a disturbing sluggishness in the entrepreneurial body of the province that all the hectic promotional to and fro had not, of course, touched. Then concern arose that the investment community's bad image would hurt growth. (The exact opposite policy, the tightening up of securities regulations in Quebec, was undertaken in the early 1960's, as part of an exactly opposite cultural effort — the attempt to escape a long, dark age of corruption and backwardness and to create a modern economy.)

Similarly, in one of the most crucial phases of our entrepreneurial history — post-World War II to the mid-1960's — the mining promotion ritual was endlessly and elaborately staged in and around the Toronto Stock Exchange, sustaining in Canadian bystanders the spiritualism of gung-ho risk-taking and its peculiar sectarian expressions, like faith-in-the-Timmins-area worship, or the uranium-in-the-North fetish, while in the real and secular world of economic development, unopposed by Canadian entrepreneurial devices of real vigour, U.S. capital was subjugating the Canadian economic heartland, and the hinterland with it.

In particular — especially in British Columbia, the main refuge of mining promotions today, and also in Quebec, as before in Ontario (up to the Windfall scandal) — this frayed ritualism serves as a device for keeping public enterprise out of mind, when public enterprise is the one proven way Canadians have found of facing up to the corporate challenge of outsiders.

Appropriately, this works by incantation. The chanted words themselves are the effective element. The Quebec minister of financial institutions, for example, will ask how else, other than through a "risk-capital market," can Montreal be made a lively commercial centre, without which "we'd have separatism." A broker-dealer spokesman in Vancouver will ask how else Canadians are to participate in developing their economy, if not through such promotions. The president of the Vancouver Stock Exchange will ask how else the capital for western Canada's natural resources industry is to be raised, if not through his exchange. Investment writers from a national financial weekly will ask how else areas like Quebec and British Columbia will catch up to Ontario unless they have more lenient regulations than Ontario, which is the wealthiest province and doesn't have to take the risks that other provinces do? These questions are duly propagated and repeated, as they have been also in the past, from whence they come. One answer, of course, is crown corporations (as Shaffer, to his credit, points out). But in this ritual, the question is put just so the answer does not have to be given. The answer must not be given. That is the point of it all, to make sure the public enterprise possibility, which is sensed to be everywhere around, is not considered.

Also, the transactional activities of mining promotions in those regions, marginal as their productivity is, prop up their stock exchanges and the bureaucracies that go with them. The Vancouver Stock Exchange is in large part dependent for its livelihood on speculative mining stock. Before the loosening up of regulations in Quebec, the Canadian Stock Exchange, scheduled to be merged shortly with the Montreal Stock Exchange, was on the brink of insolvency. These propped-up exchanges occupy cultural space that could be much better used by public enterprise, or almost anything. They are meant to offset Toronto's dominance in financial matters (after New York). In fact, they serve mostly to hide just how subservient their regions are.

This brings us directly to public enterprise as a pioneering vehicle, and as a vehicle of regional self-assertion, in exploration and mining development. Without such "rational" exploration vehicles of our own, other peoples, with their long-standing and productive economic forms, have the advantage over us in our own country and reap the rewards. Regions that are now hinterland are the most vulnerable.

Scandal and magic never were substitutes for enterprise.

*   *   *

Alas, what goes for queer mining promotions and quaint hinterland stock exchanges also applies, in a less sharply defined way, to the Toronto Stock Exchange and to stock exchanges generally in Canada; to the unlisted markets in industrials, as well as the mines and oils, surrounding them; and to the bureaucracy of brokers and investment dealers sustained by them.

They are a backward, inadequate, and in practice, marginal vehicle for financing entrepreneurship and innovation in this country. But stock exchanges historically, as we've seen, have battened on to entrepreneurship — have been a bureaucracy after the fact — rather than playing a pioneering role.

Among other things, this has meant that the investment community has steered Canadian money to U.S. markets, which are more developed and which offer both investment firms and their clients better possibilities, exporting investment capital from a country whose pioneering entrepreneurship has often been desperately short of it.

As for the scene in general, the old totemism remains in religious pockets, removed as ever from the practical world.

The authors of a book aimed at saving the small investor

(John G. Doherty and Timothy Pritchard, *Bulls, Bears and Sheep*, 1971), for example, write that "the stock market has some appeal to whatever entrepreneurial instinct people possess." What instinct are they really talking about? Shaffer mistook raw greed for the entrepreneurial spirit; Doherty and Pritchard's appreciation of the investor's acquisitiveness and calculations as the "entrepreneurial instinct" at work is only a less crude version of that notion.

Any connection between the narrow habit by which a small investor ("Charlie Chump," "Sheep" — their words) trades in stock, on the one hand, and the culturally impregnated entrepreneurial spirit which has expressed itself in myriad, richly creative ways in countless societies (not excluding American capitalism), on the other hand, is incidental to entrepreneurship if not antithetical to it, as it is now in Canada.

In the same spiritualist vein, the authors refer to the choices for investment made available by stock exchanges to the small investor ("the smug middle-class investor," to quote them again), as "capitalism's sanctifying grace". . . which is to damn capitalism with faint sanctity indeed. Any alleged connection between stock exchanges and "sanctifying grace" should be investigated by the Sanctity and Exchange Commission.

CHAPTER 8

The Canadian Monopoly Culture

Another central tenet of free enterprise ideology and of the American-ideology-in-Canada is that competition means efficiency and that without it, the Canadian economy would bog down in a perniciously wasteful and sluggish bureaucracy. The economic theory taught at our universities revolves around competition. The Economic Council of Canada works hard at promoting competition. The Department of Consumer and Corporate Affairs, with its combines investigation branch, goes through the motions to ensure competition. And if it can't have competition, it tries for respectable oligopoly.

When we actually look at our own experience, however, instead of repeating what we have been told, we can't help suspecting that all these people are living their ideological lives in another country. In Canada, in key sectors of the economy, monopoly has meant efficiency and market competition has meant pernicious waste. Monopoly is the economic model. Monopoly suits us, and always has.

We have an aptitude for monopoly, in a world where monopoly, with a dynamic beyond competition, is coming into its own as a creative entrepreneurial form. Yet being in thrall to the colonial ideology, we force unnatural and contrived competition on ourselves. We cannot accept our monopoly culture because others won't accept it for us.

The monopoly culture has deep and tenacious psychic roots in Canada. It goes back almost to the beginning — to the economic era following the conquest, when the fur traders began to suspect that the American dream of competitive free enterprise was impractical revolutionary dogma, not least of all because in pursuing it they were killing each other off and decimating the native population, which was the fur trade's equivalent of a labour force. But the conclusive reason may have been the Hudson's Bay Company's monopoly over the short trading route via Hudson Bay, which lent itself naturally to a monopoly culture in the trade itself. Free enterprise was impossible in the context, and was seen to be impossible.

Even before the Montreal traders had it out with the Company, the mechanics of competition proved bloody and financially intolerable.

In 1786, Peter Pond, a North West Company trader, murdered one of the partners of a rival organization in the Athabaska country. A year later, a merger was arranged. In 1800 the XY Company was formed. Gustavus Myers, looking back on the period a century later, wrote that "employe often murdered employe in disputes over furs and territory. . . . Indians were incited to pillage and fire upon canoes of the XY Company . . . attempts, often successful, were made to debauch and entice away its employes; and its property was destroyed by treachery and other underhand acts." Not all historians offer such a colourful account. But it is agreed that, financially, competition was damaging.

The North West Company alone used 16,299 gallons of rum in trade in 1803 as compared to an annual average between 1806 and 1810 of only 9,700 gallons for the two companies after merger. Competiton was uneconomic in another way: important fur areas were becoming exhausted, and relations with the Indians had deteriorated along with the deterioration of Indian society. Only four years after the XY Company was formed, the North West Company absorbed it. It was after this competiton ended that the North West Company and the St. Lawrence fur economy had their greatest success.

The consequent near war between the North West Company and the Hudson's Bay Company, on the other hand, revolved around the latter company's monopoly charter over Rupert's Land and the North West's contrary campaign to keep the territory open. The killing of the governor of the Selkirk colony and 19 of his followers by a column of Metis, supporters of the North West Company, at Seven Oaks in 1816, was only the most dramatic of the many belligerent incidents. Kidnapping, physical combat, embargoes of pemmican and other food, seizure and destruction of forts and records, miscellaneous trespass, plundering, false arrests and counter-arrests, forced contracts (once with the aid of liquor), and the occasional death by unnatural causes are also part of the record. While competition in trade lasted, it again proved financially ruinous to both sides. Negotiations for a division of territory had begun as early as 1811. Gradually the Hudson's Bay Company tightened up its organization of the superior Bay route and gained complete dominance.

Taking the fur trade as a whole, the uses of competition

were few. It forced expansion and a certain administrative efficiency on the Hudson's Bay Company. But the dis- economies of bloodshed, high costs, insufficient profits, over-trapping, and debauchery of the Indians loomed larger. In the end, the cautious, bureaucratic, centralized, miserly, but scrupulously consistent Hudson's Bay Company won, and with its monopoly charter unchallenged, established a tradition. The brawling, cheating, generous, adventurous, decentralized North West Company, optimistically distri- buting dividends instead of building up reserves — the prototype of the individualistic, aggressive, "boomer" Ameri- can frontier spirit — could not adapt to conditions of stable or declining trade, and lost.

As with the North West and XY Companies merger, the major efficiencies occurred after, and only because, competition had ended. Duplication of posts and personnel was eliminated; transport was improved and closely scheduled; expensive presents and liquor to the Indians were reduced (cuts were also made in wages and free equipment to company employees); a more detailed and systematic cost-accounting system was introduced; at posts in the interior, self-sufficiency was encouraged in food supplies and equipment in an attempt to reduce incoming cargoes; administration was rationalized; fur resources were conserved in areas which had been over- trapped during the period of competition, while they were systematically exhausted in areas along the American frontier which might have attracted competition; a quota system was instituted in the most exhausted districts under company control; prices were adjusted to favour the trapping of animals other than beaver, as a conservation measure. Most of this would have been impossible without monopoly control of the trade.

But the lessons of the fur trade era were lost on the Canadians of the railroad-building era.

First came the Grand Trunk's duplication of the Great Western line from Toronto to Michigan, in which the first inadvertently committed suicide while murdering the second by splitting traffic, and which inevitably ended with a merger of the two corpses after the damage had been done.

None the wiser a generation or two later, Canadians then perpetrated their famous "railroad folly." If the building of one Pacific railroad was considered at the time an act of "insane recklessness," the construction of second and third Pacific railroads, sometimes on top of each other, should defy description. Is there anything in human inclination beyond insane recklessness? Well, there is: ideological perversity.

In the light of the Canadian market contradiction, the granting of a monopoly to the CPR was lucidity itself. Even in the vastly richer market of the United States, competitive railroad construction and railroad operation had resulted in costly waste and overbuilding, which the United States is only now sorting out. A second, pioneering line opening up new territory north of the CPR just barely made sense, given all the mitigating circumstances of reckless optimism and political expediency. But the allowing of a third line has baffled historians.

There was another factor. The fur and railroad monopolies were economically logical. But in private hands they also were arbitrary and oppressive. The Hudson's Bay Company for decades tried to suppress the free enterprise spirit of the Red River settlement, whose inhabitants insisted on smuggling furs and otherwise carrying on trade with American middlemen. The CPR grew strong and prosperous at the expense of the western farmer. Both were "evil" monopolies, with superior power unto themselves. The people of Manitoba had running battles with the two companies, culminating in a face-to-face meeting of volunteer CPR and Manitoba armies west of Winnipeg over an attempt to lay tracks across the CPR line that stopped just short of a fight and bloodshed. The British Columbia government was exceedingly generous to the Canadian Northern, by way of bond guarantees and other considerations, as their contribution to breaking the CPR's stranglehold. What puzzles historians is why the Laurier government didn't try to bring the CPR under control by regulation — didn't at least make the attempt — before underwriting a competitor.

And the question of the third line, the Canadian Northern, remains. Why didn't Laurier force the Canadian Northern to merge with the Grand Trunk? Why was the Laurier government so generous to Mackenzie and Mann when Laurier distrusted them so much? Why should otherwise shrewd and practical politicians behave in such incomprehensible ways? Nobody has satisfactorily explained these minor mysteries of Canadian history because nobody has ever explored the ideological web binding the minds of these ideological men, as all men are ideologically bound.

That was not the end. In the booming 1920's, when new agricultural settlements were opening up in the West along with branch lines, there were invasions and counter-invasions by the CPR and CNR into each other's territory. Each built a large hotel in Halifax just to spite the other. In 1929, the presidents of both railroads decried the wasteful competition, but a clear apportionment of areas of activity was impossible. The competitive ethic, played out in this case in a political-mercantile butting against each other of two transcontinental giants, had too much momentum inside them.

They did at least, after a fashion, realize how wasteful competition was, and actually did something about it. In 1929 the two railroads bought and jointly operated the Northern Alberta Railways into the Peace River country. Union Station in Toronto was opened in 1927. But even when the depression struck body blows to both lines, which made the waste of duplication in trackage and services obvious to everybody, and when the need to economize was drastic, the country still was caught in the old ideological vise — or vice, as you see it.

The CPR was forthright in calling for unification and in attacking "the tremendous waste caused by maintaining duplicate services in a country which can no longer afford to pay for the duplication." But a CPR monopoly was out of the question. Even joint ownership was seen by some as a CPR Trojan horse.

What was the obstacle, though, to a public monopoly? Ontario Hydro had been surpassing all expectations for 20 years, and was one of the few organizations in Canada taking the depression in its stride. The prairie telephone companies, the first of the government-owned regional systems on the continent, had been in existence for a quarter of a century. Beyond that was Canada's continuous history of centralized economic organization, unAmerican in spirit and conception, underwritten by the force of politics, the whole dictated by the economics of staple production and Canada's great distances. I say "continuous" because it had never been interrupted, as it had been in the United States, by a competitive era. Monopoly should have been as much a part of our inclination as the RCMP was part of our symbolism, the North West Mounted Police having been formed in the first place to protect our sovereignty by protecting the Hudson's Bay Company monopoly, and having done the same again by guarding the construction of the CPR.

Amalgamation in the 1930's would have brought savings of upwards of $60 million annually, according to Edward Beatty, CPR president. The half-hearted attempts at co-operation that actually took place — particularly half-hearted on the part of the CPR — produced instead a saving of just over $1 million in 1933. Compound similar waste over the years to the present and you have a pretty high price to pay for an inappropriate ideological prejudice.

Nevertheless, the Canadian dialectic would not be denied. Certain passenger services were pooled in the 1930's. Telecommunications have now been consolidated. Recently the CNR and CPR bought controlling interest of a computer time-sharing company. The two companies are involved together in Metro Centre Developments Ltd., organized to develop railroad property in and around Union Station, Toronto. But the existence of the two railroads side by side, instead of one publicly owned system, remains a bizarre anomaly. When René Lévesque refers to "the mess in railroads" in Canada, he knows, and we know, that he is not referring to messily operated railroads, nor just to unnecessary duplication, but to a paralytic irrationalism in Canadian life.

But the lessons of the fur trade era were lost on the Canadians of the railroad-building era. And as I am going to argue, the lessons of the fur trade and the railroad-building eras were lost on the Canadians of the air transport era.

We can ask, in a preliminary way, why does it go on like that? Well, people sometimes learn from experience. We Canadians often don't, because we don't trust our own experience. We're continually looking to somebody else's example. That cultural imitativeness, far more than any overt subservience, is the mark of the colonial condition.

A student of Canada's idiosyncratic colonial pathology could do worse than to look into its manifestation in the culture of air travel, drawing up a case history of how our colonial penchant for imitation destroyed one of the soundest manifestations of our practical genius for monopoly.

In 1958, the Conservative government invited Stephen Wheatcroft, a British air transport economist, to do a study on Canadian air transport. The terms of reference for Wheatcroft were solidly fixed in colonial dogma. George Hees, the Minister of Transport at the time, had proceeded "on the assumption that competition is a valuable stimulus to more efficient operation and to the provision of better service to the public," although in particular cases where there wasn't enough traffic, competition might not be justified. Wheatcroft's job was to see whether competition on the domestic mainline was desirable. Up to that point the transcontinental route was a Trans-Canada Air Lines monopoly.

The Wheatcroft Report was ill-starred from the beginning. The Canadian drama is like no other drama. Anyone who wants to play in it has to go through a period of acculturation. Wheatcroft did not, and was miscast. He was, in the first place, an outsider whose ideological reference points came from another place. And, secondly, he was an economist without training in getting out of himself and into the culture and ideological imperatives of other peoples, so that during his short stay in Canada he remained an outsider. If the Department of Transport had been seriously interested in getting to the bottom of the Canadian airline puzzle, it would have hired an anthropologist.

Wheatcroft did a detailed analysis of TCA's transcontinental service and discovered that it was as good and as efficient a service as anywhere in the world, although it had no competition on the route. There was, nevertheless, one serious deficiency in the service. "A highly vocal section of the Canadian public" refused to believe that TCA was as good as it was. Without the choice of another airline on the route, transcontinental travel for them was psychologically unsatisfactory and sometimes even psychologically painful. This was at a time when statistical checks showed that TCA's percentage of error in reservations and baggage handling was very low, in fact lower than similar figures for U.S. airlines. TCA's safety record was also exceptionally good. Technologically, TCA was well on the way to having the first all-turbine fleet of any carrier in the world. In the case of the Viscount services (then accounting for 64 per cent of seat-miles), TCA had "set a standard on domestic and trans-border routes which has unquestionably been some years ahead of the rest of the industry." G. R. McGregor, the airline's president, recounted later that "that airplane [the Viscount] was the happiest thing that ever happened." Just at the very moment of the Wheatcroft Report, the spring of 1958, TCA was riding high in both senses of the phrase.

And just at that time, the "highly vocal section" of TCA's customers was indulging in seemingly "irrational behaviour," mostly by magnifying small grievances into major failures. The one investment that TCA was not getting adequate returns on was expenditure on advertising (public relations).

Wheatcroft explained this in terms of consumer hostility towards a monopoly producer — to an unquestionable desire by the travelling public for the right to choose between carriers — which is the kind of questionable cultural assertion which an economist should never make. All kinds of consumers live in all kinds of situations with monopoly producers without magnifying small mistakes into monumental issues and longing for competition, particularly where a monopoly is publicly owned and is seen not to be gouging the public. But what alternative explanation for the "otherwise irrational behaviour" was available to Wheatcroft, other than that some Canadians were in fact irrational?

"Eureka!" cries the anthropologist of the mining promotion culture, knowing the answer where the economist does not, and could not, know it. "As I've already discovered, Canadians *are* irrational. When it comes to public enterprise, these odd people are driven by a web of cult beliefs and superstitions into ritualistic self-abasement."

I remember flying in one of the old North Stars from Edmonton to Toronto in the fall of 1958. For a reason I can't recall, the plane was diverted en route to an air force base in Manitoba. It reached Toronto late. Then a connecting flight to Montreal was delayed because of engine trouble. There was loud hilarity by a group of businessmen over what they saw as TCA's characteristic incompetence. None of them mentioned safety precautions, a rational explanation. None of them mentioned monopoly either. (In fact, in 1957, 85 per cent of TCA's route mileage, responsible for 50 per cent of the airline's revenue, was subject to competition.) For them, TCA wasn't able to do anything right because it was government-owned. It was a familiar ritual that was to become even more familiar later on.

The irrational dissatisfaction with TCA's service by the "highly vocal section of the Canadian public" wasn't so much a "psychological matter," as Wheatcroft saw it, but an ideological, or better still, a cultural matter. To people for whom the indigenous public enterprise culture was second-rate, because it couldn't be any other way, the idea that TCA's service was as good as any, and better than most, would bring on something in the order of mild culture shock, to be exorcised by ritualistic stomping and shouting, when the opportunity presented itself, at boarding gates and baggage counters.

The hardest flying that TCA ever had to do was through thick ideological fog.

Wheatcroft's second cultural mistake was to accept Hees' assumption that competition was the ideal, if it was at all practical. Hees' full position was close to, almost a copy of, the "presumption doctrine" enunciated by the U.S. Civil Aeronautics Board in 1943, with its "presumption in favour of competition," even if this meant a (not unreasonable) increase in total operating cost. Note the language. "Presumption" and "doctrine" are words of dogma and arbitrary theory, not words of experience. Why should Canadians be so foolish as to adopt other peoples' theology? The presumptive, and presumptuous, doctrines of the British, and then of the Americans, have always been our undoing.

But to Wheatcroft, the doctrine would seem perfectly natural. In his report, he takes it for granted that competition is the motor force of service, technological progress, traffic development and efficiency — the categories in which air transport analysis is made. So that when he discovered how effective TCA's monopoly was — and even singled out as reasons TCA's internal tradition as the national airline, competition on international routes, and vulnerability to public criticism — he did not bother going further into the matter to elaborate on the dynamic of Canadian public monopoly. Consequently he never did find out that, in the light of the long Canadian experience, the U.S. doctrine was backward, ethnocentric doctrine, if doctrines are your game.

TCA's domestic monopoly excelled in service and efficiency, but nobody bothered to pursue the matter. Some irrational customer behaviour was observed, but instead of suggesting that the ideological, or psychological, syndrome be remedied by empirical education, the consultant saw in the irrational behaviour the "strongest argument" for changing the air transport system around it, which meant, as it turned out, making the system irrational. ·

There is reason to believe that Wheatcroft gave undue weight to the "psychological" dissatisfaction, as he saw it. Only four years earlier, when there was a shadow of a cause for being critical of TCA because of insufficient capacity, an economic historian, in a full-length study of the economics of Canadian transportation, had written that "on the whole Canadians are satisfied with their pubicly owned airline."

Transcontinental competition was introduced not for practical but for ideological reasons.

But experience confounded dogma again. Within a few years, the cost of acquiring new jet aircraft, coupled with excess capacity, involved both TCA and Canadian Pacific Airlines in losses. The press and the civil service began to talk of the benefits of a merger as if they had come up with a new idea. Doing away with duplication would bring substantial savings, they said. Internationally, a single airline would be able to make maximum use of existing routes. A domestic monopoly would also allow a more rational distribution of flight times, and mean better service. And so on, all over again.

Excess capacity above all has plagued the Canadian air transport industry. According to Wheatcroft, a passenger load factor of from 70 to 75 per cent on scheduled flights best combines optimum use of capacity with fully adequate service to the public. In 1957-58, TCA's domestic load factor was from 70-73 per cent. By 1971, it had fallen to 59.3 per cent, its lowest in the intervening period, before rising again substantially the following year. CP Air's low point was 53.1 per cent in 1968 (53.2 in 1970, 54.6 in 1969 and 55.1 in 1961 were the next lowest). In none of those years, up to and including the rise in 1972, did the domestic load factor of either airline reach 70 per cent, and only in 7 of a possible 28 cases — all TCA-Air Canada: 1959-61, 1965-67 and 1972 —

did it reach 65 per cent. Their international load factors were even lower. The inefficient waste endemic in the U.S. air transport industry came to saddle Canadians as well with higher costs. (Wheatcroft estimated that a fall of the passenger load factor from 75 per cent to 65 per cent would involve a cost per seat-mile pro rata increase of 16 per cent. He also pointed out that no other factor has such a direct influence on costs.)

If you adhere to inappropriate doctrine in the face of contrary empirical evidence, you pay for it. But then, both the U.S. Civil Aeronautics Board and Wheatcroft ("The [policy] judgment will also depend upon the price . . . thought worthwhile to pay for competition") regularly linked oligopolistic competition with higher total costs, a practical realization which did nothing, however, to separate them from their presumption favouring it.

I should mention that Wheatcroft wasn't joking when he wrote that the largely psychological matter of having a choice of carriers was the "strongest argument" in favour of competition. Open capacity competition leads only to excess capacity, raising costs all around. Price competition, which also could influence traffic volume, becomes, at a certain point, self-defeating to all parties. Both these matters are regulated. Wheatcroft himself stressed the crucial role of regulatory boards. But this very oligopolistic nature of the industry, in turn, as Wheatcroft pointed out, leads to undesirable competition of a purely "product differentiating" and "quality inducement" nature, which also raises costs, and calls for further regulation, or higher prices.

Each theoretical advantage of competition cancels itself out with a practical disadvantage, until only the psychological matter remains. Later, in 1966, after a second study, Wheatcroft· found no major improvements in efficiency or new traffic — an understatement — just "a wider public satisfaction (J.W. Pickersgill's paraphrase). That was all Wheatcroft needed to recommend more of the same.

It has been in this contrived world of trussed-up waste

"competition" that Air Canada and CP Air have lived their product-differentiating, excess-capacity, added-cost, govern-ment-regulated lives, where one airline's "competitive" efforts can perversely help the other, as when Air Canada boosted earnings and volume on its transcontinental run in the mid-1960's, from which CP Air also reaped the reward by being granted extra flights.

*   *   *

In one case where state-owned and privately owned airlines fought it out openly, in Australia, the operation of the state-owned line threatened to force the private line to the wall; after which the government rescued the private line, first by government loan guarantees, then by imposing an exchange of aircraft to equalize fleets, under a policy of "co-operation," then by binding both parties to similar dates for aircraft acquisition, then by ensuring roughly equal cost structures, and even to allowing daily flights between Melbourne and Sydney and on other routes to be run at identical times (called "frequency parallels"), thereby restrict-ing frequency of service. At one point, according to a critic, the government had almost as great a monetary interest in the private line as in its own line. Except for a reduction in parallel scheduling, this policy is still in force. In those circumstances, competition can manifest itself only in absurd product differentiation, as in the Ansett advertisement, in *Aircraft* magazine, which tries valiantly to establish that "yes, there is a difference between airlines." How does one know? By looking into the eyes of the hostess.

A reporter for the *Vancouver Sun* ("Two might just as well be one," April 4, 1972) put the difference to the number of sugar cubes that come with the coffee. He compared the service available on the Australian lines unfavourably with service in New Zealand, where the New Zealand National Airways Corp. (NAC) has had, except for a brief period, a monopoly of the country's domestic air routes. CP Air, in the same position as Ansett, also uses affected, stewardess-linked fantasies of manner ("When they smile at you, they mean it"; "It has to be there, inside"; and so on) to differentiate itself.

* * *

Not that there weren't proponents of merger from the private enterprise side in Canada — merger was all right on their terms, and forget about competition — only that they never did come to grips with the monopoly culture. Like wary soothsayers not too sure of their powers, and not wanting to get too involved, they did an ideological tribal dance around the proposition instead. The monopoly they accepted, but the attendant culture which makes monopoly work, and gives it its edge of efficiency, they could not or would not accept.

When talk of merger arose in 1962, Grant McConachie, the president of CPA, giving way to logic, proposed a plan whereby CPA and TCA would share ground facilities, aircraft and even routes — but would retain their separate identities, which was holding fast to illogic. "Not quite a wedding," read the headline in the *Financial Post*. "Only copulation," the reader might have concluded. Later, in 1969, merger talk again arose. The *Financial Post* did an article on Alitalia, the product of a merger, to show that a private-public line could work, and recommended to Canadian federal planners that they take the example to heart.

In the previous year, 1968, Alitalia had flown 5,600,992 passenger kilometers (15th largest in the International Air Transport Association) compared to 8,934,436 passenger kilometers for Air Canada (7th largest, and largest outside the U.S.). "Shareholders can be a nuisance sometimes, but they keep you on your toes," the *Financial Post* quoted Alitalia's president as saying, yet has any airline kept on its toes, and been kept on its toes, as much as Air Canada (TCA) during its domestic monopoly days? Small shareholders are the weak link in modern economic cultures. And Alitalia was Italian. Air Canada was Canadian, and had mastered the most difficult international and domestic route pattern in the world. Why not take the remarkable Canadian example as a model? Why go to Italy, of all places? Or anywhere else? "There is a strong case for a national airline backed by private enterprise . . ." stated the *Financial Post* in an earlier editorial, without bothering to state what the strong case was.

The federal government would be accused of creating a public monopoly and dealing a blow at "good old private enterprise," G. R. McGregor, Air Canada's president, admitted ruefully in 1965, when repeating again the advantages of merger under public control. We had not come much farther than the days at the end of the 18th century when the XY Company and the North West Company maintained parallel portage roads at Sault Ste. Marie.

Just as we were destroying the indigenous entrepreneurial form in air travel, because it existed outside the American-ideology-in-Canada, the Americans, back home in the metropolis, were discovering the value of the Canadian outlook, and departing from their own model, although not without a bit of ideological obscurantism to make it easier for themselves, and incidentally mystifying imitative colonials like us as they went along. There we were, and are, caught in the ideological double fault again.

In 1968, John D. Barriger III, the president of the Missouri-Kansas-Texas Line, one of the legendary figures of the U.S. railroad industry, gave a press conference in Vancouver where he was meeting some of his B.C. customers. While he described himself as a devout "free enterpriser" (his bit of ideological obscurantism), he praised Canadian railroad policy for preventing what he termed "destructive competition," and also for allowing the railroad industry to diversify into other transportation systems. Although against nationalization in principle, he was convinced that the U.S. should follow the Canadian lead and eliminate duplication by reducing his country's 76 class one railways and nearly 400 smaller ones into two transcontinental railways and regional feeders.

This was before the Penn Central, the U.S.'s largest railroad, and sixth largest corporation, went into bankruptcy. Seventy per cent of the Penn Central's business was done as interchanges for other railroads. One of the cultural obstacles in the way of efficient railroading has been America's historical commitment to competition and to anti-trust laws to protect the public interest, instead of turning to consolidation under public ownership. It took 11 years for the Interstate Commerce Commission to allow the merger of the ailing New York Central and the Pennsylvania. American railroading has been the prisoner of ideological fetishism, the same fetishism which made the domestic air monopoly in Canada taboo — taboo in the literal sense of superstitious accursedness.

According to an Associated Press report, a guarded suggestion by the Transportation Secretary that nationalization of railroads might be necessary if large scale federal aid were not forthcoming, drew a reluctant and sometimes angry response from a House of Representatives committee. Nevertheless, Congress did approve the nationalization of inter-city passenger trains. The CNR and other nationalized railroads began to be mentioned in the U.S. media as models for American transportation to follow.

At the same time, 1970-1971, conditions of static or declining trade plunged the U.S. air transport industry into heavy losses, just as similar conditions had cut down the North West Company in the fur trade era. The airlines complained of excessive competition and attacked the Civil Aeronautics Board for letting it happen, which is like criticizing the pregnant girl after having destroyed her contraceptives and seducing her. A raise in fares was demanded. One of the overseas carriers, Pan American, asked for transcontinental routes to integrate its service despite excess domestic capacity. Mergers and merger talks got underway. The industry desperately sought to match capacity to demand and to eliminate duplication, both of which Canada had achieved with the TCA domestic monopoly *back in 1958*, and in a sophisticated, innovative form, in which service, technological progress (new aircraft) and traffic development went ahead vigorously.

Since then, domestic air travel in Canada has gone to the oligopolistic dogs, in the oligopolistic American doghouse. Air Canada and CP Air have simultaneously gauged their fares to cover the cost of their chronic excess capacity — chronic since the monopoly was dissolved — recent fare cuts notwithstanding. The division of international routes among the two carriers, who are also domestic competitors and "political" competitors, hinders the most effective utilization of route structures and overheads, and hence the development of services and of international sales. For Canadian carriers to compete against themselves, making them less able to compete against American and other carriers, doesn't make much Canadian sense.

Competition also hinders the maximum utilization of the jumbo jet. Monopoly allows the best possible combining of flights, and the best possible distribution of flight times, to take advantage of the more efficient large airplanes without diminishing service. Monopoly has always allowed for the most efficient configuration of equipment and flights.

"[The Boeing 747] is a good airplane," said the president of TWA in 1971, "but it's simply too big." It's only too big because the list of competing flights is too long. False presumptions . . . costly configurations.

These are only particular instances of impracticality. Underlying them and more grievous is the dissolution of the monopoly culture and its symbolism.

When Air Canada and CP Air jointly applied for identical fare increases in 1968, 1970 and 1971 (in one case at least, using a joint press release for the announcement), they were granted with little or no public debate or counter-movement. By contrast, had the domestic routes been an Air Canada monopoly, and had Air Canada been guilty for over a decade of costly excess capacity, considerably above the limits put down for Parliament by their transport consultant, public debate and indignation would in all likelihood have blocked such fare increases and forced a more efficient configuration on air travel. Wasn't public indignation in the 1950's part of TCA's equipment, like radar and flashing lights?

When Wheatcroft interviewed TCA's management in 1958, they were already aware of the advantage of having a second carrier to serve as a means of comparison, which would dispel chronic indignation and leave them, and the industry, in peace and quiet. They were against it anyway. They were right on both counts. The existence of the two airlines facing each other, and providing comparison, allows each of them to perpetrate impracticality together – or to push each other into impracticality together – in public silence.

There is a smaller but better example. International air fares are calculated in U.S. dollars but set down in Canada in both currencies, and quoted here in Canadian dollars. When the Canadian dollar was unpegged and allowed to float on June 1, 1970, it quickly went up in value compared to U.S. currency and stayed there, theoretically making international flights cheaper for Canadian travellers. Both Air Canada and CP Air, however, continued to quote the old Canadian price unless specifically asked otherwise, and went on doing so for six months until the Transport Commission imposed a new exchange rate. On the other hand, if a customer were aware of what had happened, went to a bank, bought U.S. currency, and then purchased his ticket, he would have saved himself upwards of five per cent in the process, which on overseas travel in particular would amount to a considerable sum. The airlines, by agreement between themselves, would not volunteer the information.

Although it was a matter of international fares, would that have ever happened with a domestic monopoly in existence? First, the financial position of the airline would have been strong, since the domestic structure of the industry would have been strong. The carrier would not have drifted into trying to turn a penny any way it could. Secondly although ultimate authority for a change in price listings lies with the government and IATA, the airline likely would not have dared let such an anomalous situation continue for so long, because critical interest would not have let it. Thirdly, it would not in all likelihood have countenanced such gouging, regardless of the unexpected decrease in revenue, because such unfair practice would have run against the grain of the monopoly's service ethic.

The culture of Canadian air travel was a different, better creature in the domestic monopoly days.

Bad money may or may not drive out good money, but oligopoly sure as hell drives out the monopoly ethic.

Oligopoly is the most obliging of covers (the Executive Cover) for bureaucratic malpractice.

The ideological double fault also fixes colonial journalists and intellectuals in abstract backwardness.

In 1967, *The New Industrial State*, by John Kenneth Galbraith, was published and was read assiduously by interested Canadians. One of the leading ideas of the book was that ownership of a mature corporation was no longer a determining factor in its operations. Another was that in the world of mature corporations, the free enterprise mechanism, or the market mechanism, had been superceded by planning and technology, the whole protected by state investment and pervasive propaganda (advertising).

"Prices, costs, production and resulting revenues are established not by the market but, within broad limits . . . by the planning decisions of the firm." These corporations could no longer be considered "private." Where governments were the principal buyers, as in the defence industry, "private" corporate activity was really disguised socialism, or "semi-nationalized" industry.

The implications for Canada, if Galbraith were right, were obvious. We had always had difficulty raising investment capital privately, but never too much trouble raising it, and organizing it, through governments. If ownership were no longer a determining factor, why not expand our economy with public enterprise? Also, if the free market had been superceded by planning and technology, with state and cultural safeguards included, and if "industrial planning is in unabashed alliance with size," why not make the most of Canada's small domestic market by promoting the monopoly form, where planning and technology could flourish?

If, however, you think in terms of the American economic culture, you will reach opposite conclusions. Galbraith had argued that ownership had been alienated from the managerial technostructure not only in the United States but also in the publicly owned industries in western Europe and the communist countries, because only with policy-making autonomy and freedom from social control, did such enterprises work well. "Public ownership of industrial enterprises . . . is no longer a political program," Galbraith wrote, "but an overture to nostalgia." Bruce Hutchison, editor of the *Vancouver Sun*, biographer of Mackenzie King, historian and chronicler of Canadiana — a fair example of the acceptable intellectual drift in the country — seized on this.

"Socialism doesn't worry [Galbraith]," Hutchison observed on the *Sun*'s editorial page. "He considers it irrelevant and meaning only 'government by socialists who have learned that socialism, as anciently understood, is impractical.' "

A year later, Hutchison took up the same theme. "If . . . we take the Left to mean socialism in the form of government ownership of industry, the general movement is Rightwards, the good old simplicities of Marx and the Regina Manifesto being almost totally discredited except, perhaps, in China."

So the strictly economic case for more government ownership in Canada — the argument flowing out of Galbraith's thesis — was lost on Hutchison and others. But the important question is elsewhere. Why should we in Canada accept any of Galbraith's arguments about ownership in the first place? Galbraith's thesis was constructed largely with American data, and on certain phenomena in Europe and elsewhere. In the whole of Galbraith's book, Canada was mentioned only once, in a footnote, in a collective reference to unified railway systems, where, as it happens, there is indeed public enterprise. Yet Hutchison referred to Galbraith's analysis of the "North American economic system." Nowhere in the two columns he wrote on the book was there a reference to a particular economic phenomenon in Canada.

A people which looks to outsiders for its seminal ideas, and reports them with adulation, without putting them up against indigenous circumstances, is a colonial people.

As I pointed out in Part II, who owns what is important in Canada, particularly to the entrepreneurial function. But it also is important in the United States, and everywhere else, to a lesser or greater degree. A highly motivated manager in the technostructure of General Motors is identifying not simply with a corporation, but with a corporation inside a culture — with its history, symbolism, ideology and ritual — of which the mythology of private ownership and private enterprise is a part. If the culture is fragile and deteriorating, the symptoms will show up eventually in the technostructure. Similarly, if the culture is nationalist, or innovative, or humane, or authoritarian, that will show up too. No corporation exists isolated in technostructural space.

For example, I can't imagine anybody in CP Air declaring that "airlines, whether private or public, are semisocial instruments; their interest must be weighed against the interests of Canada as a whole," although I can imagine Yves Pratte, the chairman of Air Canada, saying it, as he did. I can't imagine the president of an American airline saying the equivalent, but I can imagine his muttering under his breath that what is good for the airlines is good for the country. To conceive of airlines as "semisocial instruments" evokes in Canada a whole cultural outlook linked to the role transportation has played in creating nation and identity. This is the kind of commitment to social goals which Galbraith was hoping might come out of the autonomous corporate technostructure in the

United States, once its connection to the state was demonstrated. But how could this be accomplished without a radical change in popular notions about ownership, and about the rights of shareholders to maximum returns — a change equivalent to cultural revolution — and without symbolic changes in the form of ownership itself, to legitimize the revolution?

The nature of ownership also can affect the structure of an industry. When Stephen Wheatcroft discussed the circumstances in which domestic airline competition could be successful in Canada, he underlined forcefully the responsibility of the regulatory authority to keep capacity in line with demand. The Civil Aeronautics Board (CAB) has had the same responsibility in the United States, and the International Air Transport Association (IATA) for international carriers. None of them has succeeded — both the CAB and IATA have fallen into disrepute, for good reason — because the dynamic of "competition," even under regulation, even under price-fixing, even under oligopolistic arrangement, is different from the dynamic of monopoly. If a regulatory board ever got to the point where it was regulating the airlines successfully, it wouldn't be regulating them, it would be running them.

Now, while in the colony we were being told that our public enterprise tradition was irrelevant, because Galbraith in the metropolis had said this and that, and that government ownership of industry had been "almost totally discredited," Galbraith himself, forced by his own country's experience, seemed to have changed his mind about ownership, and in an interview for the Canadian public, September 1970, cited the Canadian public enterprise tradition as a model for Americans to follow:

> . . . I was thinking of socialism in the sense of public ownership of the means of production. I am persuaded there are substantial areas of modern business enterprise, notably the railroads and the weapons firms, as well as

sectors of the housing industry, which do not function
effectively or efficiently under private ownership. . . .
My own feeling is that as long as liberals in the United
States are elaborately explaining they are not socialists as
they have in the past, they won't take hold of these
industries and have pride in some areas of public activity,
notably the Tennessee Valley Authority.
There is a parallel here with Canada. There has never been
in Canada quite the ideological resistance to public ownership that there is in the United States. The political right
in Canada has never campaigned with quite the fervor
against public ownership and socialism as the American
right has. Therefore, the position on public ownership of
the railroads, public ownership of electric power production, public ownership in the grain trade and so forth has
always been pragmatically acceptable.

As could be expected, he was all right until he got onto
Canada. Our political right has not been less perfervid than
the American political right. It has been different, because
the Canadian continuity runs on a different plane than the
American continuity. In Canada, the political right fought *for*
public ownership of power in Ontario and, in a quieter way,
for a publicly owned Welland Canal, and took passionate
pride in these areas of public activity, as against American
principles. As George Grant has reminded us, the Conservatives, in the days when they used to constitute a right, also
established public broadcasting in Canada (although much
of the political impetus for public broadcasting did come
from the left). The right was in power when the CNR was
established. The right (of a sort) also established the Bank
of Canada and the Canadian Wheat Board. The right took
over telephones in Manitoba. The right also finished the
Pacific Great Eastern (B.C. Railway) and took over the Black
Ball Ferry Company and appropriated B.C. Electric. The right
also rescued and renewed the Sydney steel mill. The federal
Conservatives, in opposition, also attempted to save Research
Enterprises Ltd. Even the Diefenbaker government, which
savaged and tore asunder broadcasting and air transport,
stood behind Polymer at a crucial point in its history. The

right is, or should be, proud of all of those things. Without public ownership, Conservatism in Canada is only a hollow shell of a dead past.

If American reality had approximated ours, the U.S. electorate would have overwhelmed attempts to block public ownership. As it is, public ownership, with some exceptions perhaps, has never seriously been put to Americans, from any direction.

Galbraith did suggest in one paragraph in *The New Industrial State* that a public corporation may be more appropriate to the new world of overwhelming social imperatives, because "the nature of the legal ownership" makes it more amenable to social goals. But that too is to miss the point. What counts in the case of a public enterprise is not so much the legal structure as the culture in which the enterprise is brought to life, and the ethic which is internalized in the enterprise in a way that transcends legal relationships and economic analysis.

Here, Galbraith is just fishing. While his analysis of the new American state is perspicacious, solid, and rich in allusions, the avenues for change that he suggests have almost no verisimilitude, because there is so little for him to go on in the American experience. *On the other hand, the internalization of a public style in our most vital enterprises is the indigenous Canadian experience.* One of the most excruciating ironies of the ideological double fault, which is the anguish of being a colonial, is suddenly seeing that the long indigenous experience has become valid, and yet seeing at the same time that we spurn this experience, while waiting timidly for the metropolis to show us the lead, *a metropolis which has none of our aptitude*. To plunge ourselves into backwardness again, when, after 200 years of backwardness, we were finally becoming creative!

When we broke up the domestic air monopoly, we not only struck a blow against better service at lower cost (which is practical foolishness), we also made our economic culture the less (which is historical blindness). Like the insecure Irish who could not make room for some of the greatest literary giants their own culture produced, we colonial, prejudice-ridden Canadians cannot accept our indigenous economic genius, and must suppress it, and must block off the new possibilities it opens up.

CHAPTER 9
___

The Colonial Oligopoly Culture

We know that a good part of our manufacturing is inefficient. What's more, we know how it's inefficient. What's more, we hold back on making it efficient, because being prisoners of the American-ideology-in-Canada, we cannot bring ourselves to act on our own calculations. The colonial ideology does, however, allow us to ruminate, which we do endlessly — slowly and with measured pace chewing on questions of economies of scale, sufficient production runs and rationalization.

Of all this analytic fodder, the one item regurgitated the most is the illustrious case of the refrigerator industry. The details sound like a dirge, they have been repeated so often. The smallest efficient plant size has been estimated variously from 200,000 to 500,000 units a year, with efficient production still possible at 700,000 units annually. The need to produce different sizes and models, and to finance technical development (where it is not available free from a parent company), biases optimum scale upwards; new production techniques might bias optimum scale downwards. In any case, Canadian shipments of domestic models in 1972 totalled 559,912 units, enough for the cheapest production possible. This does not include substantial imports. The market, however, is divided primarily among eight manufacturers, producing many sizes and models each, functioning at higher cost because of short production runs, and, even behind a 15 per cent tariff (until recently 20 per cent), losing an increasing share of the market to imports, mostly American.

In a competitive situation, companies would fall by the wayside until only one, or perhaps two producers were left. But each is wary of a protracted price war. In addition, most of the firms are American-controlled, whose parents' financial and technical strength makes it difficult for anyone to win a competitive struggle, most of all an independent Canadian producer. Also, the U.S. subsidiaries, whose purpose is to amplify corporate operations as a whole, may not want, or may not be able to enter into mergers. They come to an oligopolistic settlement at a higher price level instead.

The entry into the Canadian market of so many subsidiaries, for whom even a small volume and marketing outlet may add to the profit of the larger corporation with its base operation and technology already in place, is to a great extent responsible for this "market fragmentation" in the first place.

Refrigerators are not the only, nor necessarily the best, example. The smallest efficient plant size in oil refining is 140,000 barrels a day (the size of the projected Imperial Oil refinery in Edmonton). Costs per unit continue to fall as capacity increases to 200,000 barrels daily. According to one calculation, 500,000 barrels daily would fully realize all economies. In British Columbia where I live, there are seven refineries, four of them close to each other in the lower mainland. The biggest has a capacity of only 37,000 barrels at the outside.

From the available data, it appears that chemicals, rubber tires, television sets, electric ranges and other major appliances, pharmaceutical products, textiles, polyethylene, nylon, some machinery and equipment, electronic components, furniture and fine paper all fall, in whole or in part, into this same inefficient structural pattern, although the fault is not always the result of the presence of American subsidiaries. A complete list would likely be considerably longer. For all but a relatively few main product lines like automobiles and typewriters, and often then only the production of more complex parts and exotic materials, the Canadian market is large enough to sustain the smallest efficient plant size. At least this was the case in the mid-1960's when most of the work on economies of scale was done. Moreover, in most of those instances, enough of that market is concentrated in the Ontario-Quebec urban axis to absorb at least one such efficient plant. But since the market may be divided among two or more producers, Canadian manufacturing is riddled with inefficient plant sizes and inefficient production.

Add to that, as well, the phenomenon of excess, uneconomic model proliferation (one recent count turned up 36 models of "made-in-Canada" toasters and 300 varieties of automobile mufflers). This is also largely influenced by American subsidiaries with their derivative production ideas, and by American cultural patterns superimposed on Canada by subsidiary advertising here and by advertising spillover.

One of the results is that productivity in manufacturing in Canada is an estimated 15 to 20 per cent less than in the United States. The cost to Canadians, in higher prices, lower wages and wasted capital has been estimated in the billions of dollars annually. There are other charges on the Canadian people. High-cost industry means fewer export possibilities and stagnant technology, as often as not low profits and poor tax returns, and also vulnerability to imports, which further reduces domestic production, in turn compounding the problems of scale.

The disclosure of these structural inefficiencies in our economy has resulted mostly, over the years, in a . . . repetition of the disclosure of these structural inefficiencies. The production of the analysis of the refrigerator industry has particularly flourished, although it is losing ground now to the analysis of such things as the television set industry and the microwave equipment industry. Inventive jargon, like "miniature replica effect" (describing the imposition of American production patterns on the smaller Canadian market), has been coined for the purpose, much like a new machine tool might be devised in a workshop to aid production flow. There have been a good 15, perhaps 20, years of honest colonial application here.

The first official analysis was produced and displayed in 1957 for the Royal Commission on Canada's Economic Prospects; the refrigerator industry, of course, was a component. Since then, the Economic Council of Canada has elaborated on it. So has the Task Force on the Structure of Canadian Industry (1968). So has the Science Council of Canada (1972). Economists have amassed chapters and books by delving into it. Polemicists have cited it. The men who manage our factories, and work in them, and distribute their products, live with it every day. To judge from the comments of the western sales manager of Canadian General Electric, they have always known it for what it is: industrial sickness. Other peoples who wouldn't permit such inefficiency to go on at home, like the Japanese, must wonder at it. The high cost of manufacturing in such significant sectors in Canada must be to them, on their trips to North America, one of the wonders of the world, along with the Aurora Borealis and the Grand Canyon.

Yet there is, and always has been, an empirical solution: the consolidation of this largely American settlement under Canadian public enterprise, so that we have one producer of refrigerators if necessary to benefit fully from economies of scale and specialization, one refiner of gasolines in areas like southern B.C., and so on where appropriate, at prices equal to, or lower than, U.S. equivalents; just as in domestic air transport, where we have one dominant public enterprise carrier, prices have been as low as, sometimes marginally lower than, American prices.

The data on the optimum number of plants in relationship to market size of course changes as markets and technology change. For example, it appears that for some of the major appliances, the increasing market in Canada might support two producers of efficient scale. On the other hand, a single producer, with a larger volume and more resources, might have more leeway for technical innovation, and for the development of components either within the firm or by suppliers. In any case, the argument, as will become clear, goes beyond the immediate financial advantages of Canadian public monopoly, to the cultural possibilities.

The mechanics of nationalization and payment to bring about this consolidation — the financial aspects — are the easiest, not the most difficult, part of it. The acquisition and integration of fragmented plant pays for itself quickly. In the private sector in the United States, it happens as a matter of course. It is seen to be rational and desirable. In Canada, the colonial ideology stops us again, and stops us from doing what the United States did for itself decades ago (in the case of oil refining, almost a century ago): another ideological double fault. John D. Rockefeller, reminiscing with old friends about his role in rationalizing the U.S. oil industry, summed up with emotion: "I discovered something that made a new world and I did not know it at the time." We "dumb Canadians," 103 years after the formation of the Standard Oil Company, still don't know it. Not all of the data of royal commissions and the studies of economists and the earnestness of politicians have made much difference.

The blindness to public enterprise provides only part of the explanation. Canadians can easily imagine a government takeover of Bell Canada or of B.C. Telephone. The economic case for public monopolies in refrigerator and washing machine production, where savings are to be had in structural reform, is much stronger. But the ideological block against it is inversely much larger because the pressure against conceiving of consumer goods that way — that is, in terms of the Canadian monopoly culture rather than of the American oligopoly culture — is so much more intense.

This has not, of course, come about in a vacuum. We have been caught here in a massive cultural struggle, involving legions of men and women and vast sums of money.

On the one side are the dominating, well-equipped forces of the colonial army. The ranks include all of our advertising agencies, all of our daily newspaper publishers, all of our few publishers of popular magazines, all of our television and radio stations (save the few that do not run commercials), and a good part of our film makers, writers and artists. Our elected representatives and economists are camp followers. Together with the producers of our gasolines and refrigerators and detergents, they constitute a sort of oligopoly-cultural complex.

Using the most advanced technology available, they bombard Canadians incessantly with images, slogans and sequences in which consumer products are linked to the symbols and style of the oligopoly culture, most of which has its origins in the American imagination. Brand name differentiation is its artistic core. The culture depends on it. We are culture-bound by it. The display of brand names fills up our environment and holds us to it. Hypothetically, a single producer marketing the same product under different brand names would be acceptable to us.

The workings of the oligopoly culture are not, very often, far removed from that. As we are now realizing is the case for a large variety of contending products, much of the choice is only a choice of images. The "highly vocal section of the Canadian public" that carped against the Trans-Canada Air Lines domestic monopoly in the name of what Stephen Wheatcroft called "an unquestionable desire . . . for the right to choose" got little or no additional choice in prices, routes, aircraft, airports, crews and auxiliary services, only a choice of names. We haven't heard from them since. Grant McConachie's proposal for integration of Air Canada and CP Air but with a retention of separate identities was administrative nonsense but cultural cunning.

So that while we accept a single symbolic description of our telephones, the notion of having a parallel monopoly in gasolines, for example, argued in economic terms only, is hard to assimilate. It "shocks" us. It comes at us with the tangled promise-threat of financial savings and cultural dislocation. Since man is primarily a social and cultural animal, and only in a secondary, linked way, an economic animal, we pay the higher price for our Shell and Gulf and Westinghouse and General Electric products, and stay hooked to the old culture, and shout out whatever ideological rationalization is at hand.

It follows that by the nature of the colonial occupation, political radicalism without cultural radicalism isn't enough. It hasn't been enough. It follows, also, that members of Parliament with cultural imagination will help more to bring down our refrigerator and washing machine prices than members with legal or economic imagination. Given our present members of Parliament, it follows further that we are still paying through the nose!

If all the lawyers in the House of Commons were poets instead, those hurrying cretinous men in running shoes, and the light bulb with a better idea, and that insufferable mother who made a sock used as a rag come out smelling fresh again, and her son who was thereby overjoyed, and their whole monumentally crass and phoney family of relatives who keep our prices high, would be hooted out of existence. The members' cultural good sense would get the best of their political dogma. Poets have better ideas.

*   *   *

The cultural occupation has another demoralizing effect. Since the Canadian entrepreneurial mainstream in public enterprise stands outside it, it adds to the feeling, noted in Part II, that as regards a wide range of manufacturing activity and innovation, we are capable of very little on our own. A cheap and serviceable electric kettle taken by itself, as a physical embodiment, is simple enough. As a cultural embodiment of General Electric and Westinghouse and Sunbeam, against whose cultural mystique nothing Canadian with equivalent force is offered, it can be humbling, although an equally cheap and serviceable kettle from a Canadian producer may be sitting next to it on the shelf (not to mention larger contrary examples elsewhere, from telecommunications equipment to nuclear reactors). In a cultural zone like automobiles, where constant blocks of visual and verbal sequences are catapulted at the public by American, Japanese, Swedish, German and other foreign producers and their agents, but where there are no Canadian participants, there is not even a nominal Canadian cultural presence.

So that a neighbour, in a branch of wholesaling, should tell me of the American, and German, and Japanese products he handles, and then, his anger escaping him, should announce that Canadians don't seem to be able to make anything. My plumber, when I asked him about the companies making bathroom fixtures, should reply with sarcastic astonishment that they were American, and what else could they be? A sales officer of a U.S. appliance subsidiary, despairing of Canadians' ability to produce efficiently in his field (although the market in Canada, taken as a whole, is no problem), should suggest, seriously or sarcastically, I'm not sure, that "maybe we could manufacture lace or some other specialty like the Belgians; maybe that would make us world-famous." Again, counter-examples are no good here. These are deep-rooted feelings conditioned by skilful cultural repetition, without being offset by an adequate response from the Canadian community, which is the entrepreneurial problem at the beginning.

*   *   *

Against this omnipresent, technically advanced and expensive "imperialist" oligopoly culture, however, lies an opposing force which, without apparent resources in dollars and technique, nevertheless does it in, in the end — namely, indigenous circumstance. The same dialectic which induced us to build the Welland Canal and the CPR, and which broke the North West Company, is pushing us now in other sectors.

Where we have gone into public enterprise and monopoly, as in electric power and transportation, our industry has been as efficient as any, and in the forefront of technology, and has benefited by our creative ability. Where we have refused to elaborate on the Canadian market contradiction — where we have adopted or received the ill-fitting American model instead of creating one of our own based on the indigenous circumstance — our industry has been inefficient and second-rate, and worst of all, imitative. In that latter process, the rich public enterprise culture of service and craft, along with its larger potential for participation, has been set back. The elimination of the Trans-Canada Air Lines monopoly model was such a cultural step backward. Ontario Hydro has become culturally stagnant. B.C. Hydro, growing up in an oligopoly frontier at the edge of a free enterprise wilderness, has been culturally shallow. The tradition is there, however, buried, waiting for a renaissance.

E. P. Taylor used to talk fondly of the "wasteful vigour" of competition in the Ontario brewing industry, and journalists marked him down as a philosopher. To the indigenous mind, "wasteful vigour" is just wasteful, plain and simple. The high cost of consumer products in Canada is described as "the price of being a Canadian." But we don't have to pay that price. If we were true to the Canadian experience, we would not be paying that price. "The price of being a Canadian" is really the price we pay for being Americans-in-Canada.

While we go on masochistically, stubbornly paying the price, our neo-classical economists, trained in the assumptions of the American-ideology-in-Canada, and masochists in their own special, cabbalistic way, go on butting their heads against a prosaic fact of life whose villainy they sustain for the purpose, namely the tariff. This also, in the colony, plays a useful social function. As long as they keep the tariff problem alive, we can escape into it, and avoid facing up to our condition. All this time, the tariff has been the procrastinator's and dogmatist's best talking point. Nothing very much happens. Nothing much can happen. The masochism endures.

In the bold terms of the anti-tariff doctrine, Canadian tariff policy is a fraud, and John A. Macdonald's National Policy is the Great National Failure, perpetrated on Canadians by a narrow-minded, provincial, smug, chauvinist, petty, protective economic elite, who guarded *their* British imperial preferences and *their* profits, and who attempted to convince the Canadian masses that they were far better off being poor British cousins than money-grubbing American ones. This Bay Street gang were marked by other characteristics. They were really and truly unenterprising, afraid to face up to American competition, and to competition in world markets. Their anti-Americanism was mean and underhand, stemming from a deep-seated inferiority complex. Not having accomplished anything worthy of genuine national pride, they refused to acknowledge that American exuberance and imagination were something more than materialistic crassness. They could not stomach American mass society, which offended their conservatism. Yet they themselves were infernally jealous of the Americans, and watched their games and followed the gossip about their presidents. Their overweening Britishness and conservatism was only a convenient, self-serving screen by which they lined their own pockets and maintained their social power and self-respect, meanwhile keeping the rest of the country down.

More than that, Canada's tariff policy, in the terms of the doctrine, is a crime against progress and civilization. Free trade is the vehicle by which mass-produced goods, at lowest cost, will eventually free the world from inefficient local production and poverty, and incidentally, by spreading the mass consumer culture, break down parochial, feudal enclaves and divisive nationalisms.

Even now, economic nationalists, and particularly tariff nationalists, are still occasionally described as inward-looking loyalists — throwbacks to the Tory nationalists — although that old British-infected loyalism died long ago. The Tory rump army, led by its fleet-footed generals, has long since gone over to the other side. Only a few peevish intellectual batmen stayed behind. And yet, in the face of the internal logic of the doctrine, the tariff remains, as it always has, through anti-American Tory and pro-American Liberal governments alike.

The support of the Ontario voter for tariifs, on the grounds of provincial self-interest, is understandable. But in the rest of the country, including the West and the Maritimes, where grumbling about tariffs is a chronic habit almost as old as Canada itself, there has never been a serious anti-tariff movement either. If the price of being a tariff-bound Canadian is so high, why do even the biggest losers go on paying it with only token opposition?

The answer is that Canadians are not losers by the tariff but winners by it. A Canadian, like everybody else, is not a walking, waking bundle of economic impulses, but a social creature linked to a culture. And a culture that leaves itself open to powerful economic forces outside its control instinctively feels itself vulnerable, with justification. Mixed exceptions, like Switzerland, only prove the rule. Far from incorrigible backwardness, Canada's tariff policy confirms us in our human nature.

The experiences of the peoples of the world with free trade are strewn with cultural tragedy and dislocation.

The entry of cheap manufactured goods from Europe into the coastal ports of China virtually extinguished traditional rural industry in accessible regions, while the western hammerlock on Chinese sovereignty prevented her from protecting a nascent capitalism. This precipitated the economic deterioration of the Empire which led, along with other factors, to the chaos and notorious famines of the Age of Confusion.

The permanent underselling of hand-woven cloth in India by Lancashire machine-made piece goods effectively destroyed the cohesiveness of the Indian village community. This also left the people vulnerable to famine and degradation since the traditional village economy no longer existed to store grain and to distribute it in times of difficulty. In even more devastating ways, the economic culture of Europe helped to demoralize and then shatter the Kaffir of South Africa and the North American Indian.

In Europe itself, where nations were more culturally

prepared for the Industrial Revolution, and maintained their momentum and retained the basic elements of sovereignty, societies in distress were able to build tariff walls instead.

Only for a hardly perceptible moment, between 1860 and 1875, was something like unrestricted free trade and free capital movement in force, regulated by the "semi-automatic switchboard" of the free trade power, Great Britain, *but excluding the United States, which remained systematically protectionist throughout.* Then in the late 1870's, a general movement of protectionism got underway. The disruptive strains of free markets and free trade were too great for men to tolerate. Labour sought protection in unions and social welfare. Employers, to meet their workers' demands, sought protection from competition from low-wage countries. Nations as collectivities sought protection from the vicissitudes of the international market. Agricultural interests sought protection.

In particular, industrializing economies set up tariff walls against Great Britain, without which their own development would have been stifled. There was never much doubt on this point among national economists in the United States and Germany, for example. Behind their tariffs, in the 19th century, they flourished (as Japan would also, in a protected climate, after World War II). India, on the other hand, prevented by British rule from doing the same, languished and suffered as a manipulated, de-industrialized hinterland.

An attempt was made to re-establish free trade after World War I, but that ended in such severe dislocation that it created an extreme defensive reaction towards protectionism, and in many European countries towards totalitarian government as well. At that point, international trade dried up. Then came war, genocide, the drawing down of blinds.

The countries most doctrinaire in preaching free trade would also break the faith when it suited them. While cloth was still hand-woven, British textile-makers secured the prohibition of foreign "calicoes." Later, when they were making cheap factory cloth, they turned about and imposed a market for their products on India and wherever else they could. Nor did they hesitate to manipulate tariffs on yarns and finished goods, to prohibit the export of machinery and migration of skilled workers and technicians, to impose inland duties on Indian textiles within India from which British traders were exempt, and to otherwise inhibit Indian textile manufacturing, in order to protect Lancashire's markets at home and in the colony. After all that, Britain put on its liberal face. Unassailable, it could by then afford in colonial matters what Gunnar Myrdal has called the "luxury" of greater laissez faire. Free trade and "Free Trade" became the order of the day.

But after World War I, with her industry obsolete, Britain turned naturally to tariff protection again (in the case of automobiles, long before the official burial of free trade) and this was in fact an important period of economic reorganization for the country.

International free trade was the doctrine only as long as it favoured the nation espousing it, which realists in all countries well knew.

The United States, the most powerful of nations, has also hewed to the human rule. Tariffs grew up with industry (or vice-versa), from the beginning of the 19th century. The explosive industrial expansion during and after the Civil War took place behind new protective tariffs. In 1866, in the middle of this phase, the U.S. abrogated reciprocity in natural resources with Canada. In 1922, tariffs were the highest in U.S. history although the United States was the leading industrial nation of the world and also its chief creditor. In 1930, the U.S. reverted to higher tariffs just like most other countries at the time, cry as the critics might that it was virtually "a declaration of economic war against the whole of the civilized world."

Throughout the 1960's the world became familiar with another side of American commercial practice — a manipulative, strong-arm side. The U.S. government became notorious for interfering with the free flow of capital and goods for the sake of the national interest and at the expense of other countries, by legal and "illegal" orders to multinational corporations. But the corporations themselves, in also notorious ways, could display their American nationalism. It wasn't too much different in spirit from the imperialist administration of the British Raj in India on behalf of the Manchester Chamber of Commerce and the rest of the manufacturing interests that dominated British life.

"We welcome competition, because America is at her greatest when she is called upon to compete," the president of the United States declared in 1971, and then went about sabotaging free comeptition with export subsidies and other commercial and diplomatic manoeuvres and pressures so that America would be at her greatest. But other countries are not free trade innocents either. The human condition remains the same.

When the international trade structure began to break down in the interwar period, trade theorists let go with angry, impassioned sermonizing at the unfaithful. Yet the idea that societies would willingly suffer serious and even traumatizing dislocation from unhindered free trade, and ignore their own problems, and keep their hands tied on the premise that it was best for them in the long run, if they would only stick it out, was a hopelessly extravagant, utopian presumption, particularly when so many historical examples of eventual betrayal by other parties were on hand. And once intervention began here or there, reciprocal intervention occurred. The system was perilously fragile. No arguments that protectionism was irrational and insane, backward, retrogressive, tribal, autarchic, no argument that it led to inefficient, unsuitable local production, particularly for small countries, which was indeed the case — no such argument would avail.

No argument that Canada, with its limited global power, should open itself up to the United States, with preponderant global power and a notorious self-centred nationalism — no such argument can avail either. That kind of leap of faith is too much even for Canadians' irrationality.

Meanwhile, the scholars of free trade go on elaborating their otherwordly theology.

Story has it that during the Middle Ages, preceding the dawn of empiricism, when dogmatic scholasticism reigned over intellectual life, a group of monks fell into intense argument about how many teeth there were in a donkey's mouth. They hunted assiduously through the scriptures for an answer. Not finding one, they began to elaborate theories and counter-theories based on indirect clues. One monk suggested they go to the stable and look inside a donkey's mouth. He was thrown out of the monastery.

Our free trade scholars are such scholastic monks. They promote pious study organizations with sound theological names like The Private Planning Association of Canada. They effectively solicit charity, to keep them running, perhaps even from great sinners against the principles of free trade. Their doctrinal treatises and calculations fill catacombs and study cells. The University of Toronto Press is up to volume 13 on a series of books on Canada in a free trade North American or North Atlantic area. Since history is endless and numbers infinite, and since the monkish life is psychologically self-sustaining, that series may go on forever.

Or perhaps the proponents of free trade, as zealous preachers to the natives, are best described as latter-day Black Robes. I say that because the venerable chief missionary of North American free trade during the sixties, Harry G. Johnson, a professor of economics at the University of Chicago, really is a resurrection of the black-robed pemmican-eating Jesuits who, from St. Louis and Chicago, preceded the boomers and wolfers and free traders into the American northwest, to proselytize the native people and, as it turned out, to betray them. And the small business propagandists of continentalism really are resurrections of those free traders, happily beating the drum of Manifest Destiny, and never admitting to themselves that the materialist utopia which they envisioned was as firmly tied to the wiles and evils of a self-interested establishment as were the old cities which they couldn't tolerate, and the old families with whom they had nothing in common.

The essence of the missionary doctrine is economic determinism — that the selective rationalization of the Canadian economy by Canadians for Canadians isn't even worth thinking about, that the decisions of responsible governments to protect collectivities against the commercial march are primitive and irrelevant, because American economic domination of Canada is inevitable. As Professor Johnson himself put it, the U.S. will not "sacrifice its own economic interests to those of Canada when the two conflict." Canada's role is — must be — to submit.

One can almost hear the Black Robes in the 1860's patiently explaining to the natives the practicality of surrendering to what was essentially a commercial and cultural, and only incidentally a military, invasion; or Captain Mullan of the U.S. Army pronouncing his famous dictum, not without a touch of sorrow: "The Indian is destined to disappear before the white man, and the only question is, how it may best be done . . . to produce to himself the least amount of suffering, and to us the least amount of cost."

In those frontier days, the missionaries chiefly argued the virtues of non-violence, and of respecting treaties, although they knew from repeated disappointments and abuse that their ministrations were not taken seriously by the white man himself. Yet they kept on preaching to the red man because he was theologically naive and susceptible to religious persuasion. Economic integrationists· like to preach to Canadians for the same reason. We have no Adam Smith, no Karl Marx, not even a J. K. Galbraith of our own — no economic theology based on the Canadian experience. We are a glorious field for American economists hooked on a messianic vocation, but ignored by their own kind, except that unlike the plains Indians, Canada has half a chance of coming back.

The tariff, then, is normalcy. Growing up in the West

I was led not so much to despise the tariff as to take pride
in the fact that it was we in the West who were paying for
it, and not some arrogant, patronizing, self-centred Toronto
manufacturers, and to never let them forget it.

The abnormalcy is not that we should go on paying for
the tariff, but that we should go on paying such a high price
for it when we don't have to.

Once freed from our obsession with the tariff, we
make an astonishing discovery: that the creation of public
monopolies in many of these consumer goods industries in
Canada would mean more competition rather than less.

There are primarily two kinds of competition. One is the
competition of liberal economic theory, where protagonists
fight each other endlessly with low prices and entrepreneurial
stratagems, cutting margins to the bone, and where the weak
fall by the wayside and the strong survive, to be challenged
in turn by new entrants searching after some of the profit.
All of them are servants, or slaves if you like, of market
forces.

That kind of "price competition," or "perfect competition" (the theoretical expression), or what might be
described as "basic market competition," can be economically
destructive. Farmers set up marketing boards to eliminate it.
Professionals and others form associations. Large companies
combine into cartels or trusts, or gain monopoly or oligopoly
advantage in the market by consolidation, and with the aid
of expensive cultural propaganda and other oligopolistic
devices. Price accommodation among firms is the corporate
rule rather than the exception. And if Galbraith is right, a
certain management of prices and demand is essential to
safeguard large investments in technology and production.
In an earlier age, in the last quarter of the 19th century, the
burgeoning trust combinations, for all their anti-social evils,
also served a purpose, particularly in the U.S: they brought
order and scale out of competitive chaos. The countries that
allowed or encouraged such concentration of industry — the
United States and Germany — forged ahead into new fields

of technology and business administration. Great Britain, caught in the legacy of her Industrial Revolution and disinclined to concentration, was eclipsed.

"Perfect competition," wrote Joseph Schumpeter, as if to put down the theory once and for all, ". . . wastes opportunities . . . is not only impossible but inferior, and has no title to being set up as a model of ideal efficiency." That was a generation ago.

Basic market competition can be anathema to progress. One might more appropriately call it "market shackled" or "market tyrannized" competition.

More generally, the uncertainties of such competition (the possibility of losing money and even being run out of business), and the uncertainties of markets (the possibility of prices, particularly commodity prices, falling through), go against the grain of human nature. "People of the same trade seldom meet together, even for merriment and diversion," wrote the original liberal economist Adam Smith, "but the conversation ends in a conspiracy against the public or in some contrivance to raise prices." Against that, the anti-trust philosophy, even the doctrinaire and dogmatic American code, has been relatively useless.

It goes without saying that not all forms of competition in the marketplace end there. Companies compete by innovation, on a technical basis, for example, or with product differentiation and other customer inducements, which are innovations of another sort, or by organizational innovation. According to Schumpeter, the possibility alone of competitive innovation can keep even a monopoly alert and energetic, especially in manufacturing. This has been the effective motor of creativity and productivity in the modern American economy, the argument goes. The freedom from the limitations of basic market competition helps rather than hinders the process.

However, such competition by innovation is not necessarily forthcoming. And when it does occur, it is not always meaningful or constructive — superficial product differentiation, for example. In that sense, it is wasteful and uneconomic. Or it is not exceptional enough to disrupt the protective arrangement which oligopoly or private monopoly represents. In other words, it has little disciplining effect. Further, a breakthrough giving clear superiority to one firm can lead to its own abuses. In cases like the Canadian subsidiary economy where rationalization has gone begging, an organizational innovation that is obvious and whose merits have been demonstrated elsewhere is not accomplished because of an oligopolistic stand-off. In all instances, the margin afforded by the absence of basic market competition is in the background, ranging from a loose understanding at a low price level in a technically progressive sector to flagrant gouging and restrictive practices by a traditional cartel.

So, in different contexts, to different degrees, the oligopolistic settlement is made, by hook or by crooks. But if made too well, there is little to control abuses of price arrangements and manipulation of the public. The system lurches on by itself, like a runaway tractor.

But there is another general sort of competition, a sort which is natural to the human condition, in which men vie with each other in thoroughness and excellence, for self-affirmation or social approval. In most cases, this has nothing to do with market competition or profits. More likely, the competition takes place within a framework of collective pursuit, or of peer values, in which individuals vie for recognition from the group or collectivity, like George Stephen, who, in the bitterest days of trying to raise money for the CPR against Grand Trunk machinations, pawned his fortune, although it was "simply absurd on any kind of business grounds," and wrote to John A. Macdonald that "personal [profit] interests" had become a "secondary affair" for him. No simple market competition would have made him do so much. Or men will compete in generosity, and compete with great ardour, even unto outlandish extremes, as in the Kwakiutl potlach, where the incentive was status. Or groups or communities will compete, not necessarily for gain, as countries compete in world markets, but for group affirmation. Or individuals will compete, quite simply, for adventure, to meet a challenge, like mountain climbers and chess players.

Anthropologists have found that it is this kind of socially bound competition, not the market-bound kind, which is among the usual incentives to economic effort, and of course it is this kind of vying for excellence in performance which is the motive force behind Canadian public enterprise.

Maintain the tariff along with the present industrial structure in Canada, in that whole range of products from drugs to refrigerators, and you maintain a high-cost, low-grade oligopoly. Remove the tariff, and Canadian industry becomes part of the backward, American oligopolistic settlement. Maintain the tariff, and organize public monopolies behind it, and you create the kind of situation of which the real stuff of competition is made.

Under public monopoly, the tariff would still prevent disruptive market-bound competition, thereby assuring industry of the stability for technological and cultural innovation. But there would also be great public interest and pressure in bringing our prices down to, and below, American prices, as well as an intense subjective impulse on the part of the enterprise itself to bring prices down and to raise quality, stemming from the compelling, historically inbred urge of Canadians to prove themselves next to Americans.

What could be more compelling? Was there ever, in Canadian business history, an episode of competition so bitterly intense, and absorbing, as the battle of technology and efficiency waged by early Ontario Hydro against the New York power companies, although they weren't in the same market at all? The performance of American industry becomes a challenge and a yardstick. The until now traumatizing proximity of the industrial United States is turned to advantage, although, as it might turn out, the proximity of an intensely creative Canadian public enterprise style — of a Canada in a creative phase — might have a traumatizing effect on United States industry, as Ontario Hydro did have on American privately owned power producers, in its halcyon days.

The much-abused tariff, lo and behold, enhances competition.

In the meantime, the blind (economists) go on leading the blind (the rest of us).

Trained in the market-bound dogma of the American-ideology-in-Canada, our economists are constitutionally incapable of elaborating the possibilities of monopoly. Their methodological tools are cut for the wrong country, in the wrong century.

The economists' concepts of "perfect competition," "imperfect competition," and "monopoly," for example, should for many sectors of the economy be replaced with the culturally derived ideas of "public monopoly," "imperfect monopoly" and "market-bound competition," with "market-bound competition" at the bottom and "public monopoly" as the theoretical ideal. It makes far more sense, for example, to describe the co-existence of the CPR and the CNR as "imperfect monopoly" rather than as "imperfect competition," as the merging of telecommunications and the division of passenger services indicate, and as Edward Beatty, as president of the CPR, realized back in 1935. Domestic air transport is also now an "imperfect monopoly," after having been a "perfect monopoly," and a perfect "monopoly" model. The practical possibilities of elements of Canadian manufacturing are also, as we have seen, best understood by describing those sectors in terms of "imperfect monopoly," with all the implications for cultural striving to monopoly that the phrase touches off, rather than in market terms of "imperfect competition."

That has to do with the particular Canadian situation. As I am going to argue in Chapter 15, the concept of monopoly culture also lends itself well, as a theoretical model, to development in all advanced countries.

Similarly, economists, instructed in competition only in its exceptional and fragile market-bound sense, inevitably call for the abolition of tariffs to increase competition. The tariff is necessarily seen as a defensive, reactionary instrument. On the other hand, taking competition in its more substantive culture-bound sense, and seeing that in many sectors of the economy, market-bound competition cannot culturally hold, least of all in Canada where price fixing from drugs to farm machinery is notorious, Canadian historical man is equally obliged to see the tariff as a creative, ingenious instrument for stimulating competition.

Economies are cultures. Economists are culturally backward. Economics is too important to be left to the economists.

The two unique dialectics which have created the contrasting economic cultures of the United States and Canada work themselves out in all aspects of the culture — in consumerism, technology and the media, as well as in production — and will continue to produce contrasts as they unwind.

Ralph Nader, for example, visits Canada, and finding the absence of a vibrant *Consumer Reports* and of multitudinous citizens groups across the country involved in investigation, disclosure and court action, is perplexed at the weakness of the consumer movement on this side of the border. Coming from the dense and heavily populated economic culture of the United States out of which that creativity arises, that is how he inevitably sees consumerism.

In the U.S., Nader can draw on student and graduate idealism. In Canada, two student activist groups organized at McMaster University and the University of Windsor after a Nader visit, quickly fell apart from lack of interest. "Traditionally, a lot of the reformers [in the U.S.] were lawyers," Nader has pointed out, but in Canada, the lawyers just "don't look to the broader consequences of what they're doing."

"What we're looking for," he says, "are Canadians with guts." One gets the impression that he's not expecting to find too many. Canadians seem to be afflicted with an inexplicable listlessness and indifference. Nader despairs, we are told, of being able to do anything for us.

Coming from the smaller Canadian population, which is divided as well into two language groups, a reformist Canadian equivalent listens to Ralph Nader and, noticing in his solutions the absence of any coming to grips with the private ethic of American industry, is perplexed at the weakness of the consumer movement on the other side of the border. In Canada, consumer independence has expressed itself in just such realistic ways — in the passionate, broad-based movements behind public power and public broadcasting, whose citizens' involvement Naderism hasn't even come close to approaching. One thing that would never be even hinted of Adam Beck or of Alan Plaunt (of the Canadian Radio League) was that they didn't have any guts, or that they were listless or indifferent.

Those profound, illuminating experiences in consumerism and the public good have been suppressed because the American-ideology-in-Canada has no way of accommodating them. An altogether Canadian boy like Ken Dryden, ex-goalie of the Montreal Canadiens, will give up his summer holidays to work free for Nader, will approach Nader, on leaving, "as if he [Dryden] were an Italian peasant having an audience with the Pope," in the words of *The Canadian Magazine*, such is his respect, and will return to Canada with a Nader-inspired project in mind; yet he will probably have no inkling, not the slightest suspicion, of the strength of Canadian originality when it expresses itself in its own way. That current in Canadian history, slowly and fitfully pushing against the colonial mentality, is still, nevertheless, inching the country forward.

Nader, himself, is an unmistakably American creature. His strategy of attempting to decentralize industry and to promote honest-to-goodness competition is hopelessly American romantic. Nader's Raiders are Easy Riders turned inside out. In the same way, Nader's achievements in the United

States are so encouraging within the American context, and American romanticism is so congenitally blind to collective differences, that it would likely never occur to Nader that creating "a few model involvements in Canada," or taking on Canada, or despairing of the difficulty of doing anything in Canada, carried hidden away in itself the same assumptions about peoples that were harboured by the Black Robes of the 19th century, and the drummers of Manifest Destiny then and now, although it unmistakably does, and that these assumptions have in them the seeds of humiliation and dislocation for other peoples.

In Canada, for all of the imitative Naderism that is starting up in our newspapers and cities, the real challenge to the oligopoly scandal is coming again from public enterprise with the entry of Saskatchewan, Manitoba and British Columbia into automobile insurance, the establishment of public exploration companies (also the momentum building up across the country for more direct public participation in resource development), the creation of the B.C. Petroleum Corporation to capture windfall profits in natural gas, the prairie telephone companies whose rates provide at least a rough standard of comparison for charges elsewhere, the land bank and land-use programs and the beginning of an exploration of crown entry into the manufacture of consumer products, the most frequently mentioned possibility being generic drugs (at the retail level, Saskatchewan has begun a program of bulk purchase of hearing aids for clinic distribution).

When a royal commission confirmed the existence of excessive profiteering in farm machinery from price-fixing and corporate manipulation, which Canadian farmers had long known about, the Canadian Federation of Agriculture did not go after anti-trust prosecutions in the Nader style. It asked for a crown corporation for selling farm machinery instead. When Nader's controversial book *Unsafe At Any Speed* was published in 1965, from which point in time Naderism began, it was a Canadian public corporation, the

CBC, among the continent's mass media, which had the freedom and the internalized spirit to interview him first, an occurrence Nader has never forgotten because the interview was also seen in Detroit.

It's a matter of the Canadian temperament. The public enterprise vehicle suits us. On the other hand, we can't uphold American consumerism in Canada because we have no masses of Americans to uphold it.

The same contrasts between the Canadian monopoly culture and the American oligopoly culture show up in technology. Would a comprehensive system of electrical inspection have come out of Canada (in the 1920's) if Ontario Hydro had been a privately owned American subsidiary? Would the introduction of safety belts have taken so long, or would we still be without a truly safe car, or a car designed for Canadian winters (one of J. J. Brown's grievances), if automobile production all this while had been a Canadian public monopoly instead of an American oligopoly? For the future, the public enterprise ethic of service and design, in the monopoly culture and elsewhere, lends itself almost perfectly to the production of goods "that have greater reliability, durability, safety, efficiency and esthetic value," to borrow from Pierre Bourgault's instruction in *Inovation and the Structure of Canadian Industry.*

The affliction of consumer product oligopolies is that they can focus competition on economically wasteful, culturally narrowing product differentiation, and drag all firms together in the same technological direction. The public monopoly culture opens up other, different technological possibilities. For that matter, if life insurance, realty services, gasolines, the marketing and in some cases manufacture of drugs, hearing aids, detergents, margarines, breakfast cereals and so on, were public monopoly cultures, would we be paying the high costs of excessive marketing structures and product differentiation that we are stuck with now? And what new consumer possibilities would monopoly culture open up in such areas, liberated as they would be from the culturally stultifying oligopolistic stranglehold?

Similarly, most calculations of optimum plant size are based on American oligopoly experience. Polymer, working with a smaller domestic market as a base, nevertheless extended technology to produce more varieties of rubber inside its single Canadian plant without a telling loss in efficiency. Public monopolies in household appliances and other areas might be faced with the same challenges of producing variety inside production runs, or of combining production runs of different but related products. Just conceivably, had we been deeply involved in these kinds of problems in the past, the hand-arm machine, which was invented in Canada, might have had the capital for a strong patent fence, and might have been elaborated on here instead of in the United States, and we might have gone on to take the lead in automation technology.

Now imagine how the uses of the media would change, to reflect the indigenous monopoly culture in full elaboration. The oligopolistic American culture of incessant, unbalanced, needless, trivial, dehumanizing product differentiation falls away — these manifestations are not synonymous with a consumer culture, only synonymous with American consumer culture and its imitators — and a familiar, community-oriented, environment-oriented, appropriate Canadian personality rises to the surface, in television, film, graphics, print, sound and product design. A stranger coming across the border from the United States would not have to bring an anthropologist with him to discover why Canadians persisted in their belief that they were different.

So the tariff, as well as enhancing competition, also enhances technological and cultural innovation by nourishing the full range of economic cultures in the world, out of which can spring the greatest variety of practical ideas. These economic cultures touch each other in a process of cross-fertilization. Without the American economic culture, where would European and Canadian technology be today? In the same way, the more the American culture intrudes into western Europe in the guise of corporate organization, the poorer and less various the world's technology will be tomorrow.

Not unnaturally, our contribution to this process as regards North America has sprung from our public enterprise character, with the monopoly ethic of public service in the background, although often hedged in and imperfectly expressed. In railways, in public power and in public broadcasting, in the 1967 world exposition, perhaps also in automobile insurance, Canadian public enterprise has helped to fill the blind spot in the American psyche. It is this kind of participation in North America which has exciting meaning, and which advances practical civilization. Beside it, free trade participation is trivial.

Until now we have never taken our monopoly culture seriously. (We have been told we were a free enterprise nation, and we believed it.) Utilities, transportation and communications have been considered exceptions to the rule (although both their assets and their revenues are enormous), and have suffered from being so considered. As a result, we have overlooked the rich possibilities flowing out of the monopoly culture, which means that we have overlooked some of the rich possibilities in ourselves.

CHAPTER 10

Some Other Examples of Economic Masochism
(In Which the Canadian People, Having Been Stood on Their Heads by Colonial Ideology, See Public Enterprise Upside Down and Accordingly Act Backwards)

All of these cases stem from a defensive, somewhat absurdist antipathy to indigenous public enterprise caused by inappropriate perceptions of Canadian entrepreneurship.

(a) *Missing the entrepreneurial woods for the entrepreneurial trees.* Research Enterprises Limited was a wartime Canadian producer of optical glass (including filter glasses and glasses in platinum), finished optics, fire control devices, radars (including light airborne radars, heavy models for ships, large mobile tracking assemblies and cathode ray tube production), and instruments (including range finders, artillery directors, binoculars, telescopes, periscopes, dial sights and precision level bubbles). It produced the first microwave (radar) gun-laying equipment in the world, and was the first mass producer of radars generally. Its admiralty fire control clock was made up of 6,000 parts, 3,000 of which were high precision small gears. It substituted cerium oxide for rouge in glass polishing in North America, cutting polishing time in half. Sufficient ceria not being available, it also developed its own special extraction methods to produce it. For manufacturing graticles (scales on glass), its technical staff designed a novel multiple pantograph machine using altogether new principles.

In putting together its instrument division, the company had to build up a completely integrated operation from scratch, starting with the raw materials for glass-making and ending with the delivery of many types of finished equipment. Canada had little experience or skill in this field. Moreover, there was almost a complete absence of printed information on large scale production of this type. British instrument technology, which the company drew on at first, proved to be unsatisfactory. The company had to do its own work there too. Optical systems were also redesigned.

Research Enterprises was established in late 1940 at the instigation of the National Research Council to produce optical instruments, although the nucleus of the plant wasn't completed until June 1941. The NRC did much of the instrument development work, and supplied the company with a senior physicist from its Optical Department to serve as Director of Optical Shops. The council was also working on detailed radar design (the specifications came from Britain), and radar soon accounted for the best part of the plant's production, measured in dollar volume. Research Enterprises was, in a sense, the council's manufacturing branch.

The production of optics in the three years 1941-44 increased ninefold, which exceeded by more than double the anticipated volume. The microwave gun-laying equipment, although its reputation at first suffered from disbelief as to the effectiveness of a Canadian-designed and manufactured unit, came to have a performance even beyond early expectations. Comparisons between Research Enterprises equipment and British equipment were almost always in favour of the Canadian-made product (although no true economic comparison was possible since the cost of the British equipment was not disclosed).

In the few years in which it was in production, Research Enterprises made shipments valued at over $220,000,000, and had up to 7,500 employees, 15 of whom were specially skilled men from Britain and the U.S. By the fall of 1945, operations were already being phased out. By September 1946, the creative momentum incarnate in Research Enterprises passed out of existence. "The workers with their new skills had been scattered," J. J. Brown noted sadly, "and we had gone back to the old system of buying our scientific equipment from the United States, Germany and Japan."

How did it happen?

It seems that C. D. Howe, who was ultimately responsible for the company, was not so much of a pragmatist after all, that he was an unblinking adherent of some of the dogmas of science and commerce at the time (which not even the explosive entrepreneurial blossoming of the war could offset – and nobody was closer to that awakening than Howe), and that underneath his skilful use of the crown corporation form lay an amorphous cultural resistance to it. Howe probably never understood what made public enterprises go, not even his own most cherished creations like Trans-Canada Air Lines. He could not fully accept them for what they were: a practical expression of a cultural aptitude.

Answering criticism in the House of Commons about the

closing down of Research Enterprises, Howe pointed out that the peacetime Canadian market for radar and optical instruments could absorb only a tiny fraction of the company's capacity, and that without sufficient volume the use of such a large plant wasn't justified. Export possibilities were not mentioned. Discussions among Howe, the NRC, the Department of Transport and the president of the company about keeping Research Enterprises alive apparently took place within those fixed limits of products, market and plant size.

Howe posed other problems, Optical glass had been manufactured by a British process on loan for the war only. A licensing agreement would be necessary for continuing. In any case, the Americans had a different and cheaper process. If in 10 or 15 years large scale production were to be taken up again, a new process and new equipment would have to be acquired. . . .

Howe's argument proceeded in that vein — optics and radar, radar and optics, again and again.

The potential of Research Enterprises, however, was at altogether a different level, where technological imagination and end products are not locked in tightly, and out of which new work evolves. Such new work may be only tenuously related to previous production. This is how economies diversify and renew themselves, and where Research Enterprises' real promise for the future lay. In a relatively short time, the company had become an animated amalgam of science, engineering, administration and inventive workforce, livened by collective purpose. In other words, it had *cultural substance and openness*, by which entrepreneurship flourishes. Howe talked about tools and buildings instead.

He kept on missing the entrepreneurial woods for the entrepreneurial trees. The official historian of the Department of Munitions and Supply remarked that Research Enterprises was the "ideal structure" for such remarkable accomplishments in wartime radar and optics production. He did not record that it was also the ideal culture for remarkable accomplishments in other circumstances.

Howe did protest too much, and thereby gave us some inkling of the true nature of his resistance. As if sensing what the real issue was, he would not let any cultural description of Research Enterprises stand. The ability and dedication of the company made him proud, but ingenuity, a sure sign of cultural liveliness, he seemed to want to keep out of the picture.

He insisted, for example, that Research Enterprises was "a manufacturing plant and nothing else; . . . that is the function of the plant; it is a manufacturing plant; the tools needed are manufacturing tools," although a considerable amount of development engineering was done in the course of operations, including the multiple pantograph machine and the substitution of cerium oxide for rouge.

Most of the product development work was done in the NRC laboratories in Ottawa. This too, of course, was an essential part of the operation. It was not disconnected. That was the beauty of it all. As well, many scientists worked "between the research council and that plant," as Howe himself mentioned. Of the other scientists at the plant, most, like the Director of Optical Shops, were on loan from the council.

Howe insisted on separating this scientific side out. He argued that "on the strength of the plant itself there were not many men who qualified as pure scientists," rather than arguing about the strength of the enterprise in which many scientists were deeply involved. He spoke of the great wisdom of having the manufacturing plant in Toronto, away from the development laboratories in Ottawa. This was also council dogma at the time. He did not consider, in his Commons speech, the possibility of scientists attached to the enterprise developing new products, or of the converse possibility of the enterprise attached to the council animating new science. This culturally debilitating separation of technique from use (of science from service and manufacture), debilitating to the culture of entrepreneurship, that is, would come back to haunt Canada a quarter of a century later amid bitter cries from scientists themselves that Canada had become an abject colony of another entrepreneurial culture from elsewhere.

Howe also failed to see the entrepreneurial possibilities in the cultural aptitude of the work force. He argued that most of the employees "were men who acquired their skills in a short time, and who could readily convert those skills to other types of production." This was by way of pointing out that their dispersal was not such a serious matter. But such adaptability and quickness were exactly the characteristics that promised efficiency for any new venture a peacetime Research Enterprises might have undertaken.

(Some of the possibilities mentioned for Research Enterprises in the debate in 1945 were household appliances, surveying instruments, scientific apparatus, aeroplane engines, light passenger aircraft, prefabricated houses, motorcycles, business machines, measuring instruments, cameras and photographic equipment, motion-picture projectors, hearing aids, television sets, automobile and aero instruments, medical and dental equipment, electronic equipment, control instruments, electrical and radio test equipment and commercial radio sets. It is quite possible that if Research Enterprises had been kept alive, it would have gone into different fields altogether.)

The CCF spokesman in the House (Alistair Stewart) was moved to say that as regards optical glass and instruments, Canada had the world as its oyster, because of the plant. The Conservative spokesman (Donald Fleming) called Research Enterprises "one of the marvels of industrial enterprise wrought by Canadians." Howe considered it was "a great experience to be associated with the plant." It wasn't until 1970, however, when Polymer entered industrial housing and computer time-sharing — only indirectly related to synthetic rubber and plastics, if at all — that a crown corporation showed in practice what Research Enterprises might have become if its public enterprise culture had been sustained. By then, Howe was long since dead. And where are our Research Enterprises now? Who remembers Research Enterprises? For that matter, when was the last time Canadians considered they had the world, even their own world, as their oyster?

(b) *When is a state enterprise not a state enterprise? When it is a foreign enterprise.* For many years now, oil exploration in the Canadian Arctic by a French government-controlled company (Elf, formerly Petropar) has been welcome. So has French government participation in oil exploration and production in Alberta and elsewhere (Aquitaine, most notably the Rainbow Lake field). So has refining and oil and gas exploration and production by the British government (through British Petroleum [BP]). But up until the recent creation of Panarctic Oils in December 1967, the idea of the Canadian government even nominally doing the same thing in its own country was automatically put down.

Unlike the Entreprise de Recherches et d'Activités Pétrolières (the French government's holding company) and British Petroleum and the Ente Nazionale Idrocarburi (ENI, the Italian government company), Panarctic has no mandate to acquire, by purchase, producing wells and refineries and distribution networks. Any proposal to establish a crown corporation for that purpose has been scorned or set aside. So that while British Petroleum, controlled by the British government, can control in turn an exploration company (BP Oil and Gas) and take over a refinery (in Oakville) and acquire by merger a distributing system (Supertest) in Canada, a Canadian crown corporation cannot; that is, there isn't one to do so. Similarly, while Snam Progretti, a member of the ENI group, can contract to build a 200,000-barrels a day refinery in Nova Scotia, there is not even a Canadian crown corporation in the field to bid against it.

By the same token. Britain's government-owned British Steel Corporation can buy control of Slater Steel (steel bar manufacturer) in Hamilton, but no Ontario or federal crown steel corporation can, because there isn't one. Ontario in particular does not believe in that kind of thing, but made no effort to stop the takeover of Slater by foreign government enterprise. Ontario does not believe in stopping such foreign takeovers either.

British Steel, through Slater, also owns 25 per cent of the issued shares of Interprovincial Steel and Pipe Corporation (IPSCO) of Regina. When the government of Saskatchewan recently increased its holdings to 23 per cent from roughly 14 per cent, the leader of the opposition questioned the transaction on the grounds that the company had already shown it was extremely viable and had an excellent future. The opposition apparently does not believe in Saskatchewan investing in such things, although the British Steel acquisition, through Slater, was not objected to.

Similarly, W. A. C. Bennett, in the days of his Social Credit regime in British Columbia, would regularly campaign for re-election with attacks on the "heavy hand of state socialism." After one such victorious campaign, promoters of an alleged copper property in the interior brought in a group of Czechoslovakian officials who announced, according to a press release, that they would recommend to their government a joint partnership to develop the property and to build a multimillion dollar processing mill, using heavy equipment built in Czechoslovakia and assembled under Czechoslovakian direction. The officials were from Inter-project, Czechoslovakia's engineering design bureau, which is a subsidiary of the Skoda Engineering complex. Skoda Engineering is as close to a "heavy hand of state socialism" as any company will get. The whole affair dissolved into thin air. But while it lasted, no stentorian complaints were heard from the provincial government, nor from the small but noisy private business community in Vancouver. There were no cautionary editorials in newspapers and no hostile statements by Chambers of Commerce.

A state enterprise from the outside can psychologically be kept at a distance. The Atlantic Ocean exists, or is thought to exist. The enterprise is thereby psychically neutralized.

(c) *Wasting good money on poor culture.* When a federal spokesman says that it costs more to create crown corporations for slow-growth regions than it does to provide subsidies to private investors, he may be making an honest and earnest observation. But it's upside down.

In the case of crown corporations, profits and assets accrue to the public purse, defraying the costs of investment, and then providing additional moneys. In the case of subsidies to private investors, the subsidy and the profits and the assets are lost to the public purse. Over an appropriate time (and all investment is measured in such time), the first is cheaper than the last.

But if you look at the establishment of a crown corporation across the American-ideology-in-Canada, you do not see it as it is in the indigenous circumstance (an investment in economy over time) but as it appears to be an artificial ideological space (a government handout that comes to an end when it is handed out), so that the last does appear to be cheaper than the first by a kind of ideologically induced psychic inversion.

But in the short run, it may be asked — in times of a threat from without (as in war) or of overwhelming pressure from within (as in bitter regional disaffection) — doesn't the organization of capital and enterprise for crown corporations take too long? Isn't it more expedient to subsidize private enterprise in order to get the job done quickly?

C. D. Howe, when he was in a desperate hurry in World War II, was guided by an exactly opposite, right-side-up reasoning, and opted for crown companies instead. Howe was right. In five years, the Department of Munitions and Supply put together 28 crown companies (as well as organizing 26 departmental branches and 19 control agencies). The investment in industrial plant from this one department alone (of which 75 per cent went into plants wholly owned by the crown) surpassed by more than half the war industrial expansion undertaken directly by private industry. Among them, Polymer, Research Enterprises, Eldorado Mining and

Turbo Research were on the frontiers of technology for their day, but machine tools, cutting tools, aircraft, explosives, guns and gun carriages and small arms also were involved. The war was also an important formative period for Trans-Canada Air Lines and the CBC, already established, and for the National Research Council.

Crown corporations are not only cheaper in the long run, they are also quicker for the short run.

Notice how capital is easily found in such cases, as if it were automatically making itself available, as it should in a healthy economic culture. As in the case of Polymer, the crown corporation can quickly become self-financing, or can raise large sums of money for capital projects on the basis of its assets and entrepreneurial vigour. All vigorous firms are able to undertake new projects or make acquisitions in that way, and they do. Privately owned companies can even use the assets provided by government subsidies as leverage for borrowing. Depending on the case, the amount of initial outlay for a crown corporation may not be much greater than the amount of a subsidy to a private one.

But even total capitalization is no problem. The culture makes an adjustment for it. Public enterprise does not spring up in a vacuum. It takes shape in a context, ideally amid intense public debate. This entrepreneurial thrust works on the context, changing its priorities and its financial modes, as it did during World War II. Before the entrepreneurial tumult takes hold, it may be impossible to see where the money is going to come from. By the time it works its way into the culture, the money is already there. All allocation of capital, in the U.S. as elsewhere, is at root a cultural process. By the same token, in a colonized economic culture this process is stifled, so that while adequate capital may exist, it seems out of reach.

Our ideological topsy-turviness as regards subsidies has a far more serious consequence, however, than the costly forfeiting of profits and assets. Subsidies to private enterprise are a relatively ineffective generator of entrepreneurial energy in Canada, which is the crucial factor in economic growth, so that in slow-growth regions the entrepreneurship is liable to stop where the subsidy stops. We are wasting good money on poor culture.

Canadian public enterprise, on the other hand, can be a potent generator of entrepreneurial energy, as we have seen. Since it is culturally appropriate, it can animate society as a whole, by nourishing the spirit of inventiveness and reinforcing practical application. It does not merely create employment here and there. It arouses practicality. Investment which has this creative, cumulative, differentiating effect on the entrepreneurial culture is cheap at almost any price.

The subsidy of U.S. investment is consequently the costliest of all such subsidy. In terms of entrepreneurial animation at the basis of economy, it is a giveaway to another culture, and detracts from our commitment to our own culture. The cost in lost profits and lost assets is serious enough but the loss from cultural quietism is altogether destructive.

This stems again from the misunderstanding that entrepreneurship is essentially a financial and technical phenomenon rather than a cultural one. Technique may be good and administration may be competent, but if the culture enclosing them is prosaic and imitative as the indigenous culture of private enterprise is in Canada, or if technique cannot draw on cultural strength by fitting itself to cultural strength, as a private company cannot draw on the public enterprise dynamic, then subsidizing such enterprises is subsidizing shallowness, which has been the case.

The only practical subsidization policy — and I use the word "practical" in its ordinary, literal sense — is to subsidize cultural vitality (and enterprises which contribute to that vitality). Anything else is gamesmanship. It is fully expected to have a real effect, but it is culturally limited and has a superficial effect instead.

(d) *Building on weakness instead of building on strength.* Technological innovation is a combination of research and entrepreneurship. The problem in Canada is to put the two together. The Senate Special Committee on Science Policy (the Lamontagne Committee) addressed itself to this predicament.

The committee heard from Northern Electric that "industry in Canada suffers from a low entrepreneurial coefficient." This was not contested. Spokesmen of foreign subsidiaries in chemicals and electrical manufacturing even pleaded feebleness in their industries in Canada as an excuse for not committing themselves to more vigorous research programs — all the more disturbing when one recognized the role of entrepreneurship in leading the innovative process in so many cases. The committee also heard from J. L. Gray, president of Atomic Energy of Canada, that unless industries do take such initiative, "all the government support in the world for 'industrial research' will be an exercise in futility." This was not contested either. The committee, in summing up, referred to the "incipient stagnation of Canadian manufacturing," "the low innovative capacity of Canadian industry," and to "secondary manufacturing . . . rapidly reaching a structural dead end."

Dealing with government-funded research laboratories, on the other hand, in particular the National Research Council, the Northern Electric brief commented that the "NRC's designs have consistently high technical merit." The capability of the NRC was not questioned. One major problem was "the reluctance of [private] industry in Canada to interest itself in NRC's patents and new products." On the other hand, industry played "a relatively unimportant role in establishing NRC's projects." The brief called for closer liaison. The Senate committee, for its part, concluded that the NRC had overestimated the value of long-range research in creating new technology and innovation, to the detriment of its involvement in specific short-term industrial projects. Whatever the arguments, the connection between research and entrepreneurship,, or between entrepreneurship and research if you like, was not being made.

Those were the given elements. Private entrepreneurship was weak. Public research was strong.

The question arises: do you build on strength or do you build on weakness? Any community in its right mind builds on strength. An ideological colony, which cannot perceive what its own strength is, may build on weakness instead. All manner of proposals were put to the committee for building up the "desperately weak" research and development dimension of private industry by increasing government subsidies and by subordinating or taking over the NRC's and other government laboratories' development work. And that was basically the position the committee took in its report. But nobody suggested, or even hinted at, taking a more indigenous approach — creating a multifaceted entrepreneurial dimension of the National Research Council by making new sums of capital available to it and, where appropriate, by taking over some of what is now private industry's • manufacturing and distribution work. Such an NRC Group of Companies would not just develop technological possibilities arising from the independent work of laboratories and take greater advantage of the NRC's varied technical capacities — two areas where Canadian private industry has been remiss. It would extend the culture of public enterprise in Canada — open up new entrepreneurial directions that derive from a public and Canadian sense of practicality (which, I detect, is part of the NRC's tradition). This would be a substantial cultural process, Canadian style. As history would have it, the NRC once did have such an industrial dimension — Research Enterprises Limited — formed at the instigation of the NRC itself. The combination was exceptionally productive. It astonished the whole country. Research Enterprises was not discussed before the committee, however. The American-ideology-in-Canada screens out such public enterprise examples.

The same applies to Atomic Energy of Canada. The committee underlined criticism of AECL for not involving private industry more in its development work (a spokesman for an American subsidiary, Westinghouse, was particularly importunate), whereas the indigenous solution is to involve AECL more in industry. Whatever the industrial difficulties incurred in AECL's heavy-water reactor program, and many of those difficulties can be traced to inexperienced private suppliers (but everybody on a technological frontier is inexperienced), they do not begin to detract from AECL's overall technological achievement. And whatever the industrial capacity of private corporations in Canada, it does not begin to subtract from their overall innovative underachievement. Again, do you build on strength or do you build on weakness?

The committee noted in passing that the British Atomic Energy Authority, given industrial freedom, had moved into new fields like desalinization, ceramics and non-destructive materials testing. AECL's cobalt teletherapy units and its research and industrial irradiators, manufactured by its Commercial Products Division, and both first commercially produced in the world by AECL, are excellent instances of the progression from research to development. But they were not discussed before the committee. The American-ideology-in-Canada screens out such public enterprise examples. Narrow observations from Harvard and M.I.T. and London and Washington were cited instead.

Similarly, the committee's now notorious misjudgment of AECL's nuclear reactor program was no simple accident but stemmed from a pervasive ideological inability to understand AECL's real strength.

So went the proceedings. "Between March 1968 and February 1970," according to the committee's report, it "held 102 public meetings and more than 20 *in camera* meetings to plan and prepare its work in addition to its visits abroad [to the United States, Sweden, West Germany, France, Switzerland, the Netherlands, Belgium and the United Kingdom]. It received the views of 325 groups and individuals in Canada. Well over 1,000 scientists and science administrators attended the hearings, either as witnesses or members of the audience. More than 10,000 pages of evidence were accumulated. As the inquiry proceeded, the Chairman and other members of the Steering Committee spoke at about 30 special symposia and annual meetings of Canadian associations across the country on science policy issues." As well, a long list of distinguished experts from abroad (the U.K., the U.S., France, Belgium and Japan) were invited to the initial round of hearings. Spokesmen of U.S. and other subsidiaries in Canada, even the most vacuous apologists among them, were listened to attentively. Is it surprising, however, that the committee did not look into the history of Polymer, although there was perhaps no better illustration of the entrepreneurial leadership that the committee was searching for in the difficult Canadian circumstance?

One of the serious gaps in our knowledge, pointed to by the committee, was the lack of understanding of the indigenous environment surrounding innovation as compared to the extensive documentation of the "U.S. system." In the United States itself, analysis of the innovative process went back only 10 to 15 years. During that period, in 1962, when such work had just barely begun in the U.S. much less in Canada, E. J. Buckler, Polymer's vice-president, research and development, was presenting a paper on Polymer's R&D method and organization to the U.S. Industrial Research Institute (published in *Research Management*, New York, Vol. IV, No. 4, July 1963). The construction of Polymer's research laboratory in 1953, and its extension in 1958, coincided with the opposite, increasing surrender by Canadian private industry of manufacturing facilities and the power to innovate — the calamitous beginning of the end of "the élan of '44," to use a phrase from *Galt, U.S.A.* of Robert L. Perry. Had the committee examined Polymer's history, they might have discovered how the public enterprise current contributes to a general bent for innovation, even in the origins and mandate of such a "private" kind of crown company. But again, the American-ideology-in-Canada screens out such public enterprise examples. (Unfortunately, Polymer's only participation in the hearings was as a member of the Canadian Chemical Producers' Association, which presented a brief.)

In the same way, reviewing the various possibilities for innovation in Canada, in the second volume of their report, the committee contrasted private firms on the one hand with government laboratories and universities on the other. That was all. By the kind of outrageous trick played on grown men by ideological dogma, the public enterprise culture at the centre of Canadian existence, expressed particularly in crown corporations, was made to vanish — poof — like that, people, physical assets and all.

The committee sought out its answers in foreign models instead of looking into the vigorous character of Canada itself, because in terms of the received ideology, Canada has a feeble character. So it missed the most instructive examples of what it was after. Its discernment of strength and weakness came out exactly backwards, as did also the federal government's subsequent science policy, borrowed as it was from the committee's own borrowed perspectives.

"Know thyself," goes the dictum. But an ideological colony is incapable of knowing itself, least of all its practical self.

The committee, of course, isn't alone. We have already noted in Part II the general blindness to the culture; also how J. J. Brown overlooked Polymer, and crown corporations as a form. Similarly, the CBC and the *Financial Post* did a television co-production on the problems of financing development and innovation in Canada without mentioning crown corporations, even to dismiss them. Alexander Ross did an article in *Maclean's* on innovation and development, straining hard to find something in Canada that might, by a large stretch of the imagination, be compared to the American venture capital firm, praised fulsomely as a prototype. But nowhere did he mention the crown corporation.

Sometimes the "invisible" economic form makes itself present willy nilly. Doherty Roadhouse & McCuaig, the brokers and investment dealers, ran a series of advertisements showing an analyst and his secretary-dispatcher at the scene of the action. The two items entitled "Because we're looking into tomorrow . . . you can too" featured the Pickering nuclear power station and the ill-fated CN turbotrain, although there are no shares of AECL or the CNR to be traded. Pierre Bourgault, in *Innovation and the Structure of Canadian Industry*, automatically repeats the assumption about "our western free enterprise society" without asking (a) whether it exists, and (b) whether Canada is in it; then, searching around for some examples of Canadians' creative genius, he mentions nuclear energy and basic research in medicine.

The *Financial Post*, in its annual listing of Canada's 100 largest companies, 'excludes crown corporations and includes U.S. and other foreign subsidiaries as a matter of ordinary practice.

On another matter, the free tradition and multidisciplinary aspect of the National Research Council may be ideally suited to the development and manufacture of new products.

Jane Jacobs argues, in *The Economy of Cities*, that when new work arises upon existing work, it often cuts ruthlessly across old categories. However, large organizations, with exceptions, tend to get stuck in their own mental categories. With "sterile" divisions of labour and integrated patterns of organization, they cannot in these cases bring themselves to such category crossing. They grow by acquisition instead.

This pattern, if it becomes too dominant, eventually leads to a wider stagnation. Research and development departments, for their part, are limited "surrogates" of the great body of sterile divisions of labour. Even within those limitations, the new work that the researchers find it logical to develop "frequently turns out to be irrelevant or hostile to the interests of the organization as a whole," and is neglected.

Another aspect of creating new work that cuts across

old categories is that it often appears to be inefficient. Category crossing breaks out of rationalization and organization. It also involves the financing of unproved production. A certain kind of "inefficiency" is a sign of economic progress, then, and a certain kind of "efficiency" is a sign of economic decay. Moreover, old economic activity is entrenched. New economic activity is in conflict with it, and everything else being equal, loses out to it, unless government gives the people whose interests are in new economic activity a hand up. At least that is the situation now, where large corporate organization is the rule.

Perhaps because of Mrs. Jacobs' American experience (and her examples draw heavily although by no means exclusively on that experience), she does not touch on the possibility that given different cultural modes, large organizations may be quite capable of, even conducive to, category crossing. A public monopoly, for example, is as open or as closed as the public which sustains it. If it is rooted in an open and lively culture, the cultural turbulence will break down the mental categories of the monopoly, and its fixed structure, and "liberate" it for innovation (see Chapter 15). The use of radio receiving sets in parlour cars by the CNR (half a duopoly) in the 1920's, and then, from there, the creation of broadcasting stations and network broadcasting and a full range of programming, was just such a case. The CPR, on the other hand, with a history of narrow operation for private interest, didn't know what to make of radio. Not until the innovation had been made and accepted and might be acquired, did the CPR seriously commit itself. By then, for the CPR, it was too late (see Chapter 11).

But aside from all that, the National Research Council, with its "inefficient" multi-category tradition, and the absence of a narrowing organizational pattern, fits Mrs. Jacobs' conditions perfectly, once the entrepreneurial connection is made. Atomic Energy of Canada, for example, is an NRC spin-off.

There is good reason to suspect that the reluctance of

private industry to take up licences on NRC patents and new products is not necessarily because they are commercially impractical, as even the Council's supporters like Northern Electric suggest, but because private industry cannot always cross into the NRC's categories. First, some licences are in fact taken up on NRC and other government agency work (through Canadian Patents and Development Ltd.) but mostly by smaller firms, which is consistent with Mrs. Jacobs' observations. Secondly, Canadian private industry is dominated by American and other branch plants, whose categories are borrowed from elsewhere, and whose branch-plant function, as Mrs. Jacobs points out, is not conducive to creating new kinds of work. Cultural incompatibility, not practicality, is perhaps what keeps large industrial organizations away from the NRC. This isn't surprising when the one side is a crown corporation created from within the indigenous experience — "a Canadian social artefact," as an historian of the NRC has called it — while the other side is a privately owned configuration culturally dominated by another nation's experience, and often captive, through subsidiaries, to that other nation's imperatives. From a different perspective, J. J. Brown writes that the "big corporations have their own research laboratories and are usually financed by their parent corporation in the United States, hence they do not want tax money spent on research which will inevitably bring in new products that will be open to all companies in Canada."

Finally on the Senate committee: their report took note of a lack of motivation among university science graduates to go into industry, or to do industrial research as opposed to research in pure science. Everything else being equal, a culturally appropriate entrepreneurship is more likely to shift this bias than the arbitrary shifting of government funds for science to a second-rate, derivative, borrowed entrepreneurship.

(e) *The Canada Development Corporation is also upside down.* One of the early steps taken by the CDC was to purchase Polymer and Connaught Laboratories (the latter from the University of Toronto), as a beginning of profitable holdings, in order to help attract the capital of the small private investor later on. In all of Canadian economic history, this small investor has been a feeble and sluggish, that is, impractical participant in Canadian entrepreneurship.

The CDC also has under consideration Northern Transportation, the public share of Panarctic Oils (45 per cent) and Eldorado Nuclear for possible acquisition from the federal government.

Also, the CDC, whose pioneering motive force was a powerful public mandate, and whose crucial original financing came from government, will be devoted to sustaining the culture of Canadian private enterprise, whose motive force has been feeble and sluggish, relative to the challenge, which again is why the CDC was created.

By contrast, the CDC will not, of course, be creating crown corporations in turn, although the public enterprise culture – in its vigorous egalitarian base, in its rewarding of the enterprising risk-takers (the community) rather than the lethargic and undeserving (such as the propped-up small investor, the tariff-protected manufacturer), in its monopoly innovations (as opposed to wasteful, costly, backward competition), in its animated relationship to Canadian nationalism and Canadian regionalisms, by which entrepreneurship flourishes – is exceptionally creative and practical, and is, paradoxically, also at the base of the CDC itself.

Also paradoxically, the addition of private investors planned for the CDC, which according to the received ideology is supposed to add to the animation of the enterprise – which is taken as the normative way – only detracts from this animation, since the culture of the small investor (written into the CDC's mandate) is nowhere near as creative as the broad interests and egalitarian enthusiasm of a democratic public.

In other words, the practical (public enterprises) are absorbed to support the impractical (the small private investor) so that the practical (the CDC's public impulse) can support the impractical (the imitative private enterprise culture) while not being able to support the practical (the public enterprise culture), all in the name of the highest practicality.

The CDC skirts the native practicality because while the ideological colony recognizes that public enterprise devices are useful, it is unable to accept that the culture itself is legitimate and desirable, and perversely seeks to diminish the culture as it feeds on it.

*   *   *

What of the particular cases where the public enterprise culture is involved in the CDC's acquisitions?

The CDC's strategy has been described variously by its leading officer as "identifying and bringing to fruition major development projects"; "reinforcing strength . . . where a unique competence can be developed or encouraged"; creating "teams which are willing to assume risks heretofore too often left to non-residents"; trying where possible "to confine our purchases of existing assets to those situations where we need a base for building up major new enterprises," and in the long run even selling "holdings which have matured, in order to free our resources for more aggressive investments."

Polymer (Polysar), in 1972 when it was acquired, was already a series of major enterprises, was a mature corporation, was bringing major development projects into fruition itself, was a past master of developing unique competence, and had for all of its history a team willing to take risks. The CDC's acquisition of Polymer, made especially available to it by the the federal government, was entrepreneurially passive.

Looked at another way, Polymer, in its years of public ownership, had built up its own "special management skills and ... diversified base of operations," to borrow again from the language of the CDC's objectives. Imagine an entrepreneurial fight to the finish between a crown-owned Polymer and the present CDC management: who would end up as whose subsidiary?

Connaught Laboratories was established in 1914 to counter the high price of drugs, particularly diphtheria antitoxin imported from the U.S. at as much as $20 to $80 for the large dosage required. Many patients were dying because antitoxin was not available or because the cost of adequate doses was beyond the means of their families. Connaught supplied the antitoxin to public health authorities for free distribution. The price in 1917-18 was 15 cents per 1,000 units. The previous retail price was $1.25 per 1,000 units — these latter figures are from a Saskatchewan government report. Similarly, in the early days of World War I, the Department of National Defence paid $1.35 for a preventive dose of tetanus antitoxin, and supplies were hopelessly inadequate. The Antitoxin Laboratory, as Connaught was then known, supplied all the serum that was needed at 34 cents per vial.

Insulin has since become its most important product. The price has increased only once since 1921, from $1.10 to $1.30 a bottle in 1967. The price in the U.S. is about 50 per cent greater. These figures are from an article in the *Toronto Star* by Margaret Weiers. Connaught files up to 1955 show the price decreasing rapidly from $10 per 100 units in 1922 to 75 cents in 1924 and then gradually to 20-24 cents in 1942.

When Salk polio vaccine was first distributed, in 1955, Canadians paid $1 for a double dose and Americans paid $3 to $4. The difference, according to the *Toronto Star* article, was that Connaught, "with low operating costs and no selling expenses, made the Canadian vaccine; in the United States, the drug companies had to meet high costs including large advertising and sales promotion budgets." Dr. J. K. W. Ferguson, recently retired director of Connaught, puts the difference to pricing policy: "Good vaccines tend to put themselves out of business by preventing the disease against which they work and thus decreasing demand. Some U.S. companies set an initial price designed to recover development costs in two to three years. Connaught has traditionally opted for a more modest initial price counting on a longer life for a good product."

According to the CDC, "Connaught represented an underexploited Canadian opportunity in that its aboslute size had been virtually unchanged in recent years while other — mainly non-resident controlled — companies in the industry were growing vigorously. This acquisition should enable us to create a really effective Canadian-owned presence in the marketplace as we infuse new management with entrepreneurial qualities and sound commercial, financial and administrative skills into [the] organization." It was also suggested that Connaught's operating costs were too high and that the company was not price-competitive enough. Subsequent to the purchase of Connaught, the CDC broadened its position in the pharmaceutical and paramedical products industry by further Canadian investments and a major partnership with a large Danish firm.

Dr. Ferguson comments that "Connaught's prices have often been higher than those of competitors — usually European competitors in foreign markets. . . . Connaught was never to my knowledge a very cheap producer of anything. High quality and low cost are not easily combined." Further, "Connaught has never been a 'drug company' in the usual sense. It has never produced synthetic chemical drugs which have proliferated so stupendously during the last forty years... Connaught has specialized in biologics — usually related to preventive medicine." He points out that while there are considerable year to year fluctuations due to unpredictable sales abroad, the trend "has been generally up from 1949 to 1971, e.g. in 1971 the sales were 6.6 times those in 1949."

Another factor to note: Connaught, not itself politically aggressive, yet touching a combative private enterprise milieu, was constrained by its university ownership. According to the *Toronto Star* again, the laboratories "tried to keep a low profile so as not to anger private industry [against the University of Toronto] and tried not to sell drugs that were being made by anyone else."

This brings us finally to the question of entrepreneurial culture. Connaught was an expression of the Canadian tradition of public service. The CDC purchase pushes Connaught into the American tradition of pharmaceutical private operation.

The difference goes back to Connaught's early history. Dr. J. G. Fitzgerald, the founder of the laboratories, saw their purpose as threefold: research, teaching and medical public service. This broad commitment to preventive medicine is where Connaught's animation came from. Even when personnel resources were strained, courses in public health were taught by members of the lab. Fitzgerald himself wrote a badly needed textbook of preventive medicine. The medical research program was also considered essential to the whole. The supply of biological products was just a facet of a larger medical aim.

Despite some early opposition from druggists, Connaught pioneered the idea of free distribution of biological products by governments, to which it sold the vaccines at wholesale. rates. This was the laboratories' big contribution to reducing the price of diphtheria antitoxin — an innovation in preventive medicine by entrepreneurial device which began to save lives immediately. Plans for distribution involved the participation of provincial departments of health. Some 55 years after Fitzgerald's program was organized, a provincial minister of health (in this case, from B.C.) could still declare, following a conference on the high cost of drugs, that "when Connaught comes out here it doesn't send a salesman; we get professionals to help us."

Perhaps the case of the insulin patent sheds the most light on Connaught's entrepreneurial character. Patent monopolies are the kind of device which allows a drug manufacturer to mark up his product 1,000 or 2,000 per cent (one Swiss tranquillizer in Canada was being marketed recently at 2,300 per cent of cost of production). They lend themselves naturally to the practice of recouping development costs within a short period, and to providing the overhead for expensive marketing by which a company consolidates its mercantile position. By contrast, Connaught, in the case of insulin, as with the diphtheria antitoxin and the Salk vaccine, quickly passed on decreases in price to the purchaser. The usefulness and improving quality of the product over a reasonable span of time were counted on to underwrite development costs.

Indeed, Frederick Banting, one of the co-discoverers of insulin, at first refused to participate in any patent application, but changed his mind when he realized that others might obtain patents in certain countries and monopolize the product, and also that without control by patents there would be no control over the quality of production. The patent rights were assigned to the University of Toronto and administered by an insulin committee which assured an economical retail mark-up that still prevails. The insulin committee also facilitated the use of insulin patents elsewhere, in particular by transferring the administration of patents to public or semi-public authorities in areas outside North America where a competent organization could be located, and by assisting manufacturers.

Connaught exports, which began with diphtheria and tetanus antitoxins during World War I, followed the pattern established at home. The laboratories sought to supply government departments and institutions directly or through accredited agencies and to prevent exploitation in distribution. In its last years under university ownership, Connaught served as a consultant for the World Health Organization as part of a campaign to eradicate smallpox. Connaught's job was to upgrade existing laboratories in South America and Central America where smallpox vaccine was already being produced, since the purchase of quality vaccine from developed countries was beyond WHO's financial resources. Connaught also agreed to establish an isolated testing laboratory for vaccine samples. Another consideration was the stimulus to the technical competence and national pride of the countries involved which home production would induce. This consultative function extended to production and control of other biologicals. Connaught had previously provided similar assistance to foreign laboratories in the manufacture of insulin, penicillin and several other vaccines. This advisory work meant, in some instances, helping competitors outside Canada to establish themselves.

That was Connaught's style.

On the other hand, the new president of "Connaught Laboratories Ltd.," installed by the CDC, is a former executive of a U.S. drug firm, and we can expect the different style, "carried out in anticipation of profit and in the best interests of the shareholders as a whole," to cite Section 6 of the CDC enabling legislation.

Which entrepreneurship in pharmaceutics is more practical to build upon? That is to say, which one would bring lower prices, draw best on indigenous creativity, and contribute to a forward culture of pharmaceutics use: a CDC complex whose prices remain "reasonable and competitive" in a market rife with high prices and price discrimination, with the overheads of such a market including advertising and sales promotion budgets, and bent with its competitors on changing prescribing habits of doctors to increase sales rather than for independent scientific reasons, with possible abuses of misuse and overuse that go with it (I am projecting ahead here in general terms); or an entrepreneurship based on the Connaught example but extended in full elaboration, in the indigenous tradition of public awareness, careful education of users (in this case, doctors and governments), technical advance and service at cost, shared technology abroad, and eliminating unnecessary overheads?

Of other publicly owned companies mentioned in connection with the CDC. Northern Transportation is a public service monopoly, which is the last kind of enterprise to be transferred to the CDC.

Although Panarctic Oils is not a "public enterprise" at the moment, the changing energy situation, and the changing relationship of society to energy and environment, call for a new entrepreneurship of energy rooted in the public interest ("embedded in social relations" in Polanyi's phrase) rather than an entrepreneurship of private marketing. All enterprise in Canada is backward on this score, but the Canadian public enterprise monopoly, as a form, is particularly well-suited to such a new entrepreneurship, which is the entrepreneurial frontier (see Chapter 15). The CDC, on the other hand, is particularly ill-suited to it.

*   *   *

The creation of the CDC does not liberate the indigenous economic culture, wherein our entrepreneurial genius lies. That requires a different kind of creation.

Let a thousand crown corporations bloom. Let a thousand public enterprises contend. But not in the same market.

Peter Newman, interviewing J. K. Galbraith in 1970, reflected that he "always thought of the Canadian political tradition as a mixture of pragmatism and Manchester liberalism." (I can almost hear Laurier exclaiming "What a salad!," in the same fine 1897 colonial style.)

Let us let Manchester fend for itself for a while. What about Canada? The native reality is that a country that still condones obsolete rituals (like mining promotions), that allows an inefficient industrial structure to tax it and hold it down over several generations, that chooses diseconomies over economies despite hard lessons in the school of experience showing a different way, that is also blind to the wellsprings and modes of its practical genius so that it will even subsidize its own colonization and welcome subjection, is not a country with a pragmatic political tradition. It is a country riddled with dogma, and locked in a cultural malaise.

What Newman and others overlook is that such colonial dogma does not come at a people in the shape of brittle, patently ludicrous propositions so that reasonable citizens can easily see it for what it is. It carries with it the authority of convention. Scholars and journalists largely concur. The dogma is not altogether impractical either. It has its own practicalities which it builds on. It serves quite a few people directly, and many more indirectly, as it did in the days of the Family Compact. They have an interest in sustaining it. It modulates decision-making. It has a hold on culture. It is pervasive. In such circumstances, pragmatism is not the easy political habit of going along with whatever is going, as we have taken it for.

As long as the American-ideology-in-Canada screens the practical side of Canadian identity, pragmatism is impossible.

As happens very often in the practical life, Canadians would rather howl into the wind than take an indigenous, that is an appropriate, way. Canadians are no more pragmatic than medieval theologians, or than the Chinese peasants of old who bound their daughters' feet, and prayed to kitchen gods to hold off floods and droughts, with often disastrous results.

The Public Broadcasting Culture

CHAPTER 11

Historical Roots

No other phenomenon illustrates better the market contradiction between Canada and the United States than the
unremitting struggle for public broadcasting in Canada. No
other phenomenon has been so indigenous to Canada. And,
in the ideological colony, no other phenomenon has been so
maligned and abused. We have loved and hated our own
children most.

Almost from the moment that radio broadcasting caught
fire in North America, in the 1920's, the contradiction was
on the surface: the Canadian market was so much smaller
than the American market that as long as Canada developed
radio the American way, as a private enterprise adjunct of
the market, Canadian radio, in quality and distribution,
would be hopelessly feeble.

There followed another prospect. Since a tariff on
radio waves was unimaginable, American radio might simply
overwhelm Canadian broadcasting, just as the construction
of the Erie Canal had dealt a body blow to the St. Lawrence
economy almost a century earlier until the Canadian collectivity, in its own way, financed canal and railroad construction.
So that if Canadian broadcasting were to follow the American
model, there might not be any significant Canadian broadcasting at all.

A writer in *Maclean's* in 1924 estimated that "nine-
tenths of the radio fans in this Dominion hear three or four
times as many United States stations as Canadian. Few fans,
no matter in what part of Canada they live, can regularly pick
up more than three or four different Canadian stations." In
1925 the *Toronto Telegram* ran a "Radio Popularity Ballot";
the top 17 stations were American. In terms of radio,

Toronto, at the economic centre of Canada, was a sluggish, provincial backwater, incapable of even modest competition. Frank Peers, in his history of Canadian radio (*The Politics of Canadian Broadcasting 1920-1951*), points out that even by the end of the twenties, not only were Canadian stations still small, "but their schedules were irregular, the hours of broadcast few, and the average program unexciting." French Canada and the Maritimes were particularly ill-served and many rural districts were not served at all, although rural areas accounted for nearly half of the population and 40 per cent of the radio receivers.

While broadcasting in the dense American market "was becoming a big business, and Canadian listeners were responding to it . . . no businessman in broadcasting [in Canada] believed that the scattered Canadian population could make larger stations profitable." And since "broadcasting in Canada was not yet regarded as anything more than a business," Canada's radio consciousness was largely American.

The thin Canadian market also ruled out commercial network broadcasting. A flurry of activity out of Toronto, Winnipeg and Montreal beginning late in 1929 soon died down in the face of the depression. E. Austin Weir, head of the radio department of the CNR at the time, explained it much as if he were telling the story of the Canadian economy since 1820: "Distances were too great, population was too small, industry was too undeveloped, and wire-line costs were too high." In terms of the American model, it made far more sense to develop the Canadian market as part of U.S. broadcasting, just as it would have made far more sense, in those terms, to have built our Pacific railroad through the United States instead of around Lake Superior.

This absorption of Canadian broadcasting was already underway. In late 1929, CKGW in Toronto, with the backing of the *Toronto Telegram*, joined NBC's Red Network "to put programs on the air which it would bankrupt any Canadian station to provide," in the *Telegram's* own pretentious announcement, written by the editor. "Could there be a finer way of promoting international good-fellowship?" A year later, CFCF in Montreal became an NBC affiliate. CKAC, owned by *La Presse*, had already joined the CBS network. By 1932, when the House of Commons was considering a comprehensive broadcasting act, NBC and CBS between the two of them were in a position to expand across all of Canada, and were suspected of planning as much by Graham Spry and Alan Plaunt of the Canadian Radio League.

Within a few short years, spokesmen from all across the wide range of the political spectrum rang the changes on the Canadian market contradiction, as it manifested itself in the radio dilemma, each inevitably being forced by the contradiction to support public enterprise.

J. S. Woodsworth was the first, in 1928, in the House of Commons:

> It is only a comparatively short time before these small broadcasting stations will be bought up by big American companies. I may be afraid of handing power to any one government, but I would rather trust our own Canadian government with the control of broadcasting than trust these highly organized private commercial companies in the United States.

R. B. Bennett, in introducing the Canadian Radio Broadcasting Act in 1932, was outspokenly nationalist and, necessarily, outspokenly in favour of a public system:

> First of all, this country must be assured of complete Canádian control of broadcasting from Canadian sources, free from foreign interference or influence. Without such control radio broadcasting can never become a great agency for communication of matters of national concern and for the diffusion of national thought and ideals, and without such control it can never be the agency by which national consciousness may be fostered and sustained and national unity still further strengthened. . . .
>
> Secondly, no other scheme than that of public ownership can ensure to the people in this country, without regard

to class or place, equal enjoyment of the benefits and
pleasures of radio broadcasting. Private ownership must
necessarily discriminate between densely and sparsely
populated areas. . . .

Then there is a third reason. . . . I cannot think that any
government would be warranted in leaving the air to
private exploitation and not reserving it for development
for the use of the people.

The Royal Commission on Radio Broadcasting (Aird
Commission), 1929, starting with the proposition that
"Canadian radio listeners want Canadian broadcasting,"
inexorably came to the conclusion that the interests of
Canadian listeners and of the Canadian nation "can be
adequately served only by some form of public ownership,
operation and control behind which is the national power and
prestige of the whole public of the Dominion of Canada."
Former Conservative prime ministers Arthur Meighen and
Sir Robert Borden — Borden was the one who had been so
sceptical and down-in-the-mouth about involving the government in the CNR — also backed a "government owned
national broadcasting system," also driven by the same logic.
Ernest Lapointe, speaking on the 1932 Broadcasting Act,
supported the principle of public broadcasting for the
Liberals. In spite of an intensive propaganda campaign by
private interests, only one vote was cast against the bill, by a
Saskatchewan free trader.

Then there was Graham Spry's classic 1932 description
of the Canadian dialectic. In six words, Spry summed up not
just the pressing radio situation but the whole of our practical
history: "The State or the United States?"

Bennett, Meighen and Borden were all Conservatives
and champions of private enterprise. Bennett himself was a
former CPR solicitor, and a personal friend of E. W. Beatty,
the railway's president. Beatty, at the time, was campaigning
against public broadcasting and for a chain of high-powered
CPR stations. Quite likely, in any other circumstances except
the Canadian one, Bennett would have pronounced differently

on broadcasting. Sir John Aird, chairman of the Aird Commission, also a Conservative in politics, was president of the Canadian Bank of Commerce, and was originally predisposed to favour private enterprise in broadcasting, A visit to New York, where NBC representatives openly assumed Canada was part of their territory, checked the predisposition; a consequent visit to the non-commercial BBC destroyed it.

All proposed schemes involved large expenditures of government money. The manufacturers and advertisers advocated a subsidy for line charges. The manufacturers called on the government to build unprofitable stations in less populated areas, to be turned over later to private enterprise. The Canadian Association of Broadcasters spoke of government subsidies for programming. Amounts were mentioned. E. W. Beatty put the total figure at a million dollars annually, in licence fees. Another private spokesman suggested $1,500,000. (By way of comparison, the total budget of the Canadian Radio Broadcasting Commission in the fiscal year 1934-35 was approximately $1,400,000.) The terms of reference of the Aird Commission took government financing or subsidies for granted.

The dialectic also pointed to a monopoly system in Canada, just as it had in furs and railroads. There was no way of avoiding it. Transmission costs were too high. The American networks, against which Canadian broadcasting had to contend, had extraordinary resources. Domestic competition would inflate overhead costs, and draw badly needed revenue away from programming, dangerously weakening Canadian broadcasting in the process. Not competition, but concentration, was called for by the Canadian context.

So parallel networks, one private and one public, were ruled out by reality. The necessity of broadcasting in two languages and not just one made the reality all the more pressing. Edward Beatty, in testifying to the Parliamentary Committee of 1932, had to admit that radio was a "natural monopoly." By 1936, even the private station operators, to quote their spokesmen, had come around to favouring "a single nation-wide network system," not least of all because "network broadcasting in Canada has practically disappeared commercially on complete networks . . . because of the high cost." Only one network broadcast went out regularly across Canada — Saturday night hockey.

But why did the Aird Commission, and the House of Commons, and all the leading political spokesmen of private enterprise opt for public broadcasting instead of for a privately controlled, subsidized system under government regulation? The private broadcasters' lobby had gone to elaborate pains to show that even when the nationalist argument had been accepted, public broadcasting was not necessary or desirable. Edward Beatty had submitted, in 1932, a respectable and sophisticated proposal for the establishment of such a privately owned Canadian Broadcasting Company. *Saturday Night* favoured a similar suggestion by the Canadian Manufacturers' Association. The *Montreal Gazette*, in one of the triumphs of imaginative journalism of the time, went as far as predicting the Beatty plan would likely win out over the public broadcasting recommendations of the Aird Commission. (Perhaps what was good for the CPR automatically became true for the *Gazette*.)

What few people noted at the time was that Canada had just come through an intense coming-to-grips with the indigenous public enterprise culture, and also, for the first time, an open elaboration of the culture. In the case of Ontario, and Ontario Hydro, the 1920's had been a period of entrepreneurial legend-making and political vindication. The publicly owned railroad, the CNR, was even more in the public mind during the years of the great radio debate. The Duff Royal Commission on railways and transportation was dissecting the colossal railroad dilemma, not without a good bit of prejudice. Sir Henry Thornton had just fallen or been assassinated, either a sacrificial goat for the railroad sins of all previous Parliaments or a victim of Tory malevolence, depending on where a man stood in the politics of the land.

(Coincidentally, Thornton finally left the CNR just two months after the Broadcasting Act of 1932 was passed.) The country had been through a halcyon age of frontier optimism, symbolized by the rapidly gained world-wide reputation of the government-owned line, and then was plunged into a pessimism bordering on panic. The depression brought home with a costly vengeance the stark, dismaying foolishness of the competitive overbuilding of the "railroad folly," which the CNR had been created to resolve. In other words, it brought home, in unsparing, passionate argument over duplication, competition, private monopoly and government ownership, what it meant to live in the Canadian circumstance. A public broadcasting system fitted into this new self-consciousness. The ideology of private broadcasting did not. Canadians were ready and waiting for the public broadcasting campaign of the Canadian Radio League.

The analogy between railroad history and the consequences of overbuilding with more than one radio network inevitably was made, and made again. When Charles Bowman, editor of the *Ottawa Citizen* and a member of the Aird Commission, wrote that "it would be far more difficult [than in the case of the railroads] to re-establish a national service of radio broadcasting after private extravagance had led to insolvency," the word "insolvency" was informed by traumatic historical experience. Similarly, Sir John Aird recalled Canada's unhappy experiences "during the period of building competitive railways" in arguing for a public system rather than a subsidized private system. The ghosts of Mackenzie and Mann who, in their railroad days, had stuck Aird's bank with worthless Canadian Northern collateral — except that the government agreed to pay for it anyway during nationalization (Aird was general manager of the bank at the time) — haunted the private broadcasters' lobby. But so did the entire 70 years of manipulation, intrigue and political demoralization attendant on corruption, that had come with railroad subsidies since the first government-gilded spike went down in Canada West around 1850, and which had been put to an end, at last, by public ownership. No community which had gone into so much debt, and suffered so much anguish, to break the CPR's railroad monopoly, and which, in the depression, preferred to suffer more, rather than to give in . . . no such stubborn community was likely to give the CPR even a part of another trans-Canada monopoly, in radio.

The impassioned political history of Ontario Hydro also had an indirect bearing on the ideological approach to Canadian broadcasting. Merlin H. Aylesworth, the president of NBC, had come to that post, in 1928, directly from the National Electric Light Association. The NELA was the propaganda wing of the private power interests in the United States and, as part of its campaign against public power, had tried, by fair means but mostly by foul, to discredit Ontario Hydro. The *Toronto Telegram's* ingratiating attitude to President Aylesworth of NBC for having accepted CKGW into the network ("The one fault you may find with him is that he has been too generous in his acknowledgement of the minor part which the *Toronto Evening Telegram* has been able to play") must have seemed, to knowledgeable veterans of the public power movement in Ontario, something akin to treason. "The monopolistic interests of the U.S. power trust" was not, in Canada's case, simply an emotional phrase. It was history lived.

The ascendant public enterprise ethic in Canada contributed to broadcasting ideology in another way. One of the common characteristics of Canadian public enterprise in its entrepreneurial phase is technological openness. The liveliness of public debate, and public expectation surrounding the enterprise — the cultural electricity in the air — often passes into the enterprise itself. An imaginative opening-up-of-minds follows.

The CNR in the 1920's was in just such a technologically open period, and radio was part of it. The first linking-up of two stations in Canada, as well as the first network service, was carried out by the CNR. The initial phase of the CNR experiment involved the placing of radio receivers in train parlour cars, to attract and hold passenger traffic. (U.S. trains later copied the CNR's innovation.) A chain of radio stations across Canada was also part of the early planning. The first CNR radio station was built, in Ottawa, in 1924. The CPR belatedly entered the field in 1930, with some sponsored programs carried by private stations.

The CNR's radio years constituted a tandem *tour de force* of cultural innovation and ideological advance. The inspired genius in the CNR who originally perceived the possibilities of radio, and who acted on that perception, was Sir Henry Thornton, the road's president. Thornton was an American by way of Great Britain, but his perception was Canadian — in fact, CNR Canadian — and could only be given concrete form in Canadian terms. Had he been president of an American railroad at the time, or of an American communications company, his idea of radio would have been turned aside, to die an early death on barren ground. Even the most narrow objectives of CNR radio were linked to the public enterprise whole, which was the nation.

One of the early functions of CNR broadcasting, as distinct from the parlour car receiving sets, was to put Thornton in touch with employees, in order to build up morale and to promote efficiency and service in the system. This was the original purpose of Thornton's "fireside chats" about the road and the country. These pioneering efforts came in for some ridicule from people who did not realize, as Thornton did from experience, that efficiency was in the culture — "that the human element is the largest factor in the success of any railway." The talks, and the broadcasting policy as a whole, also meant incomparably effective advertising for the system as far away as New Zealand, Virginia and Great Britain which often could pick up CNR stations because of limited interference.

But the viability of the CNR was most dependent on the economic and social development of the country. "The success of the National System . . . is not entirely to be obtained by methods generally applied to Railways which are not producing returns, viz., improving the physical condition and operating methods — it is a matter of building up the country to support the Railways." So CNR broadcasting, willy nilly, became an instrument of national policy.

In the process, the ideology of public broadcasting in Canada was spelled out before public broadcasting was even seen to exist. CNR officials explained how part of their purpose in establishing network broadcasting was to attract tourists and settlers to Canada, and to help in "keeping content those who have to live in sparsely settled districts in the north and west." A group of Scottish journalists touring the country in 1924 confirmed the effectiveness of the recently instituted CNR broadcasts in combatting the two main disincentives to new Canadian settlement: loneliness and isolation.

By 1929, Thornton's own ideas about radio had gained in precision and insight: "It is only through nation-wide broadcasts that we shall accomplish what we regard as most important, the encouragement of a feeling of kinship between all parts of the country, to bring home to all sections more vividly our common apsirations and achievements. . . . It is essentially both a national and a local-service institution. . . . Service to the listener is the primary consideration. . . . It is not possible to please all listeners at the same time. Indeed, it would be undesirable if that were so, as great uniformity of taste is not always consistent with the development of individuality. Hence variety in programming is essential. . . ."

Thornton was also aware of the commercial possibilities of radio in an age when even advertising agencies were sceptical about the medium. Unlike the agencies later on, however, and unlike the American networks from the beginning, he was intent that broadcasting should not become an "atmospheric bill board." There was no direct advertising on CNR radio. Another part of the CNR's broadcasting effort was a monthly booklet of program information, inspired by the BBC's *Radio Times*.

The evocation of the Canadian character in all parts of the country, public service as the dominant ethos, a supplementary local orientation, variety in programming to reflect and encourage individualism, the development of Canadian talent for Canadians, a mixed attitude to commercialism with advertising allowed but deliberately kept in a secondary role — all the elements of later Canadian broadcasting ideology were there, in the pragmatic making of a network, and a railroad (and a people!), without any philosophic study, government announcement or royal commission to make it official wisdom.

The embryonic ideology did not precede practice. It was fused with practice. While Thornton was talking about broadcasting, the CNR's radio department was doing it. In relatively few years, mostly from 1924 to 1931, and with an astonishingly low capital and operating budget, the CNR created national broadcasting as we have known it ever since. Everything from special events to complete comic operas to drama were taken on, along with public service programs, children's programs and school broadcasts. The first transcontinental symphony broadcasts were originated in Toronto by the CNR, a year before CBS launched its New York Philharmonic series.

Canadian network broadcasting had a unique emotional effect because of the collective implications in a scattered land. The first cross-Canada broadcasts — three special programs to mark the Diamond Jubilee of Confederation — in which the CNR radio department played the leading role, was symbolic of what came after. Mackenzie King, prime minister at the time, gave way to unabashed rhetoric in describing what had happened ("On the morning, afternoon and evening of July 1, all Canada became, for the time being, a single assemblage, swayed by a common emotion, within the sound of a single voice. . . . May we not predict that as a result of this carrying of the living voice throughout the length and breadth of the Dominion, there will be aroused . . . an increased devotion of the individual citizen to the common weal."). The 45 seconds of carillon chimes and the striking of five by the great clock in the Peace Tower, and then the playing of O Canada — which preceded the Canadian National Symphony hour — similarly moved a well-known Winnipeg journalist to confess to unaccustomed feelings of "high-powered" patriotism, and to indulge in purple trans-Canada geographic prose.

One of the most original and indigenous projects of the radio department, and one that had a tremendous impact on listeners, was a dramatic series based on the epic stories of the early explorers and colonizers called "The Romance of Canada." The scripts were written by Merrill Denison of Toronto (Denison, much later in his career, was to write a history of Ontario Hydro). When E. Austin Weir, the director of the radio department who conceived the series, decided he would have to go outside of Canada to find an experienced producer, Thornton had only one comment, "Don't go to New York for him." Shades of William Cornelius Van Horne! In fact, it was unlikely, at the time, that New York had a competent drama producer. Instead, Tyrone Guthrie was brought in from England. After "The Romance of Canada" was over, Denison then went to New York and sold a replica, "Great Moments in History," to NBC.

I mention these programs because they played a particular role in the progression of events. The Diamond Jubilee broadcasts made a profound impression on Mackenzie King, which was likely an important factor in his decision to appoint a royal commission on broadcasting. As for "The Romance of Canada" series, E. Austin Weir recalled later that "such an impression was made with these plays and allied efforts by the Canadian National Railways that they were definitely instrumental in helping to establish nationalization of radio in Canada, it being held by many that they proved Canadian broadcasting could even compete with New York." Even in the black days in 1931 and 1932, when the Railway Committee was putting the CNR through the wringer, and when some members of the committee were after Henry

Thornton's skin, no serious criticism was made of the radio operation.

(None of this prevented a spokesman of private broadcasting from telling a House of Commons committee point blank in 1942: "It is noteworthy that up until 1932 all the pioneering, all the experimenting with the new medium, all the struggles and heartaches were borne by privately owned stations. Every bit of development was financed by private capital..." Not even Pravda could have done better in falsifying history.)

D'Arcy Marsh, Thornton's biographer, remarked that "As a direct result of Sir Henry's ability to see the possibilities inherent in a new medium of expression, the railway did for Canada what she was too apathetic to do for herself." But the CNR *was* Canada. The Canadian market contradiction, and hence the Canadian ethos, was inside the CNR. A community does not always get things done by acts of legislation. It has spontaneous ways of expressing itself.

The Canadian public broadcasting culture didn't begin with the Broadcasting Act of 1932. And it didn't begin with the CNR's first radio expenditures in 1923. It began at multitudinous, indeterminate points in the historical flow.

Another spontaneous manifestation of the Canadian impulse in those formative radio years, but in a different way, was the Canadian Radio League. The League was formed on October 5, 1930 by Graham Spry and Alan Plaunt and a few others. By November 13, the *Financial Post* was already reporting that "the membership fairly exudes names of respectable citizens . . . with nationwide reputations." By the end of 1931, the League had recruited the support of educational leaders, churches, trade unions, women's organizations, farm organizations, the Canadian Legion, a good representation of the business and financial community, most newspapers and above all many prominent Conservatives and Liberals, including a close adviser and future brother-in-law of Prime Minister Bennett. This support came from all across the country, and from both linguistic communities — a rare consensus on a matter of high national policy.

The League did not create this community of identity. It was already there. What the League did do was to elaborate on this identity in terms of broadcasting and broadcasting ideology, and in the process raise a massive popular movement. The ideological vigour of the community in a creative phase was something to behold.

Almost from the inception of radio, then, American and Canadian realities expressed themselves in unique, differing ways in their broadcasting structures.

American broadcasting conformed to the market philosophy, which is the American ethos, and strove to create an undifferentiated mass taste in order to increase its market value. Herbert Hoover's admonition in 1922, as secretary of commerce, that it was "inconceivable that we should allow so great a possibility for service . . . to be drowned in advertising chatter" was so much whistling in the unAmerican dark. David Sarnoff's conviction that broadcasting should be "distinctly regarded as a public service," free from the dictates of advertising, lasted only for a couple of years. By 1932, the American inventor, Dr. Lee de Forest, the "father of broadcasting," had already given up hope of American radio saving itself from what he considered a morass of commercial debasement. The pattern was set as early as 1925 with the formation of commercial networks.

Canadian broadcasting, on the other hand, was created to appeal to the Canadian character where it departed from American uniformity. In order to do so, it had to have relative freedom from commercial considerations (which favoured the economics of continental broadcasting), and relative freedom from commercial competition (which would hopelessly fragment Canadian broadcasting resources). Also, private commercial broadcasting could not accommodate the widespread Canadian feeling that radio should have a public service side, and should try to challenge and broaden the listener's sensibilities, as well as to entertain and flatter him. However, the commercial broadcasting argument was politically difficult to bypass altogether in the early 1930's in Canada. The whole was put together in a mixed but unified public-private system, dominated, theoretically, by a publicly owned broadcasting network (which nevertheless carried some commercials), and amplified by local commercial stations.

From the early, spontaneous divergence between the CNR radio department and New York, and given sharper focus by the politics of Canadian radio in the 1930's, of which the CBC was the outcome, two conflicting broadcasting traditions evolved, and are with us now. Both of them are "democratic," but by different definitions.

The first is "American" or "market" broadcasting, which treats the public as a mass of potential consumers of advertised products, and consequently has an homogenizing cultural influence. The constant market race to reach the largest possible audience with high commercial stakes, and therefore large budgets, has meant some enormously popular programs in both senses of the word popular — first in terms of large audiences, and secondly, in terms of entertainment style. There has never been any danger of American broadcasting becoming the "intellectual solace of a few." In that anti-elitist entertainment style — more so in that narrow sense than any other — American broadcasting can be said to be "democratic." But the same broadcasting tradition has also meant a stultifying sameness and escapism in the generality of programming, an aspect "at once excited and monotonous," to borrow a phrase from Tocqueville's appreciation of the United States in another context. The wider possibilities in drama, entertainment, children's programming, community exploration, ideological diversity, foreign programs and public affairs programming generally tend to get pushed into special occasions, or to ghetto viewing hours, or to underfinanced minority vehicles such as educational stations. The focus here is on dominant network broadcasting — in the current period, network television. The clearest expression of the tendency was perhaps television in the 1960's, when phoniness and conformity seemed to know no bounds, even to fearful interference with petty details of production.

Critical Americans striving for individualism in broadcasting have been unable, within American terms, to countenance alternatives to commercial competition as the norm. They look instead to an increase in the number of stations and to consequent specialization in programming — to an ongoing fragmentation of the audience — as an escape from the restraints of the largest-possible-audience tyranny. The proliferation of local stations does broaden the latitude for controversy and community service (open line radio shows, for example). Yet it has only a limited impact on the follow-the-leader syndrome in the uses of broadcasting, as a means to increase market power, against which individualism is struggling. Particularly in an expensive medium like television, local station owners may be even more susceptible than networks to conformist pressures of the market. (This leaves aside any assumption that station owners are naturally inclined to commit large sums of money to individualist exploration and opening avenues of dissent which, in the broad sweep of the American case, would be a foolhardy premise.) Within the dominant networks themselves, the compulsion not just to capture the largest possible audience but also to retain it throughout an evening leads the networks to block out programs in a compatible audience flow rather than in a mixed juxtaposition, which would broaden tastes but which would also mean a drain of part of the audience to other channels.

There are other restraints. Groups in the population with lesser purchasing power or buying habits (ghetto blacks, people over 50) have been discriminated against in programming schedules and the allocation of broadcasting resources. Stations and networks, with the advertisers behind them, are intent on reaching first of all the higher-spending age and income majorities. Another characteristic of the structure is the untrammelled propaganda of the commercials themselves, many of them screaming, cajoling and offending, but all of them taken together representing a manipulative anti-democratic use of media.

Schematically, this market broadcasting tradition reinforces the innate tendency in American society towards an unleavened, overwhelming majority on one side, and a rootless, dissenting intelligentsia and other minorities on the other, which, in the long run, makes for cleavages in society. In that profound sense in which a democracy should be committed to bringing out the individualism and rational understanding of its citizenry, American broadcasting is not particularly democratic.

The second tradition is "Canadian" or "community" broadcasting, or "Canadian public broadcasting" (for lack of a more precise phrase), in which the market is secondary — the community, not the market, defines the broadcasting ethic — and which assumes a continuous creative tension and dialogue between broadcasters and a larger public. Neither side can dismiss the other.

Canadian public broadcasting has never been able to overlook the immense popularity of many American programs, particularly for English Canadians. The CBC English-language service, from its early radio days, decided instead to carry the best of those programs, and sometimes the advertisements that went with them, and in the process to establish listener loyalty to the public system. At the same time, the popularity of American programs has been a constant challenge to Canadian broadcasting to popularize the Canadian character, which was one of the reasons it was brought into existence in the first place.

There have been other checks on elitism. Canada has never had a dominant, "cultured" bourgeoisie, in the European tradition, which could turn the broadcasting structure into an elitist camp. The non-elitist American example was available from across the border, and there were strong vested interests in Canada intent on extending that example here. In its origins, public broadcasting in Canada, whatever it borrowed from the BBC, was not a bourgeois carryover from the European past but the product of a widespread nationalist spirit. Without the public, public broadcasting in Canada would not survive.

On the other hand, Canadian public broadcasting does not require the system to appeal to all of the people all of the time, forcing it into a competitive sameness. And it does not require producers to sacrifice their freedom and their professional judgment in order to placate the conformist whims of commercial rule. The pervading ethos is to provide, either by the character of individual programs or by the program mix, programming with as wide an appeal as possible but without sacrificing individualism and diversity.

This is an exasperating broadcasting tradition. It necessarily evokes continuous criticism from all strata of the population (it could not function well in any other way). It is the hardest kind of broadcasting to produce. And in the long run it has a prodding, integrative effect and makes for a tolerant, cohesive society.

Just as with the economic culture in general, if we look at public broadcasting in Canada in terms of the inappropriate American ideology, we inevitably miss the point of the tradition, and denigrate it and ourselves.

Take, for example, the assumption that there is something basically malfunctioning about a broadcasting tradition that is marked with so many wrangles about censorship and outside interference, so many protests about particular opinions and programs broadcast, and so many public controversies about bureaucratic cowardice and error — a skein of occurrences stretching in Canadian public broadcasting back to the CNR days.

It would in fact be malfunctioning and disruptive in American broadcasting, which is hooked to a quantifiable standard of marketability, where no arguments about quality and popularity and dissent can go very far. Any producer who is too individualistic is put out at the door, and what can he say without being unpatriotic? The U.S.

communications official Newton Minow ended up in no man's land for calling American television a "vast wasteland." Such people *are* aberrations in America, where the market is the national culture — where it's the homeland rather than the wasteland. In that culture, smooth corporate efficiency is the broadcasting norm.

But it's the American norm, not ours. A vice-president in charge of programming who makes an attempt at smooth, corporate efficiency is killing the works in a broadcasting tradition which depends for its freedom on tension and debate. Canada's problem is not to evade or suppress conflict and controversy, so that CBC television, for example, can retain its corporate equilibrium as easily as the American networks, which can and have sidetracked even slightly controversial content without difficulty, but to find ways of legitimizing the conflict so it will add to the tradition rather than take away from it.

Although the history of it tends to be forgotten, public broadcasting, by making such conflict a matter of public concern, has enlarged freedom in the community. Canada has a long and rich background of debate over the relationship of Parliament and government to broadcasting, and on the question of broadcasting freedom in general, which is the precedent on which freedom and tolerance rests.

A preoccupation with free expression was at the base of the public broadcasting movement itself. "The free use of broadcasting by all sections of opinion" was one of the two driving motives (the other was nationalism) leading to the legislation of 1932, Graham Spry of the Canadian Radio League recounted in 1935. Leonard Brockington, first chairman of the CBC board of governors, explaining policy to parliamentary committees in 1938 and 1939, declared that "radio speech should be allowed to be forthright, provocative and stimulating . . . national problems and international problems should be discussed by Canadian citizens without restrictions or fear . . . above all there should be no preference for wealth; freedom of speech is not for sale at fifty dollars a minute on the air." A CBC "White Paper" on political and controversial broadcasting that followed reaffirmed the commitment to the "fullest use of the air for forthright stimulating discussion on all controversial questions . . . the largest possible opportunity for the expression of varying and opposite opinions . . . the air belongs to the people." There was more to it, though, than the technical right to broadcast individual views and minority opinions and, equally vital, the freedom to make use of important room for such broadcasting in the schedule. The right to individualism in programming — to a broad range of self-expression — was at stake and defended.

By contrast, the attempt to escape this conflict by rejecting the indigenous culture in favour of the straightforward but inappropriate American one makes broadcasting a matter of private, "market" decision-making (if not also a reflection of the values of station owners and advertisers), and ends up only in cutting down its possibilities — freedom to boost ratings and profits but not necessarily freedom. The American-attempt-in-Canada, in other words, is misdirected, and has a misguided effect.

The attitude of the Conservative party to public broadcasting is one such curious story. In the days of C. D. Howe and Mackenzie King, the Conservatives came to view the CBC as a mouthpiece of the Liberal party in power, with some justification, particularly in the early years of World War II. But the CBC, preceding the war, had vigorously defended its independence, and by the end of the war had regained it. The tradition was strong, and had become internalized. In 1956, during the famous pipeline debate, a decision to exclude George Drew from a series of televised press conferences was withdrawn when the head of Public Affairs threatened to resign. The Conservatives themselves, because of their vigilance and criticism in Parliament, were partly responsible for this spirit of broadcasting independence. Yet under the sway of the American model, and harbouring their old grievances, and in alliance also with private interests intent on destroying the unified system, they were unable to see how valuable their own role had been. When they came into power, they weakened the culture instead, making the besieged CBC vulnerable and defensive. Television as a whole was set back. (And as George Grant pointed out, Diefenbaker, while presiding over the destruction of the indigenous broadcasting structure and the Americanizing of broadcasting, was himself being destroyed by Americanization!)

Similarly, a falling off of contention about programming at the network television level, where public attention is considerable, may indicate an increasing acceptance by the public of a broad freedom for broadcasting. So that freedom in broadcasting is no longer the live issue it used to be. It may also indicate, however, that the questioning, individualist, experimental undercurrent in the Canadian public broadcasting tradition, that gave it from time to time an exceptional quality of freedom that had no counterparts elsewhere in North America, has given way to the limited freedom of the United States network norm, as elaborated for Canadian viewers by NBC, CBS and ABC.

But the possibility of safe escape from Canadian reality into American liberty was always a romantic illusion, not least of all because what is liberty to an American is not necessarily liberty to a Canadian.

Americans have traditionally laid great store in liberty seen in terms of the freedom of business and enterprise, which allows tremendous latitude for individualism and change in certain directions at the price of rigid, self-destructive conformity in others — the freedom of commerce, and what can be had by commerce, and what serves commerce, against the tyranny of the soul, to cite Tocqueville again. The practical application of typical American liberty in that tradition has meant in dominant network broadcasting that controversy and diversity by and large get ground down or shunted out of advertisers' prime time, or out altogether, by what Fred W. Friendly, former CBS News director, calls the "vending-machine bureaucracy."

This is not to mention the notorious direct interference in programming by sponsors in the past (this practice has supposedly ended with spot sales); the same kind of interference by network "program practices" (the euphemism for "censor"); the rejection of network programs by affiliates both for commercial reasons ("rating censorship" with a vengeance) and non-commercial ones; the pressure towards conformity put on producers by the practice of affiliate pre-screening; the cases of close identification and links to the local status quo by affiliates; fearful political practices, like the networks' adherence to blacklists in the McCarthy era.

On the related matter of checking American ethnocentrism (the miles of glacierlike "insularity" or "provincialism" — the ideological "absolutism" — that Hartz found underlying the American ethos), American commercial broadcasting still brings to mind Tocqueville's harsh observation a century earlier that "I know of no country in which there is so little independence of mind and real freedom of discussion as in America." Tocqueville did not mean that there was not open debate and fierce argument in the United States, but that it was ideologically contained. "In America the majority raises formidable barriers around the liberty of opinion; within these barriers an author may write what he pleases, but woe to him if he goes beyond them." U.S. corporate television for all its reasons is not inclined to hurdle such barriers. But on that score perhaps nothing more could be expected.

Today, in an age of prohibitively expensive network television and private industrial "governments," the myth of American liberty itself is under question.

*   *   *

Americans most engaged in American liberty are often also most bitterly aware of its limitations. Hence the declaration by Edward R. Murrow, the courageous pioneer of independent television journalism, in 1958: "If there are any historians . . . a hundred years from now and there should be preserved the kinescopes for one week of all three networks, they will find recorded, in black-and-white or color, evidence of decadence, escapism and insulation from the realities of the world in which we live . . . If we go on as we are, then history will take its revenge, and retribution will [catch] up with us." And Walter Lippman's contention in the same period that commercial television had become the opposite of free: ". . . in fact . . . the creature, the servant and indeed the prostitute of merchandising." Those passages come from Fred Friendly's account of his days at CBS, *Due To Circumstnaces Beyond Our Control*, published in 1967. Friendly was Murrow's producer, and at the end of his stay was president of CBS News.

On the larger, ideological question, Louis Hartz writes in *The Liberal Tradition in America*, "Freedom in the fullest sense implies both variety and equality; but history, for reasons of its own, chose to separate these two principles, leaving the one with the old society of Burke [England] and giving the other to the new society of Paine [the United States]). America, as a kind of natural fulfillment of Paine, has been saddled throughout its history with the defect which this fulfillment involves . . . At the bottom of the American experience of freedom, not in antagonism to it but as a constituent element of it, there has always lain the inarticulate premise of conformity." Hartz compares this to England where privacy and variety, "an indefinable germ of liberty . . . that America cannot duplicate," are part of the tradition of freedom. Does this explain why British television is "freer" than American television? For that matter, does not Canada, by fortuitous circumstances, share *both* the premise of equality in North America and the premise of variety inherited from England and France? Canadian public broadcasting was the exceptional vehicle we created to work that combination in radio diffusion. The "inward enrichment of culture and perspective" that Hartz had hoped for in 1954 (by coincidence, the beginning of the television age) to free America from its lack of "relative insight" has not been forthcoming in this medium which nevertheless probably has the greatest possibilities for it.

* * *

Private broadcasters have done their best to promote this narrow sectarian ideology of liberty in this country. But Canada never was a private enterprise nation. And, over time, as Canadians brought more and more of their non-liberal economy under public ownership and control, we felt no less free than our American brothers. The American libertarian dogma was contradicted by our own experience.

Out of our non-American past, we have tended more to identify liberty with procedures rooted in society, like Parliament, the common law, respect for linguistic and regional differences, and tolerance of opposing ideological views. Public ownership, through parliaments, has added another dimension to that mode of identification. When historical logic forced us into public broadcasting, we already had a hidden aptitude for it. In practice, public broadcasting has worked out in providing for freedom of opinion and diversity of programming, despite sad periods of fearfulness and retrenchment. Paradoxically, the system may have worked out best for French Canada, which has had the sharpest grievances within it.

The Canadian and American notions of individualism are at variance. The imposition of American individualism on Canadians in the name of a "free" broadcasting structure only constrains Canadian individualism to the point where self-expression is so curbed that Canadians are cursed with a colonial dullness, and curse themselves for it.

The arguments are in ourselves. Trying to conceive of a democratic broadcasting structure in the borrowed abstract, or by following too closely to the United States example, only imprisons us. Broadcasting freedom, like the freedom of all mass media, derives its meaning from the particular contradictions within which men strive to be free. Not that Americans love liberty less than Canadians or vice-versa, not that free expression does not suffer here from natural enemies, of which there are all too many, but that we approach it, and fight for it, from different directions, as do the Europeans, the Chinese and other peoples. By approaching freedom in broadcasting from our own direction, rather than from the Chinese or the American or another direction, we are going to get much more of it.

Another example of the inappropriateness of the American-ideology-in-Canada as regards broadcasting is to perceive of public broadcasting as a minority form, as it necessarily must be in the American context, and to point to the "freedom" and "quality" of American educational television by way of example. The suggestion is that the CBC abandon "popular" programming and cater to a "receptive" minority.

That would, simply, destroy the interaction between the individualist producer striving after quality as he sees it and the simultaneous impulse to appeal to a broad public which, when the two have dovetailed, have produced the best in Canadian broadcasting. It would also abandon the greater part of English-speaking Canadians, even more so than now, to American popular culture, or to pale Canadian imitations, and abandon creative broadcasting talent to a limited, and limiting role, after the pattern of the National Film Board. It would, in a phrase, destroy the integrative effect.

Such references to American educational television are misplaced. The American majority is dynamic and powerful, and subscribes to a homogeneous myth. In broadcasting, it generates its own lively culture, independent of any incidental interaction with less conformist individuals. And the U.S. is rich enough, and densely enough populated, that in the interstices of the dominant majority the non-conformist minorities can manage something of their own, occasionally even in as costly a medium as feature film making.

In Canada, the majorities have never been inclusive and dynamic and conformist enough, and the individualists never rich and numerous enough, to afford an escape from each other. To separate out the parts in the mass media would be culturally self-destructive for everybody. Canada is an organic, and unAmerican society. (It should be added that U.S. public television, because it has such a small place in American life and traditions of freedom, is considerably more vulnerable to outside pressures, more poorly financed, and less effective than a proper public system should be. Even in the United States, public television, to flourish, must have a larger role in the community.)

Perhaps the most illuminating of the backward effects caused in broadcasting by the American-ideology-in-Canada is the growth of unresponsiveness and bureaucracy brought on by the introduction of market competition, which is supposed to do just the opposite. Market competition, in broadcasting as in everything else, is the root ingredient of the American ideology. More market competition in a private enterprise society, among people in whom the private enterprise ethos is internalized, means greater responsiveness, and greater efficiency, with its corollary of less bureaucratic overlay.

But the introduction of market competition into a public culture, among people with a community ethos, does not necessarily produce greater responsiveness; it may bring on paralytic defensiveness and disintegration instead.

When broadcasting in Canada was essentially a public enterprise, as it was in embryo during the CNR network days, and as it fully came to be during World War II, imagination flourished and responsiveness was acute. Efficiency reigned. "I am surprised [the cost] is so small," a hostile Conservative investigator of the CNR, in 1931, remarked of the remarkably low capital expenditure on radio ($175,000). In 1938, two years after the CBC had been formed, performance relative to expenditure was equally phenomenal. Staff numbered 337 and salaries amounted to $570,000, compared to 3,600 staff and $4,400,000 for the BBC. C. D. Howe noted that the cost of producing the Charlie McCarthy program was more than the CBC had available for all of its 57 sustaining programs.

And during the war, the CBC, as broadcaster, did the impossibly Canadian by squaring the American circle. "It succeeded in attracting mass audiences," Frank Peers summed it up, "and, as each year went by, it was more successful in appealing to the discriminating listener as well." The public broadcasting ethic was heard in the actual making. The CBC news department was formed in 1941, and had almost immediate success. The 1944 Radio Committee praised it as "a service that is not surpassed in any other country." CBC "Stage" began in January 1944. Not too long after, frustrated New York producers would be putting on headphones Sunday night to listen to "Stage" from across the border. The *New York Times* called the performers "the best repertory group in this hemisphere." It was also a period of national radio forums, and through them, public participation in programming itself.

On the French-language side, a whole indigenous popular culture had come alive. The critic of the *Montreal Gazette* commented, in 1939, that some of the performers and programs had eclipsed in impact on the popular consciousness the mythic figures of the American networks. One commercial production carried by the network occasionally reached an astounding 80 per cent of the potential listening audience. As early as 1940, a survey found that public broadcasting had such a high degree of acceptance among French-speaking listeners that "it would be difficult to organize attacks upon its activities in Quebec."

By the time the war ended, the CBC had in large part regained the political and cultural independence of its early years. Revenues were secure. Psychologically, the public broadcasting culture was on a firm footing. For just a few years, the culture was free from the unscrupulous lobbying and the ideological slanging of the private broadcasters, and from the bugbear of financial starvation by Parliamentary indifference.

By contrast, the replacement of the unified public system with a modified competitive market system in television in the 1960's resulted in less freedom and more bureaucracy, contrary to all our American expectations. The origins of bureaucracy in the CBC have been traced back to the establishment of the Personnel and Administration Department (quickly dubbed the Pest and Aggravation Department) in 1944. But the 1960's were the Dark Age of bureaucratic control, when administrators in Ottawa more and more made sensitive programming decisions without being involved in the programming, with devastating consequences on the tradition of broadcasting freedom. It was a period of severe self-censorship and of the suppression of controversy and experiment. It was also the first time in the CBC's history when the nemesis of American broadcasting — sponsor interference with details of programming content — had to be contended with. The commercial tail began to wag the public broadcasting dog. Crown bureaucracy and commercial bureaucracy came together under one roof. The ideological colony had the worst of both worlds.

The native dialectic was turned around and not unnaturally, the natives proceeded to strangle themselves. In all democracies — Jeffersonian, Maoist, Canadian — widespread public criticism arising from ideological liveliness is the essential democratic key to keeping the culture free from bureaucracy. But in the case of public broadcasting in the 1960's, with the culture itself on the financial and ideological defensive, not just the malicious criticism by vested interests, but also criticism in general, had a traumatizing effect. The bureaucracy alone being able to function in a state of trauma, it strengthened its hold. Having to defend the territory without a healthy ideological hinterland, however, the CBC sergeant majors did exactly the wrong thing. Instead of confidently drawing out public criticism and using it to educate the public and the broadcaster, and to liberate them both, they tried to downgrade or sidetrack it instead, and to ride herd on individualism on the production side for fear of rousing the hinterland in the first place. Withdrawn, under bureaucratic siege, public broadcasting less and less came up with those rare broadcasting ideas which encourage creative individualism but which, at the same time, touch off popular excitement. There was a lack of quality *and* a falling off of mass appeal. Eventually, the credibility of the Canadian model disappeared. The bureaucratic structure remorselessly made its own adaptation by digging up McLuhanist cant to demonstrate that chopping up programming *and changing its style* to merge with the style of "American" commercials in a broadcasting flow was how the medium should be used, and by speculating on an administrative and technical structure by which the CBC would be an integral, minor part of a received system, which indeed it has become.

According to the received ideology, the less money that broadcasting is assured of from public sources, the harder it will have to scratch, and the more energetic, bold and individualistic it will be. According to Canadian reality, the lack of security and the forcing of market competition has broken the backbone, or bent it, of the very men on whom the independence of broadcasting depends. But the received ideology in turn prevents any empirical appreciation of what has happened. "Competition is the geritol in the tired blood of Canadian television," wrote a Vancouver newspaper critic (Les Wedman), although there was nothing tired about Canadian broadcasting until it was progressively enfeebled by the kind of competition the critic had in mind.

For anybody who had any feeling for the Canadian experience, the introduction of market competition was senseless in the first place. Inescapable cultural competiton already existed from American broadcasting. That is the competition that counts. We should have been building on public broadcasting instead. Inappropriate market competition was cultural suicide.

Canadian public broadcasting, after all, is not an artificial device. It is a living historical current having its own forceful dialectic within itself. By making the connection between ownership and broadcaster a matter of public concern, it enlarges on the meaning of freedom, pushing away the commercial notion of freedom as freedom to compete for dollars. By bringing individualists and the larger public together, and allowing for the exploration of dissent and intellectual challenge, it enlarges on the meaning of democracy. And as a vehicle of Canadian self-expression, under compelling historical pressure towards efficiency and mass appeal, it enlarges on the meaning of competition. Ignore that dialectic, cater instead to a borrowed one with feeble historical roots in Canada, and for which Canadains have no genius, where we are even bad imitators, and cultural puzzlement and dismay follow.

Always colonials, we just could not conceive that our experience had merit other than as a short-range expedient. From the beginning of organized broadcasting in Canada in the 1930's, vested interests have been allowed to take advantage of the ambiguities of the broadcasting structure to weaken it. Our governments, for their part, seem to have been ill at ease with the Canadian model, and have tended to finance public broadcasting not to make it flourish but just to keep it alive. The original licence fee was set too low. CBC station ownership was limited. Affiliates carried only a part of the CBC's programming. Commercial stations in metropolitan areas were given large boosts in power and became regional stations, contrary to original intention. Instead of publicly owned community stations at the local level, extending and elaborating the public broadcasting tradition, new licences were handed out freely to commercial operators. Public radio broadcasting was submerged.

The same structure evolved in television broadcasting. "The CBC has been maligned, misrepresented, savaged, nagged and subjected to meanness and indignities by hostile and sometimes greedy business competitors or ill-informed politicians," wrote Graham Spry, in 1961, in an analysis of the "decline and fall of Canadian broadcasting," until public broadcasting was surrounded and "hemmed in to a subordinate place in the structure," exactly contrary to legislation and to Parliament's intentions. Parliament did not have the courage of its convictions. How could it when, ideologically, Canadian public broadcasting was seen as a peculiar aberration inside the North American norm?

As the 1960's ground on, we became more conditioned than ever to believe that the CBC was chasing extravagantly after a provincial will o' the wisp. Marshall McLuhan compared the CBC to a post office. The television critic of the country's largest newspaper, Patrick Scott of the *Toronto Star*, suggested that the CBC stick to public affairs, which it could do well, and get out of drama (although when the public system was given half a chance, in the radio days, it did drama exceptionally well, and although drama in one form or another is essential to the self-expression of a culture). The heads of the French-language side were described by a public affairs supervisor as *marchands de chaussettes*. On the English-language side, former employees wrote bitter letters charging the CBC with cultural treason and with forcing them to search for work in exile.

Subsequently, the prospect of further commercial television operations in Canadian cities was opened up without any reference to the public broadcasting possibilities or to amplifying the indigenous tradition beyond the CBC, although an additional public service independent of the corporation would be the first logical step to increasing the cultural elbow room for public broadcasting in the structure as a whole, and liberating all of Canadian television.

The indigenous way was put down again.

CHAPTER 12

The Expo Experience

In the midst of this decline in the sixties, along came an elaborate happening which demonstrated that the principle behind Canadian broadcasting was viable in itself after all — that a non-commercial meeting of uncompromised artists and an open, mass public was both possible and desirable. I'm referring here to the World Exposition in 1967.

When Expo opened, Pierre Berton exclaimed in *Maclean's*, "By God, we did it. And generally we did it well." The late Pierre Dupuy told the story of how a Japanese official, on learning that Expo had no foreign consultants, exclaimed, "But then it's an Expo of amateurs!" Everybody seemed surprised, not just at the feat of construction, but at the human scale and human purpose of the exposition side, and at the relationship of the parts to the whole. Thinly populated, decentralized countries with dualistic cultures, however, do not produce a great cultural event starting from scratch.

"Would you like to see the most beautiful thing in Expo?" Dupuy asked a journalist visiting him in his Expo office. "Look at that [Concordia] bridge. That, sir, that isn't American." In selecting the congruous grace of a minor structure, Dupuy was intuitively making a major point. It is not hard to imagine Americans producing good, or better, individual works of art. The American pavilion at Expo was one of them. But it is hard to imagine Americans achieving the same integrated non-commercialism for a mass public without losing their originality. Conceivably, a non-commercial American Expo in 1967 might have drawn on a marginal, elitist style in the imperial J. F. Kennedy manner. Canadians, with their relatively limited resources, were forced to draw on something more basic to their culture — the non-elitist, non-market, collective, public style which is our broadcasting and film-making tradition.

Dupuy also spoke, symbolically, of Walt Disney's visit to Expo. Disney came to see La Ronde while it was under construction, and offered free advice on how to improve it. "I didn't abuse [his generosity]," Dupuy recounted. "Disney had inspired the New York fair. I said to myself, we're not going to do the same thing here."

There were other, more indirect, clues to the indigenous spirit. Summing up Expo for *Weekend Magazine*, Harry J.

Boyle wrote that "the significant fact, overshadowing all others during 1967, was the philosophical intent of rediscovering the importance of the individual"; and again, "What amazes is the way it evolved, and how the idea of man as an individual survived"; and again, compulsively, "We have discovered and reasserted the importance of man the individual."

But why should it be amazing? The struggle to encourage the individualism of the whole man, as against the narrowing individualism of market man, is the struggle of Canadian broadcasting. Living next to the United States, and eclipsed by American individualism, we have had to fight that struggle as nobody else has. That legacy, too, is in our psyche. So what happened at Expo was the most natural thing in the world for Canadians, just as it was natural for Harry J. Boyle, one of the free spirits of public broadcasting, to have celebrated it.

What was amazing was that Canadians, after so much browbeating and brainwashing by the massive juggernaut of imperial culture, should still have enough interior resilience to go their own way.

For failure to see that continuity, we have also failed to see the organic nature of Canadian society. J. J. Brown, for example, in *Ideas in Exile*, wrote that "Montreal's Expo 67 . . . represents French rather than English Canada in inspiration and design." The impetus did in fact come from French-Canadian politicians. Dupuy was a French Canadian. The theme "Terre des Hommes" came, via a French Canadian, from Antoine de Saint-Exupéry. The man in charge of the architectural layout of Expo was a French Canadian. And the director of expositions was a French Canadian. If we assume that French Canadians have been culturally formed apart from English Canadians — that there is no dovetailing or overlapping of psyches — then Brown is right.

But if Expo was the issue of the public broadcasting and film-making culture in Canada, then whatever French-Canadian inspiration there was in Expo was nourished by the whole. What French Canadian of the generation that conceived and illuminated Terre des Hommes doesn't have something of Radio-Canada inside himself? Even during World War II, with the bitter memory of the muzzling of the anti-conscriptionists still alive in French-Canadian minds, Radio-Canada was a powerful cultural force. And Radio-Canada, in turn, could be said to be of English-Canadian inspiration and design, if the public broadcasting movement was not, like Expo, also nourished by the whole, which is the Canadian existence.

Dupuy's own indefatigable activity on behalf of Expo was fed by that impulse. "It's necessary that Canadians know themselves better," Dupuy explained in 1967, "that they have confidence in themselves, that they stop being pessimists, hypercritical." And: "I wanted to show . . . that we had a personality different from the United States, to demonstrate our national identity: there is no foreign influence in Expo." And: Expo was a "chance for me to allow Canadians to realize they had more in common than they thought they had." And: "I had insisted that [the Expo team] have a Canadian character in the territorial sense of the word."

The dense, interrelated character of Canadian society which became visible in Expo was just as quickly obscured by colonial romanticism. An English-speaking editor reflected, with self-satisfaction, "I think we might have something to say to the world," as if Canadians had had nothing of importance to say to themselves or to anybody else before 1967. Similarly, *Weekend* exulted that "Canadians Finally Started Talking To Each Other," as if the fur trade and railroads and, particularly, public radio had not been great avenues of trans-Canada communication. The lust for communication — the historical necessity for communication — is one of the continuous threads of the Canadian experience; *Weekend* called it "the start of something most un-Canadian." *Life* magazine had a patronizing article about Canada's coming of age in which Gregory Peck allowed that Canada

had just become a "major league country." I am proud
to be a Canadian," the article cited a Russian-born taxi
driver as telling his passengers, the implication being that
a proud Canadian was something new, and was therefore newsworthy — a notion confirmed for *Life* by *Time*,
in the same vein.

Yet nothing creative comes, or can come, out of colonial
self-indulgence.

There was much talk in the winter of 1967-68 about not
letting the Expo spirit die, particularly as regards communication and environment. "Surely we are going to keep on
moving now," Boyle quoted a young Expo visitor. Boyle
himself described the experience as "the catalyst of our
century of search and sometimes confusion" and "as the
inspiration and the example." Even Lester Pearson, one of
the least confident of Canadians as an original people,
admitted cautiously that perhaps Canadians "had less confidence in ourselves, as Canadians, than we should have had."

But almost every practical inference to be drawn from
Expo involved an affirmation of the closeted, besieged native
ideology of broadcasting and film-making and the arts, and
a rejection of the American model. And in the colony, that
affirmation was not forthcoming. The continuity and interrelationships which inform Canadian identity were lost.
A young Montréalais would see no more in Expo than
he did in the anniversary celebrations of Dupuis Frères, the
department store. The Canadian roots of the Expo experience
would be spurned by the most promising generation of
French Canadians, as they would be by us all.

Far from being the beginning of a new era in Canada,
Expo was a defiant burst of creativity from out of a starved,
declining Canadain tradition, and a crumbling unity.

Only in Canada, where the people are cut off from an
accurate image of themselves as energetic creators in a public
framework by a superimposed colonial image as second-rate
creators in a second-rate market framework, could the lessons
of Expo have been so completely misread, and the cultural

basis of something like Expo have been neglected and cut down at exactly the wrong time in history.

In American terms, and these are the terms which private broadcasters have used almost exclusively in assaulting the principle of national broadcasting in Canada, Canadian public broadcasting appears to be a provincial inward-looking sluggard, outside the dynamic North American ethos. Expo's deliberate rejection of American influence, and comparison of Expo with popular cultural forms in the United States, suggests to us just the opposite — that there is nothing more provincial in the world than the American mainstream (or the Russian mainstream, or the Chinese mainstream), and nothing less provincial than the Canadian mainstream, once it unhooks itself from its colonial chastity belt. And the best case of its doing so was not Expo — a transitory, symbolic liberation only — but the passionate, involved creation of an original broadcasting structure.

Once the Expo Bacchanalia were over, though, the ideological chastity belt was locked tightly again.

Our public broadcasting experience informed Expo. What happens when we throw off the constricting American-ideology-in-Canada and relate back to broadcasting from the Expo experience?

We notice, first of all, that the American doctrine (the market tyranny) has paradoxically crushed individualism in the name of individualism, while public broadcasting in Canada has, also paradoxically, encouraged individualism in the name of the collectivity. And that as the Canadian broadcasting structure was weakened, to make it approximate the American model, this liberating, creative individualism, which surfaced again in Expo, was all but crushed as well. Not to reinforce this individualism in the broadcasting structure, but to continue to force it into exile in the continental wasteland, is to rob ourselves of pleasure and of liberty.

The Expo experience, by holding off commercial clutter,

also showed us, in bold physical, visual and aural terms, just how strident and oppressive the market tyranny is, and how suffocating its hold on our broadcasting. It was as if we had walked through a copywriting curtain into the free world.

The American doctrine has made broadcasting in North America into a vehicle of advertising. We sensed that this advertising was totalitarian, but from imitativeness and passiveness, we came to terms with it. Expo was the sensual jolt which enabled us to see clearly what was always obvious: that advertising, particularly television advertising, continuously indoctrinates the public in a parochial, limiting way of life, without the public having exposure to counter-ideology; that it is by and large mindless and illiberal; that it is high in persuasion and torturingly high in repetition but low in information and basically free from critical analysis; that it is doctrinaire; that it is as tyrannical as medieval church edicts or Confucian dogma.

All our arguments about freedom in broadcasting have been too narrowly parliamentary and political. Canadian broadcasting, and newspaper and magazine publishing, will not come near to being democratic, or to offering balanced content, or diversity, or the other side of the story, until advertising as we know it today is faced with an equally single-minded, well financed, technically skilled use of the media by the cultural opposition latent in all of us.

The doctrine is restrictive in another way. The economic dimension of Canadian identity expresses itself most forcefully in public enterprise and in redistribution (for the latter see Chapters 13 and 14). Broadcast advertising in Canada, on the oth *r* hand, draws on the American style and economic myth, and on the U.S. oligopoly culture. So Canadian broadcasting will not and can not reflect the Canadian personality until economics broadcasting (what is now mostly advertising, that is U.S.-style propaganda) goes through a cultural revolution of our own making.

Or to look at it in another way: in all the controversy about Canadian content on television, we have overlooked one of the most American, and most Americanizing, elements of them all, the advertising segments. Inevitably Canadian television loses. Instead of adapting our programming to accommodate a narrow, borrowed economic propaganda (advertising, American style) we should be adapting economics broadcasting to independent public programming, Canadian style.

Then our television would be unmistakably, vigorously our own.

The hold that American television has over Canadian viewers would loosen a bit too. Forced and phoney U.S. television commercials, and the cachet they put on the programming which they surround, could no more stand up to indigenous economics broadcasting in Canada than the expensive, systematic propaganda of the National Electric Light Association could stand up to the cultural momentum behind Ontario Hydro.

* * *

Canadian advertising agencies, including branches of U.S. agencies, play the same role in this cultural imitativeness as the fashionable literary tea parties played in the Family Compact's time, when pretentious colonials read mediocre British works while the lasting indigenous literature was being produced by William Lyon Mackenzie in the *Colonial Advocate*.

The private enterprise culture is too fragile in Canada to support much more than rhetoric and imitation, so that private enterprise nationalists become what they wrongly but freely accuse other nationalists of being — quixotic chauvinists. They want to preserve a community while bypassing one of the richest and most creative manifestations of that community — public enterprise — to the point of cultural emasculation.

Advertising being the most visible expression of the thin private enterprise culture in Canada, that is where the comic chauvinism is most noticeable. For example, the president of McKim's, one of the top five Canadian ad agencies at the time, told the *Toronto Star* in 1967, to make a nationalist point, that "it happens to be the case that French-Canadian women buy brassieres more for glamour than comfort as English-Canadian women do. That is the sort of marketing information that a Canadian agency can supply." Jerry Goodis, the nationalist president of Goodis Goldberg Soren Ltd., told the *Toronto Star*, in 1970, that "we are better than [the American agencies] are in our own country, our own milieu," and pointed out, by way of example, that such landed immigrants as "Josephine the Plumber" and "the Man from Glad," brought in by U.S.-controlled agencies, had not done a good job selling products in Canada.

I think there's a bit more to the Canadian economic culture than a dualistic appreciation of brassieres or an indifference to Josephine's method of cleaning a sink.

The advertising industry, which has a large part of the budget of broadcasting under its control, and an unmeasured leverage over media, has neither the mandate to be more indigenous nor the spirit to rebel against its provincial, backwater role, nor the imagination to do so. All it can manage, in moments of colonial disgruntlement, is to be peevish. We have come this far as a country for far more than that.

*   *   *

Expo suggests another parallel between itself and public broadcasting in Canada — in their common breaking out of the market tyranny, and their creation of cultural structures patterned after the social propensities of man, which is what liberation in North America has come to mean.

"We are just going to collapse as a civilization if we do not find ways for the vast bulk of our population to live in reasonable environments," reflected Colonel Churchill, the army engineer who built Expo. "If you don't do this then it means that you will have created not a state where the best of all possible worlds is possible, but rather you will have made the thing degraded, until people will be forced to return to the kind of living that we all look back on in Dickensian terms as awful. The environment is part of the standard of living. You have to improve it. A human is not a machine. He's a human being."

"A human is not a machine!" That itself could have come out of a Dickens novel. From the beginning of the heyday of the market system, the age when Dickens was writing, men have been slowly rebelling against their cultural dislocation and breaking the system in order to protect and express themselves. During the black days of the Industrial Revolution in Great Britain, the standard of living, measured by the market, was actually superior to what it had been before. Life, however, was bitterly inferior because the cultural cohesiveness of British society had been destroyed, leaving the mass of people in a passive limbo. Not until labour organized and withdrew itself as a passive factor in the market, and public health ordinances were passed, withdrawing the immediate environment from the market, did life take on a human face again.

As Colonel Churchill realized, looking back on Expo, and looking forward across the 49th parallel and around him in Montreal, the Dickensian horrors are about to be duplicated. The standard of living in the United States, for example, is much higher than anybody ever imagined possible. But life is becoming more and more intolerable. The urban environment has become restrictive. Even in America, the citizenry, to protect their humanity, are being forced to withdraw the physical environment from the exchange principle.

What goes for the physical environment also goes for the cultural environment. Market broadcasting is equally destructive in the broad sense of making the mass of people passive recipients of impersonal economic forces rather than encouraging their individualism. Broadcasting is inherently a cultural process. The market tyranny, by inevitably defining it in terms of private property, as an industry, distorts it and the community along with it. Market common-denominator network television, for example, separates individualists from the larger public, making more for a disjointed society than an open and various one. Its incessant, one-sided economic propaganda reinforces activity in unbalanced patterns in which the private, acquisitive sector is far richer than it should be and the community and conservationist sector far poorer, psychologically as well as financially, with all the social and environmental disintegration that implies. The broadcasting structure obeys dehumanized mercantile priorities and takes its toll in dehumanizing effects.

The parochialism of the American psyche is the last thing we should try to imitate, above all in broadcasting, even if we had a talent for it, which we don't.

The Broadcasting Act of 1932 was a great innovative move. Since then we have gone backwards.

The difficulty is that the American-ideology-in-Canada decrees (and we believe) that market television is free, although it costs money, and that it is somehow in the natural order of things — a part of natural law — because that's the way the market is itself; public broadcasting, although it may be necessary in Canada, is therefore, somehow, unnatural. After all, to establish public broadcasting requires debate, and an Act of Parliament, and arousing an imperfect humanity, and deliberately allocating funds. Whereas market broadcasting is just there, like the sky.

The truth is just the opposite. The American market broadcasting model is not one of the most natural and pragmatic cultural structures in the world but one of the most contrived and doctrinaire, whereas the Canadian model is far more typical of human experience and far more natural to man.

As already mentioned, economic liberalism, from which market broadcasting derives, was itself a revolutionary, utopian doctrine for whose acceptance secular preachers drew up elaborate ideological tracts and created mythology. There was nothing natural about an economic doctrine which descended from an abstract principle of exchange rather than from a worldly principle of social organization. The subordination of politics and of culture to an economic litany, which is the essence of the American myth, instead of the reverse, has few anthropological equivalents. Economic liberalism was a singular happening depending on a peculiar combination of historical circumstances. It was a bizarre, short-lived, liberating, degrading, immensely productive and creative, and brutalizing period. Now it is essentially no more.

Market broadcasting is one of its relics. It is sustained by mercantile agents who use it to manage demand — a sin against the true doctrine of economic liberalism but committed safely under the guise of piety. Their age of cultural interference — Galbraith calls it "organized public bamboozlement" — is coming to an end too.

Canadian public broadcasting, on the other hand, is, in its central principle, suited to our times. It has always seemed less dynamic than American broadcasting. It has certainly been financially weaker. But in spite of our neglect and our abuse, and its consequent doldrums, it represents today, more so than ever, the more valid principle on which to elaborate.

*   *   *

There is a subplot: the larcenous hoodwinking of the good-natured Canadian family by the private broadcasting industry. For sheer avarice and unconscionable hypocrisy, the private broadcasting interests could give lessons to the "parasites and sycophants" of our first Family Compact, whom they uncannily resemble. They have been real colonials.

The original Family Compact maintained themselves in power by flaunting their loyalty to the crown and discouraging the bold indigenous culture, so as to give their own superficial, narrowing imitation of metropolis culture a dominant impact. But when it appeared that loyalty to the Crown might be a private disadvantage, the Compact, like the white Rhodesians, were not above looking askance at the loyalty myth in order to retain their privileges.

Similarly, private broadcasters in Canada flaunted their loyalty to the metropolis ideology of free enterprise (and its association of freedom with a free market), as justification to encroach on, and then to overcome, the indigenous broadcasting culture. The history of their unscrupulous attacks on the indigenous broadcasting culture, and of the hypocrisy of their newspaper allies, reads like a Chaucerian tale of low cunning. But when it came to a logical application of that ideology against their own interests — the untrammelled extension of cablevision — they lost no time in piously doing a right about. The president of the private television network, the end product of this destructive opportunism in broadcasting, would solemnly, and with a straight face, condemn cablevision companies as "merchants with gaudy baubles" forcing demand, and would point out, in a burst of public-mindedness, that "the poor, the uneducated, the rural people, those who need [cable television service] most are least likely to have it." As William Lyon Mackenzie would have said, they have turned their coats and their waistcoats also.

* * *

Despite the ideological confusion, and the damping down of the indigenous imagination, the impulse is there as ever. But without a reworking of the public broadcasting and film-making ideology in the country at large, the new stratagems it forces into being — like the Canadian Film Development Corporation and the Canadian content rules of the Canadian Radio-Television Commission — flounder in ambiguity. The film-financing and distribution systems and ethos, and the broadcasting milieu, are still punishingly American-in-Canada, for all the film promoters and station owners and copywriters that come from Flin Flon or Rimouski instead of New York or Los Angeles. Such agencies like the CFDC and the CRTC end up, for the most part, desperately trying to manipulate the imitative culture.

They cannot liberate the indigenous one, even if they were able to perceive it.

The malaise in the Canadian spirit seems to be endless. The public broadcasting ethic and the public film-making ethic remain, like the country (more so the English-speaking part), in a psychic underground.

PART V

The Canadian Redistribution Culture

CHAPTER 13

Redistribution and Identity

Out of the contradiction between the small Canadian domestic market and the large American one grew the unique Canadian public enterprise style. Out of the internal contradictions between French Canada and English Canada, and between the regions and the centre, has come the adoption and the elaboration, as a fundamental mode of Canadian life, of the unAmerican mechanism of redistribution as opposed to the mythic American mechanism of market rule (free enterprise).

Instead of coming closer together over time under the force of similar dilemmas and possibilities (like the settling of the continent, the large internal migrations, the pressures of inequality), the two national characters, working on and worked on by their differing contradictions, were forced further apart instead.

Take the interrelated questions of migration and equality.

Ever since Horace Greeley's cry "Go west, young man" fired the restless American imagination — even before then — the image of men and women on the move, in groups and hordes, has marked the American identity. That, after all, was what the frontier was about. And the frontier was America, and still is sentimental America. The wagon trains and riverboats remain, in imagery and myth.

The frontier experience, however, goes deeper, to the roots of the American psyche itself. The frontier was a vast, inspiring arena in which American man could reassert his own equal standing. A worker or clerk, feeling himself bound down by the conventions of settled community, could take off for the wild west where ignoring conventions was the reigning convention. To outsiders, the depredations and violence of grasping frontier man were deplorable; to

Americans they constituted a kind of rough patriotism whereby frontier man, by force and bluff maybe, proved himself an equal to anybody anywhere in the Republic.

Americans were not just born equal. They could be reborn equal, by moving on.

Other modern societies also strive after equality. What was particular to the United States was the mechanism by which the myth of equality was sustained, namely economic individualism and the ideological values of property and free enterprise underlying it. This was the American way. Labour followed wealth, or the chance of wealth (and, on the frontier, the chance of land, the classic Lockean underpinning of private wealth). The workings of the market created opportunity and the prospect of equality, on one place rather than another, and man went after.

The frontier experience was only the most forceful expression of this enduring American way of looking at equality, that is, of the enduring American ideology. In the 1930's, the Okies, cut down and cut adrift by the workings of property and markets — resembling the dispirited beasts of Lancashire one hundred years before, only with windburn on their faces instead of coal dust or factory soot — summoned up the last of their humanity for the ride to California. The circumstances had changed. Instead of frontier optimism there was frontier hopelessness. But one would not be mistaken in taking the old patched-up vehicles, piled high with belongings and family, rolling slowly down the flat highway, as latter-day covered wagons. Americans were moving on.

Similarly, later, when the consolidation of agriculture in the South sent uprooted blacks streaming to the northern cities, at immeasurable cost to both migrants and cities arising from their dislocation and alienation, no crisis-filled national debate took place. The black community in the South was too fragmented and too weak to mount a sustained argument against the exodus. Even if they had the strength and somehow the inclination, there would have been no ideological disposition towards the argument in the mass of the citizenry to which they could appeal.

In Canada, something else has been happening. Not that there haven't been large migrations here. For almost a century, Maritimers have abandoned stagnating provincialism for Toronto and Montreal. French Canadians have left Quebec, alone and in groups, searching for prosperity as far away as the lower Fraser and Alberni Inlet. There were also great external migrations — of French Canadians and Maritimers to New England, and of all Canadians to every-where south of the border. The Prairies have lost people in all directions. The decline in population in Saskatchewan in the ten years of heavy out-migration (1941-51) was as great per capita as the decline in the hardest hit of American states, South Dakota, in the corresponding years of out-migration (1930-40), and much greater than in the other states which underwent declines (Oklahoma, North Dakota and Kansas).

But in counterpoint to these migrations, a different mode of resolving inequalities evolved, nourished by powerful regional communities — the redistribution of wealth to people rather than the opposite, mythic American way of redistributing people to wealth — and in the arts of Canadians it is this underlying mode of liberation and equality that most forcefully captures those aspirations in the Canadian character.

Goin' Down the Road, the film of Maritime migrants in Toronto, was a moderately interesting Canadian episode. But the literature of anguish from within the regions, parti-cularly from within Quebec, is the more telling expression of our condition. The Okies in *The Grapes of Wrath* set out, and made it, to California. The protagonists of *As For Me And My House*, despite their bitterness and inner despair, headed down the line from their Saskatchewan town only two hundred miles and southeast to an unnamed city resembling Regina.

Occasionally in the last 10 years, projects have been undertaken to move the poor, particularly the rural poor, out of chronically uneconomic areas, as if the American migrant experience were going to be duplicated again, and subsidized as well. But these projects towards equality are not only collectively undertaken, unlike other migrations on the continent. They are all also bound up within regions. The subsidization of out-migration beyond the region, from the Gaspésie to Ontario or Alberta, for example, where labour is in demand, although it might make sense to Americans, subverts the Canadian community. It touches on our regional anguish. Our ideological disposition runs in the other direction. We must move our economic resources into the regions and let the resettlement take place there.

The redistribution of wealth among different regions of a country is not peculiar to Canada either. Many European countries like Great Britain and France have redistribution schemes, bold in scope and explicitly argued in politics. The United States redistributes wealth among the regions in its own way on the ideological (or mythological) sly, through the pork barrel and federal education and welfare expenditures, not to mention the Tennessee Valley Authority and more recent, small-scale rehabilitation projects. Defence contracts are a favourite vehicle for such dispensations. But the culture of redistribution in Canada is so bizarre, so umbilically tied to our unique internal contradictions, that there could be no mistaking it for anybody else's.

And it's an old culture.

The Canadian style in redistribution began with the talks in Quebec in 1864 leading to Confederation, when federal per capita subsidies were arranged to bolster the province's municipal tax base, since customs and excise taxes had been allocated to the Dominion. The terms of the settlement were written into the British North American Act, where the subsidies were declared to be "in full Settlement of all future Demands on Canada." Two years later, in 1869, Nova Scotia found itself in an intolerable financial situation. A fuller settlement was made, although all of the future had just barely begun, much less come to an end. New Brunswick, by pleading special need, had already managed to wangle an extra grant of $63,000.

The entry of Manitoba into Confederation in 1870 was another particular circumstance which did not fit into the subsidy formula, but was made to fit by making it fit. The unabashed Canadians simply took Manitoba's population of 12,000, of which less than 2,000 were white, as 17,000 instead. The pragmatic British Columbians, on joining Confederation in 1871, and having noticed the demographic fiction in Manitoba's case, suggested that the province's 9,000 whites and 25,000 Indians and Chinese be regarded, for the purpose of subsidy, as a population of 120,000, as the most polite way of compensating them justly for their loss of customs revenue, and to adequately meet their needs. The baldfaced British Columbia proposition was too outrageous to be accepted by Canada . . . which arranged a quieter subterfuge to do the same thing instead. Caught in American — and English — ideology which made no allowance for such redistribution, but having to behave otherwise again because of their particular situation, Canadians took to calling a spade a club and a contract no contract to get out of their ideological fix, as if they were cockeyed liars and beggars — which they obviously seemed to be, but which they persistently pretended they were not. In 1873, the old notion of equity went under again when Prince Edward Island was allocated four times as much in annual subsidy as it would have received under the original formula. Then came Alberta and Saskatchewan, and other revisions.

What was not agreed to in the spirit of the lawyer was agreed to in the spirit of the horsetrader or, by way of federal paternalism, in the spirit of charity. Nobody had an inkling of the kind of cultural innovation that was underway.

The National Policy of tariffs and wheat changed that. What was vaguely perceived before — what was dealt with in ideological ambiguity and by convenient devices — became maddeningly clear as the consequences of the National Policy worked themselves out. The regional contradictions rose to the surface, or were pushed to the surface by bitterness and indignation. The mode of redistribution became embedded in the Canadian make-up.

The Rowell-Sirois Report, the chronicle of Confederation in good times and bad, tells the story of how the National Policy brought manufacturing and large private fortunes to Ontario and Quebec at the expense of the captive markets in western Canada and the Maritimes. Lowered freight rates and other dispensations helped to offset the unequal effects, but not by very much. Central Canada became rich, and the governments of Ontario and Quebec enjoyed the rich tax base. In 1913, corporation taxes and succession duties yielded 26 per cent of total provincial revenues but only 9 per cent in the prairie provinces and 8 per cent in the Maritimes. Less money was available in those regions for encouraging further development or providing collective services. In the next decade, the 1920's, wheat values fell twice and the tax base for prairie governments fell with them. The Maritimes still had not shaken off the debilitating post-war slump. Central Canada grew in prosperity without interruption.

In that long decade of Maritime discontent, the raw principles of a Canadian ideology of redistribution were enunciated. In 1924, a movement for the vindication of "Maritime Rights" was organized. The phrase itself was charged with ideological implications. No charity was asked for. There was none of the fine calculation and opportunistic accommodation of the Confederation period. There was only a radical demand, although it was so close to the Canadian skin that it was not perceived as radical at all.

If all the workers of England demanded, as a right, equal incomes with all other Englishmen, on the grounds that their class had been essential to the Industrial Revolution but had suffered most and been rewarded least, and that this was a callous mockery of the notion of fair play, and if they maintained their demand even when it was pointed out they had not shown as much enterprise as others, and that they had entered the Industrial Revolution from immediate self-interest anyway, the radical quality of their argument would be obvious. It might be just, and it might not be, but it would be radical. The Maritimes in the 1920's were making their claim in essentially the same style, but as an expression of a regional contradiction rather than a class contradiction.

The Maritimes argued that they had not prospered like the rest of Canada because the substance of the benefits promised at the time of Confederation had been denied them (although there was no contractual promise, only a passing historical one, and at that 60 years earlier). They maintained that they had never received their promised share of internal trade which Confederation was designed to promote, because Central Canada, through its majorities in Parliament, had fashioned transportation and tariff policies for its own benefit in callous disregard of Maritime rights (although it was all done with the stamp and seal of duly elected democratic government). In return, they demanded . . . . justice.

In looking back at the Maritime Rights movement, which ended in a near doubling of the Maritime subsidy, the Rowell-Sirois Report shrewdly avoided passing judgment on the economistic merits of the Maritime argument. For all their calculations, the businessmen of Saint John and Halifax and Charlottetown were arguing from history and expectations, not from ledgers. The report dealt instead with the ideological importance of the Maritime Rights movement. (The old Rowell-Sirois Report, in tracing and elucidating the history of federal-provincial relations, was itself an ideological event.) "It is not the present purpose to consider the justice of these claims . . . " said the report. "It is rather to draw attention to the political significance of the agitation. An entire region of the Dominion, moved apparently by a common sense of injustice, protested against the inequitable operation of the national policies." The Maritime claims, together with western demands in the same period, "announced a new era in Dominion-provincial relations, an era in which regional disparities, regional difficulties, and regional ambitions became a principal concern of federal politics."

By the time the depression hit, and the protective central Canadian national policy of higher tariffs saved Ontario and Quebec from the worst but decimated the Prairies, the culture of regional equality — the Canadian style of redistribution — already had some ideology and precedent. That was not enough to make it strong, but it was enough to make it legitimate.

The Rowell-Sirois Report, after the event, was still ideologically cautious: "When, as a result of national policies undertaken in the general interest, one region or class or individual is fortuitously enriched and others impoverished, it would appear that there is some obligation, if not to redress the balance, at least to provide for the victim." Nevertheless the basic theme was there. In the formation of the National Policy of 1879, "purely economic criteria were put aside for the creation and maintenance of a political entity." The American economic philosophy was rejected. But once having rejected that philosophy, there was no turning back. The nation needed some consensus to be workable; Canada did not have "a population of common origin and traditions, deeply habituated to think alike on fundamental issues"; the unequal effects of the economic adventure of Canada, which was devised by man and not a commitment to the rules of the market, were enough to break down consensus; redistribution followed.

The country had to be just to its parts to keep the parts in a whole, and it had to go on rejecting the American philosophy to be just to its parts.

In the course of the depression, this Canadian dialectic inevitably brought about large interregional transfers of money to offset the disparities caused by national economic policies. Money for relief payments and to prevent default on debt flowed from the less affected regions to the worst affected, particularly to the West, and particularly to the province most dependent on wheat export, Saskatchewan, whose "severity-of-burden-index," based on a national average of 100, was 367, compared to 115 for Manitoba, the second on the index, 90 for Quebec and 76 for Ontario. These payments were the cultural predecessors of the present tax equalization payments. There was also special assistance to a few badly hit industries, like wheat and coal, which, in a more indirect way, was the cultural predecessor of present regional development subsidies to industry. And there was the Prairie Farm Rehabilitation Act (PFRA), providing community pastures, farm dug-outs, stream-control dams and irrigation works mostly in Alberta and Saskatchewan — not an economically large program but, as the cultural predecessor of the regional development programs begun in the 1960's, an historically large one.

At some imperceptible point in Canadian history after World War II, all this sank into the cultural fabric as if redistribution had always been with us, as in fact it had been. Tax equalization payments were taken as part of the economic countryside. Who could say when they began? Culturally, it was somewhere back in the depression, and in the 1920's, and in the 1870's, in freight rate subsidies and false body counts and the heavy bound papers of royal commissions — in the habits of an aggregate federalist mind. Then, inevitably also, came the new wave of regional development projects — the Agricultural Rehabilitation and Development Act (ARDA), the Atlantic Development Board (ADB), the Area Development Agency (ADA), the Fund for Rural Economic Development (FRED) and then, under the force of a new imperative from Quebec as well as the old — old-beyond-despair — imperative of the Maritimes, came the formation of a Department of Regional Economic Expansion (DREE), and a frank expression of the redistribution ethic.

Again, other countries redistribute revenue, but no other country has anything akin to Canada's redistribution culture, because no other country has lived the same experiences and has buried away in its psyche the same sensibilities. Who can imagine a New England Rights movement, for example, based on a demand for economic equality, citing the Constitution of 1787, or the insurgency of 1775, as proof that New Englanders had been callously cheated, *and winning out in their protest on an acceptance of principle*? The whole thing would be absurd. The very idea of persisting as a nation of "similar participants in a uniform way of life," rather than as parts of a federal whole, was to put such a Canadian possibility out of mind. Secession and states rights were elaborated along a different axis. In the end, the South was suppressed, the Maritimes were subsidized.

There was one civil war in the United States and after it was over, the issue was more or less settled. The United States was a unitary country, whatever its federal mechanisms. There was no civil war in Canada. Confederation, off and on, just seemed always to be coming apart at the seams. Off and on, it probably always will seem so. Only a few months after Canada came into being, there was already an overwhelming separatist sentiment in one of its parts, Nova Scotia — 36 out of 38 seats in the provincial election in 1867 went to anti-Confederates — as if the symbolism of Confederation would not have been complete without its interior counter-symbolism, and the Halifax legislature felt obliged to provide it.

Has anything changed? Forgetting about separatist movements and regional disaffection for a while, where else but in Canada would a controversy break out over the constitutional status of an egg — whether for marketing purposes it was a federal or provincial comestible — as it did in the early seventies. A theatre director with little interest in politics surprised me by volunteering one day that he was following the affair with wide-eyed interest. As a marketing or constitutional problem alone — a simple chicken and egg war with smuggling and court battles on the side — it would have never come to his attention. But he had sensed it rightly as a reflection of the regional contradiction that was in his own make-up. He knew his identity was involved.

If such things didn't actually happen, Canadians would have to invent them.

The contradiction in Canada is all the more singular because of the large political and economic power centred on the regions. There are 50 states in the American union. No one of them has ascendant power. In Canada, the larger provinces — Quebec, Ontario, and even British Columbia — can break the union, and inside the union can summon up formidable pressure on the central government. They each comprise large territory. As well as revenue from mineral and timber rights, they each have economic infrastructures unto themselves, in hydro power, regional transportation and variously, in other crown corporations, covering a broad range of activities. These provincial crown corporations are expressions of regional self-assertion. In the United States, many of their functions might be assumed by privately owned national corporations. Each of these massive geographical areas and thrusting infrastructures supports a creative politics and produces large personalities at the head of demanding regimes (W.A.C. Bennett, Jean Lesage) with impact and power to dwarf the federal presence. The contradictions between the regions and the centre and between French Canada and English Canada are played out best as a clash of giants. But even the smaller provinces, and the poorest region, the Atlantic provinces, have an exceptional power larger than themselves which draws from the contradiction as a whole, so that in the 1947 tax agreements, to cite one case, Prince Edward Island, the smallest province, and all by itself, was offered a special option, because the other two options, suitable to the rest of the provinces, were not satisfactory to it.

Provincial governments in Canada provide a focus for regional loyalty, around which the collectivity can rally — "an organization already prepared for them in the sovereignty that their state is allowed to enjoy," in Tocqueville's words — and they work to sustain this loyalty to their advantage. They also provide practical leverage. And they have a legitimized role in the ritual of the contradiction by which a regionalist personality becomes a federal phenomenon, not by threatening to enter, or entering, the federal arena, which is how American governors (Franklin Roosevelt and George Wallace, for example) became federal phenomena, but by refusing to enter the federal arena, by putting the possibility that they might enter federal politics out of mind, by creating a cultural distance between themselves and Ottawa. Such is the contradiction, that they have more influence on federal politics when they are out of them than when they are in. In the more notable cases — George Drew, T. C. Douglas, Robert Stanfield — the protagonists left provincial premierships for the federal opposition. But would it make any difference if they left a radical provincial opposition, radical in the regionalist sense, for the federal prime ministership? If, by some inconceivable change of heart, during the rise of the Parti Québecois, René Lévesque had become a federalist, and then prime minister of Canada, would he have had more impact on the country as a whole, or less?

"The federal system," wrote Tocqueville, in *Democracy in America*, ". . . rests upon a theory which is complicated at best, and which demands the daily exercise of a considerable share of discretion on the part of those it governs." And: "If all the citizens of the state were aggrieved at the same time and in the same manner by the authority of the Union . . . an organized portion of the nation might then contest the central authority." And: ". . . the sovereignty of the states is perceptible by the senses, easily understood, and constantly active." But: "No one can be more inclined than I am to appreciate the advantages of the federal system. . . . I envy the lot of those nations which have been able to adopt it. . . ." What Tocqueville wrote of American federalism was laid to rest by the Civil War and the nationalist economy, with its chauvinist pan-American slogan of Manifest Destiny. It is alive in Canada instead.

By the paradoxical nature of the contradiction, also, it should follow that the most regionalist of the regions, the one with the strongest anti-centrist passions, should touch off in the redistribution culture a period of intense creative development, all the more so in a phase of separatist preoccupation. The more the contradiction is forced, the richer the elaboration.

As the separatist movement grew in strength in Quebec, that is exactly what happened. A new department was formed in the federal government — the Department of Regional Economic Expansion — and was suddenly seen to have overwhelmed in importance the great senior ministries of the past, like justice and external affairs. Massive amounts of money were poured into eastern Quebec and the Atlantic region. The Montreal region, which was unequal, though less unequal than others, was nevertheless brought into the redistribution scheme. Earlier, under the same imperative from Quebec, but in a less exciting political phase, the drawing up of a regional plan, with a concomitant ideological awakening of local communities, was undertaken in the Gaspé Peninsula by the Bureau d'aménagement de l'est du Québec (BAEQ), administered by the province and financed by both Ottawa and Quebec City.

The ramifications do not stop there. In the midst of the separatist ascendancy in Quebec in October 1970, the president of the Native Indian Brotherhood of Canada declared in a public speech that if Quebec could gain quasi-independence from the federal government, Canada's native Indians should get it too. The American black, comprising 11 per cent of his country's population, makes his argument, and makes his way, largely in terms of individual rights. The Canadian Indian, with only two per cent or less of his country's population, can nevertheless, by leaning on Quebec, make his argument in terms of a collective right.

Quebec being a region not like the others, its existence in Canada gives to the redistribution culture an unambiguously unAmerican schema all its own, totally unimaginable anywhere but in the Canadian context, just as another Quebec in the west of France, or in the southern United States, is also totally unimaginable.

The historical logic of the case is straightforward. Quebec, as the home base of the French-Canadian culture, cannot afford to lose its population and vigour to the rest of Canada. It cannot tolerate a markedly higher economic level next door in Ontario, which can draw off and anglicize its people, and diminish its own standing in the whole. *Therefore labour and community cannot be allowed to move freely to capital; capital must move to labour and community.* The possibilities permitted by the economists of the American school and its market mythology run up against a mountain of demographic calculations and historical scepticism in the minds of nonAmericans in the streets of Montreal.

Yet in the redistribution culture, historical Quebec does not stand alone with historical Ottawa. Quebec is the "strongest" region, but not the only region. Until the end of World War II, demands for economic justice against the centre were made mostly from outside of Quebec. Until then, Quebec itself as a province, along with Ontario, was at the economic centre. The skein of events leading to the anti-centrist demands of Lesage, and on to Lévesque and the Parti Québecois, is linked in unmeasurable ways, on this economic plane, to the long indignation of the Maritimes and to the bitterness of the Prairies who elaborated endlessly on the financial contradictions while Quebec was interested in other arguments.

The redistribution culture has all of this legacy of the regional contradiction and the dualist contradiction impinging on it. The black drapes on Halifax windows the day of Confederation are part of it. The separatist feeling in New Brunswick at the time is part of it. Manitoba's feud with Ottawa over the CPR's monopoly, which almost ended in pitched battle over a diamond crossing between Winnipeg and Portage la Prairie, is part of it. The periods of provincial aggrandizement, with Ontario in the lead, are part of it. The Saskatchewan farmers of the depression who declaimed against the eastern interests, and were psychologically unassailable, and knew it, are part of it. The clichés which describe these old themes, some of which were already clichés a few years after Confederation, and maybe even before, and which then kept on being used interminably until they eclipsed themselves as clichés and became elemental statement . . . they also are part of it. All the memories, prejudices, passions, habits of mind, expectations, folklore and humour which make up Canadians' *sure sense of regionalism* are part of the redistribution culture, and the culture in turn is a partial, practical, eminently civilized expression of that rich vein in the Canadian character, and always will be so, as long as Canada is so. Behind equalization payments and regional development programs is identity.

Like the public enterprise ethic, the redistribution ethic has become internalized over time so that now Canadians are psychically predisposed to it. Redistribution has come to replace the American dogma as a code of natural justice. The prime minister can declare, "This isn't a gift, that Quebec receives from Ottawa; it's only justice; the richer provinces aid the poorer ones." And nobody will contradict him. A member of Parliament from the other end of the country insists on the "basic principle that the poorer sections of the nation shall be helped by those which are wealthier." And nobody rises up to condemn the proposition as a dangerous variant of a Marxist credo. A constitutional conference can agree, with a minimum of discussion, that ending regional disparities is "an essential objective of Confederation." A spokesman for Nova Scotia even demands that a full equalization formula and a ringing declaration in favour of regional equality be embedded in the constitution, so as to codify and enshrine the ethic for all time — life, liberty and the pursuit of regional equality . . . liberty, fraternity, regional equality.

What is most revealing in all this is not that there is so much grumbling and querulousness on the part of the richer provinces — Ontario, Alberta and British Columbia at the moment — but that there is so remarkably little. For all of British Columbia's criticism that the Maritimes and Quebec are not developing and taxing their resources properly — are allowing them "to be taken away by foreigners so that we have to subsidize their provinces" — and for all of the Ontario and Alberta governments' cautionary suggestions that it doesn't make sense to "make the weak strong by making the strong weak," redistribution in one form or another as a leading principle of Canadian society is rarely in question, because to question it is to question the existence of Canada itself.

CHAPTER 14

The Social Relationships Count

The Canadian redistribution culture is dense with precedent by which the indigenous mentality can be deciphered. It also has created a peculiar language and methodology by which the natives communicate with each other. The profound emotions of regional passion are expressed in ornate demographic and linguistic tables quite unknown in American or Chinese civilizations. Bizarre locutions like "equalization payments" and "regional disparities" are used every day with common understanding and, at the right political moment, can touch off a wide range of historical associations (just as the French or the Cubans can make whole political speeches simply by shouting out dates: "Remember July 24! Remember December 2! . . ."). The culture has also produced a growing body of economistic studies and theory, best collected in long appendices under such titles as "Regional Economic Accounts" and "A Supplement on Benefit-Cost Analysis," the likes of which are equal to appendices anywhere.

The syllabic value is only part of it. In Chinese, the tonal inflection gives a wide range of meanings to the same combinations of vowels and consonants. In the idiom of regional equality in Canada, the historical inflection gives the meaning. The constitutional scholar, the late Robert MacGregor Dawson, once wrote that "this world of Dominion-provincial finance has, indeed, an air of grotesque unreality, untrammelled by logic and the ordinary restrictions and meanings of words." The delegates to federal-provincial conferences, when they are talking in dollars, only appear to be speaking finance when, as we all know, they are really speaking history. But a people who can even refuse to repatriate their own constitution, because how can any constitution do justice to their contradictions, are capable of anything.

What the redistribution culture is missing is popular ideological exposition by which Canadians can become aware of the importance of their own experience. Redistribution of wealth among culturally various regions without common history, some of them rich and powerful in their own right, is, after all, no mean experience. It constitutes the beginnings of an economic civilization proper, with all the possibilities for the practical imagination that an ascendant civilization suggests. Without ideological liveliness, however, the civilization is stunted or deteriorates.

The Canadian redistribution culture is under the shadow of the American-ideology-in-Canada. Deriving from a contrary experience as it does, this received colonial ideology makes the indigenous culture malfunction.

The American-ideology-in-Canada derives from the experience of a market system — that anthropological oddity — in which the ruling force is the Invisible Hand and the mechanics are a set of impersonal market rules. The market systems still extant today — in the United States for example — are heavily modified. Oligopoly, tariffs, subsidies, regulations, price and wage controls, monetary and fiscal policy, trade unions, welfare, the pork barrel, corruption, and taxation all subvert the impersonal market. Some redistribution is involved. But still, essentially, the notions of private ownership and of market exchange, with the economists devising modifications, hold things together. If this system, or myth, of modified impersonal rules (the Restrained Invisible Hand) does not hold, the system will malfunction.

The Canadian redistribution culture, rooted in a history of reciprocal obligations, functions by an altogether different principle. The economic modes of redistribution and reciprocity derive from social relationships. In the Canadian case, these are the relationships of interregional solidarity. All of the tinkering with the economic rules and the brilliant technical innovations by expert economists in Ottawa and the provinces will, in themselves, be insufficient. Not the economic rules, but the social relationships count. So the economists are ill-qualified, even dangerous, for the major roles in the redistribution culture. In this Canadian culture, if the *social* relationships do not hold, the system will malfunction.

The received American-ideology-in-Canada has no room for the idea that social relationships, not rules of transaction, are the basis of an economic culture, which is as much as to say that the received ideology has no room for Canada. The end effect of our adherence to it is to make us look at ourselves backwards, and to see one of the most valid expressions of our identity as a parochial aberration, which we have to cope with because we're unlucky. As with our ideological discounting of public enterprise, this has disastrous results.

The received ideology, for example, turns equalization payments and regional expansion programs into charity, which is the only way it can explain them, instead of what they are, and can only be, in terms of social relationships — expressions of solidarity and generosity. But whereas solidarity and generosity bind, charity humiliates and divides. Redistribution becomes self-destructive.

All the good will in the world goes for nought when the "ideologically correct line" is abandoned. Douglas Fisher, in his newspaper column, once had occasion to indignantly scold Toronto for whining about redistribution to Montreal. Fisher reasoned that "Quebec [province] and Montreal, its symbol city . . . must recurringly be bought to keep the merits of Confederation sustained among French Canadians." He meant to defend redistribution. But does Quebec exist to be bought, like potato futures? Canada is not the New York Stock Exchange. No wonder equalization payments and the other techniques of redistribution stick in the gullet of so many Quebecers.

This ideological dimness proliferates and abounds. A certain kind of federalist will argue that Quebec will suffer economically from lack of redistribution if it leaves Confederation and therefore separation at the moment is inconceivable; but when Quebec is economically stronger, discontent will subside, therefore separation will remain inconceivable. That is missing the Canadian point. From an indigenous viewpoint, the transactional argument means only that as soon as Quebec is fit and secure within itself, it may well leave Confederation. Why shouldn't it? The historical memory of being captive to redistribution becomes insufferable, and with a great burst of liberating energy, the ex-captive throws it off. The more money that is redistributed to Quebec to save it for Confederation, and the more such distribtuion is described in terms of the American-ideology-in-Canada, the greater the alienation, the likelier the separation.

When René Lévesque exclaims "We don't want to be supported by the rest of Canada; Quebec wants to stand on its own feet!", everybody knows what he is talking about, and· knows the just bitterness from which the protest arises· Yet in a healthy redistribution culture, such a proclamation would be unintelligible. Neither his enemies nor his friends would be able to follow him. A desire not to be stood on would make sense. But to want to stand alone, when standing together was part of the natural order of things, would not even be taken as dissent or treason. It would simply be mystifying.

(The West, at one time, came close to reflecting this. During the depression, when transfer payments were flowing westward from the taxes of Ontario and Quebec, the prairie provinces refused to accept them as charity and to be placated. If any unwary easterner suggested that the West was living at their expense, he was excoriated. Ontario always understood the calculations of redistribution but never the passion of solidarity. Ontario has always been colonial. But while the Prairies knew that as an economic region, national policy had put them at a severe disadvantage, and while movements sprang up and achieved provincial power, plain Canadian sentiment remained strong, perhaps strongest in the province suffering the most, Saskatchewan.)

By the same token, the "profitable federalism" of Robert Bourassa, with its parading of a positive transactional balance sheet with Ottawa, is inside-out separatism. What happens when federalism ceases to be "profitable" for Quebec as has been the case, it can be argued, for British Columbia, for example? The logical conclusion is for Quebecers to begin to make a transactional case against "unprofitable federalism." Indeed, the Parti Québecois has already done that using current figures. Claude Ryan touched on the heart of the matter when he referred, in a speech in Toronto, to "the spirit of friendship and cordiality that is the soul of dynamic federations, the sense of a deep-rooted community of long-term interests," as compared to the shallow, uncertain life of a federalism sustained by "strictly pragmatic calculations." The spirit of friendship is the essential basis of a healthy redistribution culture. The strictly mercenary calculations of "profitable federalism" are in the long run antagonistic to it.

As for the Atlantic provinces, they have been poor cousins for too long to see redistribution whole.

Federalists and separatists, region after region, Toronto and Montreal, they are colonials all. Few of them have ever made the indigenous argument, or even suspected it: that by leaving Confederation, Quebec, or the Maritimes, or the West would be leaving the dense and potentially rich redistribution culture of solidarity and generosity, of which transfer payments and development subsidies are only a partial expression.

They would be choosing barbarity over civilization, much as if a Confucian administrator might inexplicably choose to abandon the Empire for exile in savage Russia.

The absence of ideological elaboration affects the prosperous provinces as well as the less prosperous. If provinces like the Maritimes or Quebec, labouring under the received ideology, can be made to feel they are accepting charity, or are being bought out, or being bought in, provinces like British Columbia and Alberta can come to feel they are being taken for suckers. One of the most positive and natural acts known to man — generosity — becomes, instead, one of the most negative and unnatural acts known to man — a transactional giveaway — when defined by the colonial ideology. A Yankee horsetrader would not understand it at all.

The argument leads further. If what counts in the redistribution culture is the strength of social relationships, then changing freight rates and decentralizing banking will, by themselves, without an ideological expression of solidarity, have an incomplete or opposite effect. The idea that provinces like Alberta and British Columbia could be kept happy with Confederation by that kind of bribery would, in the end, come to be seen as insulting, as parallel transactions have come to be seen as insulting by many in Quebec.

In this colonial scheme of things, Central Canada, the dominant region, never learns. Ontario in particular, which more than any province has an immediate sectional self-interest in Confederation, and which historically has drawn Canada after its own image, sees that British Columbia and Alberta are prospering, and wonders why they have complained so much. Washington and Idaho would be tranquil, wouldn't they? But it is not so much the costs of Confederation (the tariff burden, redistribution), as the lack of cultural satisfaction with Confederation — the continuous feeling of exclusion and downgrading of the indigenous style — that has been at the heart of their discontent.

British Columbia and Alberta, unlike Ontario, do not

benefit by the tariffs of National Policy. Their industrial life has not flourished at the expense of Quebec and the Maritimes, as has Ontario's. They cannot build a Canadian statesmanship on an obvious economic self-interest as can Ontario. Their linkages to redistribution are more exclusively cultural (social, political, patriotic). Their support of redistribution underlines how strong the cultural base in Canada is, and how cultural as opposed to financial — how embedded in social relationships — redistribution is.

But cultural reciprocity (acknowledgement) has not been forthcoming from the dominant central Canadian participants. British Columbia as a rule has been treated by the culture of Central Canada as somehow exotic and unCanadian, and Alberta as a parochial outback. National radio and television give them little continuing access to correct the cultural error and to make their own sentiment part of the national culture. At the level of high politics, the federal government, as a regime, has also been removed culturally from the two provinces.

Woe be it, then, to anybody who presumes too much on their behalf.

*   *   *

Among other things, this means that when non-conformists from the West make federal-provincial forays, central Canadians have no appreciation to put them into context, and are aghast. They throw their hands up instead.

The federalist excursions of W. A. C. Bennett ("Is he real?") come to mind. When Bennett, at the constitutional conference in 1968, told anecdotes along the lines of some-of-my-best-friends-are-French-Canadians, but turned his back on the language question, he allegedly lost some of his best friends and was banished to the Chinese side of the Backbone of the World. Journalists clucked their tongues and shook their heads, laughing and crying. The whole B.C. phenomenon was cast beyond the pale. Central Canada still probably hasn't recovered.

Not much later, Harry Strom, then premier of Alberta, would tell the B.C. Social Credit League that "we in the West will continue to make our contribution to Canadian unity." (Bennett concurred; "Bennett, Strom Vow Support To Keep National Unity," read the headline. This was perfectly in character.) But "the contribution of the West has simply been taken for granted," Strom declared. Alberta and B.C. have made a constant contribution to Canada as a nation, "something which I think should be kept in mind by those who are responsible for creating a truly co-operative federalism."

The protest, although it dealt with financial matters, was more cultural than economic.

Even Bennett, a sentimental "Canadian first" but a shrewish regional demander who came to challenge equalization payments ("B.C. attack strikes at essence of federalism" read the *Toronto Star*), was misperceived. Bennett's charges that Ottawa showed continuous favouritism to Quebec (similar suggestions were made by Ross Thatcher and Strom) made little sense in redistribution terms. But favouritism in the cultural procedure of redistribution was undeniable. Trudeau and Bourassa (and Robarts of Ontario) were in a cultural circuit from which Bennett was excluded and had excluded himself. Bourassa's contention, based on figures, that Quebec wasn't Ottawa's "chouchou" was beside the point. Eventually Bennett charged there were too many Quebecers in Ottawa, Trudeau called Bennett a "bigot," Bennett threatened to go to court on equalization payments with a cockeyed suit to spite Trudeau — pie throwers in a knock-down farce out of control. Finally the Electoral Cops arrived in the summer and fall of 1972 to subdue them both.

Bennett was on the other side of a cultural line from the central Canadian circuit, and vice-versa, which was everybody's failure, going back generations.

*   *   *

In an ideologically lively redistribution culture where

social relationships are seen to be strengthened, no province would ever complain that it had to help other provinces. The whole point of the exercise is to be in a position to help. The suggestion that some provinces were dragging their feet, or getting more than their share, also would not arise. The inclination of recipient provinces would be seen to be in the other direction. Provinces would want to take only as little as they had to, and would maximize their efforts. The competition of the redistribution culture is a competition to enlarge and enrich interrelationships, to fashion solidarity, by means of the redistribution mode.

This, like nationalism and other social forces, can be a compelling incentive to economic activity. The danger of the mode of market exchange is that countries or tribes or men try too frenetically to acquire wealth at the expense of others. The danger of the redistribution mode, as the Kwakiutl Indians demonstrated, is that in periods of social dislocation men try too frenetically to acquire status at the expense of others — in the case of the Kwakiutls, by distributing gifts.

The lack of indigenous ideological elaboration has other limiting consequences. In terms of the received ideology, redistribution comes as a modification to the economic culture. Among other things, this makes absolute equality as a leading practical principle hard to conceive.

The original idea behind tax equalization payments was not to remove inequalities in any particular region, but to maintain government services at average Canadian levels so that the disadvantaged regions would not fall back altogether as communities. But the regional contradiction has been so radicalized over time that only an economic culture with redistribution at its centre is strong enough — culturally strong enough — to hold the various parts of the country together in a real way. And where no hierarchical arrangement is agreed on — and in a democracy that is out of the question — such a culture begins with a commitment to absolute equality. It cannot sustain itself otherwise.

This radicalization has occurred side by side with the growing realization that by planned entrepreneurial, technical and investment transfers (that is, the equalization of productive processes), and by extending the traditional Canadian use of transportation and communications as social, interregional instruments, the injustices of history and the circumstances of geography can be largely alleviated, if the culture is right. These are the coming mechanisms of Canadian redistribution. The changes in modern economies to new kinds of work not bound by some of the old dictates of locale widen the possibilities from one direction; the problems of concentration in southern Ontario, the Montreal region and the British Columbia lower mainland push from another.

As absolute equality is achieved, equalization payments will decline.

"Absolute equality" fully evolved in such a culture would be an invigorating process along an axis. It would be an ever-changing panorama of regional self-assertion on the one hand, and entrepreneurial exchanges of capital, ideas and people involved in equalizing currents and new directions in other regions on the other hand — a continuum of regional striving and interregional relationships. It would set the stage continuously as it went along for a lively interregional rivalry, always with its equally lively balancing modes of resolution.

By the same token, the relationships of absolute interregional equality also provide the basis for a political economy where population movements are encouraged for interregional reasons (decentralization, the integrity of the various regions) rather than arbitrary ones of economic concentration — this is already partly understood in Canadian redistribution — and also for a political economy of no-growth or of the environment in Canada. When things get that far, there might be "unequalization payments," with some regions encouraging higher economic levels in others. But that's looking to the next stage.

Meanwhile, in the present state of the culture, without

this ideological follow-through predicated on absolute equality, Canada's provinces indulge in wondrous perversity.

In the 1960's, for example, several provinces undertook campaigns of futile, mutually impoverishing subsidies and tax concessions, taken advantage of most easily by foreign investors, in order to keep ahead of each other, or not to fall further behind — providing us, in the process, with a paradigm of self-destructiveness.

The most notable cases of internecine degradation in those years are now well known:

The Manitoba government financed the total cost of a private foreign-owned pulp mill on behalf of a shady group of promoters. The complex eventually went into receivership. One of the reasons so many concessions were made was to attract the complex away from Quebec, where the group was also holding discussions. At the same time, Newfoundland handed out tax concessions, subsidized power, rights to vast tracts of mineral and timber land and hydro power resources, loans and loan guarantees. Joey Smallwood admitted that he had virtually mortgaged his province to outside entrepreneurs whom, nevertheless, he considered "not very enterprising and not very free," except in taking the government's concessions and aid. He claimed he had no choice in the face of Ontario's "forgivable loan" system, whereby millions of dollars were being handed out to giant American corporations in Ontario. But before Ontario had its "forgivable loan" program in operation, Nova Scotia was able to "steal" Clairtone Sound Corporation from Toronto by a deal which Clairtone's president called "fantastic." (Clairtone has since gone under.) Industrial Estates Limited, the crown development corporation which was responsible, offered then as now to finance 100 per cent of land and buildings and 60 per cent of the installed cost of machinery of new industry, plus special interest holidays up to three years and services as negotiator for municipal tax limitations up to 10 years. The Quebec industry minister in the Bertrand government lashed out bitterly, and in vain, at the Nova Scotia government for having supplied Michelin Tire with a $50 million preferential loan, plus $8.7 million in grants, plus unmeasured municipal tax concessions (on top of a federal grant of $8 million) — more than half the required investment — to locate its two tire plants in the province, thereby denying the plants to Quebec (the aid offer from Quebec was used by Michelin to pry the maximum in concessions from Nova Scotia). Then, about a month later, the same Quebec minister offered $50 million in financial assistance to encourage the expansion of engineering and chemical firms in the Montreal region. Then New Brunswick lured an electronics plant away from the Montreal region with its own incentives. Saskatchewan underwrote the best part of the cost of a foreign-controlled pulp mill, and committed itself to other assistance.

Michael Lejeune, an industrial commissioner writing under a pseudonym in *Saturday Night* near the end of the decade (October 1969), described how companies deliberately played off one province against another, and quoted an editorial in *Trade and Commerce* magazine that "with inducements and incentives pouring in from every part of the country, [our Canadian industrialist] figures that, sooner or later, he will be tempted by the big prize: an outright gift of plant building and equipment and a firm guarantee of profits."

(In this perverse scheme of things, Ontario, which organized its program of "forgivable loans" while Quebec and the Atlantic Region were desperately trying to catch up, and the federal government was trying to help them, was the barbarian of barbarians — not that it didn't have its philosophers, like the business columnist who wrote, "Still, you can't expect Ontario . . . to stop playing . . . the game of can-you-top-this; then the other participants would make gains." A civilized Canadian, with roots in the redistribution culture, would expect exactly that.)

Of the possible new jobs created, Lejeune wrote caustically: "Do these spending sprees add anything to our total industrial growth? Or do they simply compete against each other for the privilege of handing out billions of tax dollars to surprised and delighted entrepreneurs? There must be something good coming out of it, because we certainly don't hear any complaints from the Canadian Manufacturers' Association or the Canadian Chamber of Commerce, despite their thunderous warnings against all other forms of human welfare spending." Jack McArthur wrote in the *Toronto Star*: "Competition among the provinces in grants, loans and other aid doesn't really add much new industry to the Canadian total. It just shuffles it around inside the country."

These subsidies and loan guarantees were not just money transactions, however. They were expressions of a profound abjectness and perplexity in the Canadian people. By the very nature of the subsidies, the provinces entered into the role of supplicants after industry, and in the cases of the poorer provinces, often into the role of beggars who consorted with whatever kind of people would have them.

Philip Mathias, in *Forced Growth*, reviewing the more sensational of the 1960's experiences, described how the Manitoba government of Walter Weir was so desperate for a pulp and paper mill that they were willing to commit themselves to a group which refused to divulge the identity of its owners, and which "on more than one occasion," according to Weir, threatened to walk out of negotiations unless the government agreed to even more concessions than had been offered. Weir capitulated, and took the humility of the Manitoba people so much for granted that he could unashamedly tell the story in order to justify his actions. The Pas, where the complex was to be located, in turn made tax and pollution concessions and servicing agreements so much to its own disadvantage that it found itself unable to fulfil the agreement.

Another reflection of this abjectness was the failure of the Winnipeg newspapers to look too closely at the arrangement and to show a normal degree of scepticism — in spite of many ominous signs — for fear of finding out the worst.

This was the Churchill Forest Industries debacle, where

the principals involved turned out to be more practised in skullduggery than anything else, and which was described, in the introduction to Mathias' book, by Abraham Rotstein, as "a grotesque horror story and a scandal of international proportions."

In another case, in Prince Edward Island, the government handed out $9.3 million dollars for a fish processing plant and a small shipyard to a promoter who was an unknown incompetent of debatable integrity and who siphoned off funds to affiliated firms outside the province. The companies went bankrupt and the value of the assets was set at $3.1 million. The government had been so anxious to co-operate that it waived normal safeguards such as an investigation of the promoter, proof that his financial backing actually existed, and performance bonds and delivery date penalties on boat building loans.

In the parallel case of the inoperative Deuterium of Canada heavy water plant in Nova Scotia, the government became captive to a promoter who had a corner on the necessary technology, but who was unable to raise his agreed capital and bring the plant into production at a reasonable cost and within a reasonable time. The promoter came out ahead from selling the rights to his patented process, while the government was stuck with the whole cost, instead of the agreed two-fifths of the cost, of the resultant disaster.

But Nova Scotia and the other small provinces, with perhaps the exception of New Brunswick, did not feel able to develop — seemed barely concerned with developing — the necessary entrepreneurial and technical cadres of their own by which to control their investments. Men with small and dubious entrepreneurial talent were able to grow wealthy, or go bankrupt and still grow wealthy, at the expense of whole peoples with large talents who were too culturally traumatized to act, except to send industrial commissioners travelling about the world bearing expensive gifts and bowing to strangers.

This all happened in a country that as much as 25 years

earlier, and 50 years earlier, was able to accomplish on its own, for its own use, remarkable feats of entrepreneurship.

The "horror stories" of the sixties chastened the provinces and made them cautious, but in the malfunctioning redistribution culture, this means only constrained perversity, not the end of it. Ontario, for example, stopped offering its "forgivable loans" to large U.S. multinational corporations, and later also to Canadian corporations, not because of any commitment to interregional solidarity but because it finally admitted to itself that they were wasteful. The present incentive program, in the categories it covers, allows for low-cost loans even in the heavily industrialized area of the province. Foreign corporations will again be eligible; interest may be reduced or forgiven altogether (a grant by another name); in certain circumstances, deferrals on payment of principal will be granted. The province also may put up buildings for lease to qualifying companies, with some rental payments being forgiven or reduced. In Quebec, as of mid-1973, the largest of multinational corporations, with sales bigger than the government's budget itself, were still eligible in special sectors for direct grants and other considerations, to the cost of all Canadians. Open internecine grant competition appears to be at an end in the Maritimes, but the quieter enticing of industry by New Brunswick and Nova Scotia continues. Harry Flemming of the Atlantic Provinces Economic Council calls it "beauty contests," which may or may not be a euphemism. The Nova Scotia government boasts that it does not offer direct grants any more, leaving that to Ottawa. But it does offer a wide range of incentives in preferential loans, loan guarantees, industrial site location and other auxiliary assistance ("one of Canada's most thorough, effective, flexible and rewarding incentive programs," reads the come-on), not the least of which is showing corporations the way to the grant coffers of the Department of Regional Economic Expansion. ("In many ways," reports *The Fourth Estate*, the Halifax weekly which has followed this phenomenon from the disastrous Deuterium of Canada

days, "it represents, like much of the industry in the Atlantic
area, a giant welfare scheme for the Shaheens and the
Onassises of the world, subsidized with our money.") Or
the mutual impoverishment can express itself in the form of
low wage areas, backward labour practices and low environmental standards, by which outsiders also profit while
Canadians pay. All provinces now offer financial and advisory
assistance in one form or another; exactly how much wasteful
interprovincial competition is involved has yet to be studied.

What is more important in terms of the redistribution
culture, however, is that the supplicant syndrome which
demeans and disrupts the whole culture, and lends itself
always to manipulation, in high economic arrangements as
among bargaining children, has not been broken by experience. When the premier of Nova Scotia declares, "Let's take
the jobs we can get; we've got to scramble . . . to get what
jobs we can," his relationship to the foreign corporation and
to his own people has changed only in degree from his careless predecessors'. His visit to a yacht in the Mediterranean in
the hope that some old-style capitalist will deign to take
advantage of Nova Scotia's location and tolerant environmental regulations by putting up a refinery, or the prime minister
of Quebec's pilgrimages to New York and London with
incentives in his handbag (and his presentation polished the
way a dry goods drummer polishes his shoes) is not much
removed from the awe which some deferential Manitobans
once showed a pulp and paper gang.

Reasonable attempts to rationalize the Canadian economy or to formulate national policies can also run aground, or
be discredited, by this Canadian perversity. A proposal for a
large-capacity ethylene plant in Ontario, to take advantage
of maximum economies of scale for Canadian users and
increase their competitiveness, touches off blocking efforts
by Quebec with its own petrochemical ambitions and
arguments. Before the Middle-East producers turn the tables,
Ottawa's oil marketing policy, preventing the entry of
imported Montreal-refined oil into the Ontario peninsula,

is described as another example of how economic power in Canada discriminates against Quebec, whereas the complementary exclusion of Alberta crude from Montreal, for lack of a small tariff, while the Prairies have suffered their whole history from tariffs, is taken as one more indication of how the Canadian power structure discriminates against Alberta. The building up of Halifax as a port leads to gratuitous insults in Saint John about an Ottawa "plot" to keep the Maritimes in chains, despite large federal expenditures on the Saint John infrastructure and in the Maritimes generally. Ottawa's willingness to share offshore mineral revenues with Quebec and the Atlantic Region is resisted as an unjust stratagem by which Ottawa appropriates a share of the provinces' mineral rights, and holds the provinces down, although a Supreme Court finding supports federal ownership. The preferential freight rates for steel into Vancouver, to protect the market for Canadian producers against offshore imports, is held up by the prairie provinces as another unconscionable anomaly in the freight rate structure, notwithstanding the low freight rates for grain, which is also supported by the whole transport structure. In such cases, efforts to improve the well-being of the country come to be interpreted as attacks on the well-being of regions.

Yet without redistribution at the cultural centre of Canada's economic linkages, that is in a sense what they are — attacks charged with history. So that without financial cause, as in the old oil marketing case, Quebec will still grieve and contend. That is also a western syndrome. ("The West has been out of step with Ottawa for 40 years, from force of habit as much as from any specific gripes and grievances," James H. Gray, journalist, author and western loyalist, puts it. "It took prairie alienation a long, long time to develop and may take a lot longer to eradicate.") As for the Maritimes, their anti-Upper Canadian rhetoric has made even Lower Canada, that is Quebec, a part of "Upper Canada." Without deep-rooted assurances in their linkages with other regions, grieving also about past injustices and Quebec's long decline relative to Ontario, some Quebecers — non-separatists — will oppose a national policy simply because it is national — will elaborate a planning perspective which excludes wherever possible integration at the federal level (the more the exclusion, the greater the satisfaction).

Another expression of this perversity is the inability of the community to defend itself against economic domination from the outside, because any strategy for the whole is seen as a blow against one of the parts. Men caught up in this perversity, and all Canadians have been caught up in it, are observed to set themselves at cross purposes to even their own aspirations. They are aware of this self-destructiveness, but they have no way of checking themselves, and hurtle on:

The mayor of Calgary angrily attacks nationalist speeches on energy resources as "a kick in the teeth . . . completely negative and destructive . . . kicking the very foundation of our prosperity," although he happens to be, also, a former executive of a branch of Canada's most dramatic nationalist project, the CPR. The natural inclination to conserve our energy resources runs up against pressure from Alberta to export oil and gas..

Quebec business and government spokesmen, who should know something about the thrusting self-interested mercantile power of the United States, attack the nationalist Moore Report on the securities industry as being anti-Quebec instead. Jacques Parizeau condemns it as a device for reinforcing the Ontario-controlled financial cartel in Canada and Ontario's mercantile power. Quebec eventually welcomes the intrusion of American firms in order to build up Montreal's financial community vis-a-vis Toronto. Richard Hatfield, premier of New Brunswick, vigorously denounces even nominal legislation for controlling foreign investment, calls it a "mockery in itself," threatens to challenge it in the Supreme Court, sees no need for it in his region, explains in his reasoning how New Brunswick subsidizes and promotes its own colonization by foreign capital (oblivious to any idea that such a phenomenon is reason in the other direction), all in the name of tough New Brunswick self-assertion. Gerald Regan, premier of Nova Scotia, attacks "parasite American subsidiaries" that won't compete overseas with their American parents, but is not averse to a few such "parasites" in Nova Scotia itself, on the grounds that industrial parasites are better than no industrial sites. Robert Bourassa, speaking in Toronto, says that Quebec is an essential element for the reinforcement of a truly Canadian identity in the face of the growing U.S. influence in Canada, and that without Quebec, Canada could sink under a flood of Americanism − all of which is met with loud applause. And Robert Bourassa, speaking in New York, says Quebec wants all the U.S. money it can get, and that "not even five per cent of the people of Quebec would accept higher taxes to replace foreign investment" (although a survey indicates the contrary, but that makes no difference). He disassociates himself from nationalist Canadian policies. This is also well received. At one point, William Tetley, Quebec minister of financial institutions, defends U.S. takeovers on the grounds that French Canadians should have as much right to sell out as English Canadians.

Similarly, Ontario, which has already sold out most assiduously to the United States, commissions a nationalist task force which assails the "open door" policy (after the horse has left the barn and then some). The report recommends that *Ottawa* do something about it. Ottawa, in turn, after struggling mightily with its own committees and reports (and diversions) concludes that the extent of any federal legilsation will be largely up to the provinces ("We'll see how far the provinces are prepared to go," says Pierre Elliott Trudeau). In the end, of course, nobody goes very far.

Quebec demands that its needs for eastern Arctic gas be met before U.S. requirements. It is, after all, a Canadian province. Then, only a few weeks later, it heralds a hydro-electricity agreement with Consolidated Edison because it opens up the possibility of sales to the U.S. without having to consult Ontario or the Maritimes, or share profits ("an important step towards Quebec's economic autonomy").

Jean Marchand, when Minister of Regional Economic Expansion, says that U.S. economic domination is "scandalous to a certain extent," by way of prefacing his intention, along with the provinces, to make the scandal greater by subsidizing already powerful and profitable American companies to increase their domination. Woebegone Ottawa plays the victim as masochistically as any of the provinces alone.

There is something even more extraordinary about all this. Such strange behaviour is patently absurd, yet none of it strikes us absurd Canadians as odd, nobody is surprised, nobody would describe any of those men, including Parizeau, as unCanadian. Their behaviour too is rooted in our common experience. A new National Policy to regain Canadian independence cannot escape the legacy of unequal redistribution of the old National Policy. It must exorcise it. Ontario sows the wind of regional advantage and reaps the whirlwind of national discordance. An outsider could not be blamed for mistaking us for the Chinese in their Age of Confusion when, lacking an indigenous ideology — an indigenous way of looking at things — to meet new circumstances, they descended into warlordism and consequent economic chaos (which observers at the time considered typically Chinese), leaving them easy prey to the Japanese, the Europeans and the Americans.

Even internal free trade — one of the elementary advantages of the nation state — is made impossible. In the Age of Confusion in China, foodstuffs to avert widespread famine could not be transported about the country because each warlord feared that if he let rolling stock leave his own area, it would never come back. In Canada, internal free trade has been hindered by marketing boards and purchasing policies instead. This has been a line of defence most explicitly in Quebec. Quebec Hydro offers up to a 10 per cent bid allowance to Quebec suppliers and equipment makers. Government buyers may pay up to 12 per cent more for Quebec-produced goods. These are quasi-tariffs, and are openly praised as such in Quebec. There have been

"Buy-Quebec" campaigns to switch consumers to Quebec-owned companies. The political current of *achat chez nous* goes back at least to 1924. The provincial Créditistes at one time proposed a rebate of 10 per cent to consumers on all purchases of Quebec-manufactured products.

But again, Quebec isn't alone. Other provincial governments have allegedly long practised subtle discrimination against suppliers from outside their borders. Ontario and British Columbia, as well as Quebec, used provincial marketing agencies for chickens and eggs to protect their territory against interregional competition, and to stake out their share of production in future national marketing arrangements. The Toronto Transit Commission, at the urging of Ontario's deputy minister of transportation, bought a fleet of buses from an Ontario plant to help ease unemployment when the tender from a Manitoba company was appreciably lower. (To add to the Canadian injury, the Ontario firm is a General Motors branch plant whereas the Manitoba firm, Flyer Industries, is owned by the Manitoba government and private Canadian shareholders.)

Ontario has pointed out that the provincial "tariffs" are unfair to its producers, and that by fragmenting the already small Canadian market, the economic purpose of Confederation is subverted. Everybody loses in higher prices, less specialization, and structural weakness (and hence, also, more vulnerability to imports and less capability of exports). Quebec has countered that internal free trade is all right for Ontario for just that reason: that it's all right for Ontario. In Canada, although not in the United States, free national markets are intolerable if the advantages of the free markets do not accrue equally to all parts of the whole. And, as in the cases of the buses, Ontario itself is not above a bit of trade discrimination in a pinch.

The separatists make the analysis that such perversity is inherent in an inherently impossible Canadian federalism, and that political sovereignty is an absolute necessity to create an economically prosperous Quebec. But that is only the correct American analysis. If separation were to occur, there would be less solidarity rather than more. Without solidarity, the Parti Québecois' projected Canadian common market would have even less of a chance. Everything else being equal, mutually destructive protectionism through subsidies and incentives, low wage areas and purchasing policies would only continue, whereas the redistribution culture that exists to create solidarity by which internal free trade can flourish would have been shattered.

Paradoxically, the goal of free trade, one of the great utopian visions of liberal economics, proves possible in a lasting way only through social solidarity which, in turn, is only possible by a rejection of liberal economics. Free trade is a socially derived objective.

So our perversity abounds. Yet absolute equality by redistribution at the centre of the culture would simply dissolve it. There would be no point to it any more, even for a short-range regional advantage.

So much perversity, and so much essential simplicity in its resolution!

The answer again is in ourselves. The problem has not been that Canada is illogical, which is the Parti Québecois argument, but that its logic has been ideologically obscured. Identity is obscured with it.

The Canadian circumstance parallels the plight of the Blackfoot Confederacy, on the northwestern plains. Like Canadians, the confederacy had several levels of government, according to practical function. In the winter, the time of survival, the basic unit was the clan. The buffalo hunt was tribal. For great affairs of state and for an annual summer ceremonial, the three tribes of the confederacy came together. They were also interminable parliamentary talkers. The tribal economy was co-operative. The introduction, by Americans, of the mode of market exchange as the organizing economic principle, through the buffalo robe trade, effectively destroyed that society. At the end of their independence, the great confederacy had been fragmented in places into mutually destructive clans, so fearful of each other that they could not come together, even into tribes, even in high summer. They no longer knew themselves as Blackfeet.

Jean Marchand was wrong when he said that Canada has to pay a financial price to preserve its unity. The diseconomies of redistributing economic activity are slight next to the diseconomies of Canadian perversity. The Ottawa economics professor and former adviser to the trade and commerce department (O. J. Firestone) was wrong when he announced that equality of income standards across Canada was probably an impossible goal economically, difficult politically, and a false aim socially. But then his qualifications were wrong. The typical North American economist has no idea of the kind of economic culture solidarity is capable of, and no idea of the kind of solidarity an economic culture is capable of.

The lack of indigenous elaboration of the ideology of redistribution also blocks and frustrates the entrepreneurial possibilities which the culture offers.

In terms of the American-ideology-in-Canada, entrepreneurial man is impelled by the transcendental workings of the market, and propelled subjectively by the acquisitive impulse. Social relationships only get in the way. Redistribution is taken as a financial mechanism, or a costly but necessary bribe, to keep the infrastructure intact and modernize it, and to locate more industry, until the natives of the Atlantic Region and eastern Quebec and other relatively slow-growing regions in Canada absorb some of this compulsive spirit of what is in fact the American way of life. Then they will break out of their old economic habits and begin to generate a self-sustaining entrepreneurial zest and commitment of their own. If sufficient expertise and capital are not available, they are sent in. Foreign investment that provides employment and an increased level of economic activity is all to the good.

In terms of a redistribution culture, on the other hand,

the social relationships of solidarity and equality are the important factors in nourishing entrepreneurial commitment, while the acquisitive impulse is a minor or even destructive element.

The spirit of entrepreneurship cannot be manufactured like pulp and paper. It flows out of social ferment — a social dynamism within the community. To begin with, there must be a liveliness in society to keep the young and the talented from the Atlantic provinces and elsewhere in their own regions, and to draw them into a commitment to the difficult task of raising their regions up, with uncertainties on the way, and probably a lot of disappointment. There must be a spirited, independent press to check corruption and favouritism in government development policy in order to prevent gross waste by incompetents and political friends, and secondly, to prevent the demoralization of the populace which chronic maladministration brings with it. There must be a leavening of political life for the same reason. Somewhere in the political life there must be a vigorous party or party element that stands outside the dominant vested interests who represent the past. Old institutional barriers have to be challenged. There must be an animated exchange of information and imaginings, and new perceptions of all kinds, cultural and technical, to create a milieu of entrepreneurial openness.

There must perhaps also be an unusual degree of social cohesion, far greater than in a prosperous "frontier" province like British Columbia, so that the marginal farmers of the New Brunswick hinterland, the fishermen of the Newfoundland outports, and the small villagers of the Gaspé peninsula, caught in chronic uneconomic circumstances, can be integrated into a more productive life, and can wait out difficulties in employment and in their own projects. This touches on everything there is in the life of a community — housing, urban and town design, cultural amenities, language, class structure, all the other social linkages and behind it all, politics, by which a man relates to all of these. In such marginal economic circumstances, also, new entrepreneurial vehicles have to be fashioned which are not dependent on individual risk and which overcome the attrition of initiative and expectations from generations of poverty.

The social cohesion is necessary for another reason — to create in the mass of the populace, not just in a few restricted groupings, a spirit of resourcefulness and persistence, and an inclination to inventiveness, which can put outside capital and outside expertise to their own uses instead of being intimidated and imprisoned by them. In other words, there is required the political will to undertake long-range programs aimed at the social and entrepreneurial environment, although they may take decades, whereas the seduction of more manufacturing industry, for example, can be used for immediate political gain in an area that has grown used to dependence.

In Japan, an adaptation of the old social order has provided this cohesion. In the United States and China, the assumptions of equality, vigorously expounded in politics, have provided it. The less cohesion and cultural vitality arising from some principle of society or value system, the more exceptional enterprise has to be, unto extreme examples where, with social cohesion broken completely, there is no enterprise at all, as in the case of the culturally shattered Melanesian natives who were "dying of boredom," or the uprooted people whom Margaret Mead envisioned as perishing "painlessly beside streams still filled with fish."

From this perspective, the mythology of private risk and reward, even when underwritten by federal spending, is too weak and too unrealistic in the face of unfavourable circumstances to generate the kind of broad cultural liveliness upon which the practical life can flourish. The telltale symptom of continuing stagnation in places like Saint John and St. John's is not their relative lack of capital or expertise, which can quite easily be turned on and off by Ottawa, or their rate of unemployment, which may from time to time go down, but their chronic dullness. Expanding business and capital accumulation that are built on the back of direct federal spending in infrastructure and its effects on the local economy are by themselves culturally minor forces in entrepreneurial awakening.

Large enterprises from abroad, while providing employment, do not relieve this cultural lack. They may even reinforce it, as we have discovered in Ontario. The cultural dynamic of organizations like Michelin, deriving from outside the province, and self-contained and paternalistic, puts the local culture in a shadow. In an area like the Atlantic Region, there is little management and technical spin-off, either directly or in social interaction, and often minimal economic spin-off other than the impact of added wages. A very good manager may rise up within the company and be transferred out of the region; in that sense, branch plants co-opt leading managerial talent.

At the level of government, the dynamic of the Department of Regional Economic Expansion (DREE) has a similar, culturally intimidating effect on provincial and local bureaucracies, when it is taken primarily as a superior agent of money transfers rather than as a messenger of solidarity. (Money transfer is, of course, how acquisitive man does see redistribution. Acquisitive man, as retailer, supplier or contractor, etc., also welcomes foreign investment – may even prefer it.)

The redistribution culture, by contrast, being richly animated, generates entrepreneurial activity differently at this stage of disparities. It does this among the richer provinces by reinforcing the impulse of generosity. In the less prosperous provinces, it provides a freely given, unrestricted breathing space in which they can develop their own entrepreneurial and technical cadres, and in the process, free themselves from their abject (to put it charitably) cultural subjection to foreign entrepreneurship. It provides the economic room for Quebec to progress quickly in making French the general language of management in the province, including head offices, without fear of losing even more ground to Ontario, which, once accomplished, could generate an exceptionally creative wave of entrepreneurship. (Not economics, but cultural and political respect as expressed economically, is at the heart of the redistribution culture.) It provides, also, a powerful mystique of equality, opening up restrictive institutional patterns to a larger, energizing participation. It heightens interregional awareness and communication, and intraregional communication. Because money transfers are seen primarily as gestures of solidarity, they add cultural backing to the recipient region instead of alienating it. The principles of solidarity and equality are so rich in human possibilities that working them out in Canada will give to the sluggish parts of the whole the animation which is at the bottom of all economic creativity.

Those are two of the many ideological possibilities for approaching the economics of regionalism in Canada. The first, the American-ideology-in-Canada, draws a good deal on the culture of 19th century and turn-of-the-century America. The second is projected from the particular circumstances of Canada's regional and dualist contradictions.

The more appropriate an ideology is, the more effective are the efforts of people working across it. Until now, redistribution in terms of development aid has taken place largely across the American-ideology-in-Canada, and taught us a lot of Canadian lessons.

In the FRED (ARDA) programs of regional development in the Gaspésie and northeastern New Brunswick, extensive planning and attempts at popular participation ended up only in continued high unemployment and low income. In the New Brunswick case, when outside industry failed to stimulate the economy sufficiently, the subjects of the project simply stayed on their marginal land. The total benefits of development appeared to be less than the actual cost. The north shore area, with a narrow resource base, remained particularly susceptible to general downturns in the economy; at one point (early 1972) there were tense demonstrations in Bathurst as layoffs and wage cutbacks on the north shore triggered a chain reaction of unemployment. What was once described as "ARDA judgment at its best" (Economic Council of Canada) became, in practice, a school of uncertainty and bitterness.

In the case of the planning project of the *Bureau d'aménagement de l'est du Québec* (BAEQ) in the Gaspésie, and the program of spending that grew out of it, the process of social animation which had created high expectations devolved into disillusion and frustration as political and bureaucratic ambiguity frittered away whatever momentum had developed.

Of the larger canvas, the dependence of Quebec and the Atlantic Region on outside entrepreneurship, for which Canada continuously pays incentives, appears not to have declined markedly, while the profits from the incentives flow out of the regions. More telling, such dependence on artificial devices, whose culture is imported, detracts from the vigorous elaboration of an indigenous culture of technology and commerce from which new sorts of economic activity usually come. Branch plants could fill up the land from St. John's to Quebec City, but no real entrepreneur could be fooled into believing that these regions were not potentially static places, and that even while new factories were going up, they were not foreshadowing their own decline. Even where there is manufacturing spin-off and widening prospects, as in Nova Scotia from off-shore oil drilling, the leading entrepreneurial roles — in this case, discovery and marketing — and their future possibilities are lost to indigenous enterprise.

Entrepreneurship too, like efficiency, is in the culture.

After the mystification of the New Brunswick experience, special regional programs were directed to urban centres, on the theory that cities are more amenable to development and that revived cities would animate the countryside. Federal planners in Saint John, with a population in 1970 of 100,000 people, projected a population of 200,000 or 300,000 in 1990, at which point, they had convinced themselves, the city would start to generate its own growth. Then Montreal was included in an emergency incentive program, to keep it from going flat so that we don't all go flat, in the words of the minister. Business reluctance because of instability in Quebec was the ostensible reason at the time. But Montreal, also, had long been losing its momentum. Montreal had a population of 200,000 in 1890. Montreal was not handicapped, either, by high transportation costs to market, and had plenty of infrastructure and industry. And large cities that are culturally weak have been known to stagnate, or to suffer historical change badly, no matter all their great resources at hand, while small cities in apparently the wrong place at the wrong time with the wrong people have been known suddenly to flourish.

(One could ascertain the cultural factors behind Montreal's long decline. The takeover of the economy by American entrepreneurship with little or no historical or financial ties to Montreal was a key element, in addition to other advantages favouring Toronto and southern Ontario. The linguistic and religious isolation of Montreal's anglophone entrepreneurial class cut it off from broad public and provincial government support in influencing economic policy in Ottawa, while no such cleavage hindered Ontario's business community. In the same way, the entrepreneurial minority denied itself an important source of recruitment — the French-speaking population around it — making its continued vitality difficult. This lack of access for French Canadians led in turn to insufficient motivation for creating a modern system of education until they used their majority to challenge the barrier itself.)

But was the growth centre valid as an objective? Not so, argued A. D. Fortas, an international development specialist, in a report for the New Brunswick government. Fortas, as part of a sharp critique of the growth centre strategy, wrote that "any policy which contributes to the acceleration of urbanization can only be anti-economic and inappropriate." He recommended polycentrism — decentralization within a region — held together by rapid and cheap communication and transport. Back to theoretical questioning again.

The initial years of the Department of Regional Economic Expansion brought sundry other contrarieties to the surface. The department, whose conception was one of the greatest ideas this country, or any country, has ever produced, because the ideal of equality is so great and compelling, found itself accused in the Atlantic Region of being an imperialist Ottawa device that did not consult enough with the provinces, and at the same time was accused of not providing enough leadership. After one scathing indictment by the Atlantic Provinces Economic Council, whose region was receiving generous help from Ottawa, the minister protested that "if we give $15 million to development corporations in, say, Nova Scotia, surely it must do some good." One realized from his protesting that by some diabolical mechanism, the $15 million might not actually do any good, and might actually do harm. An angry study by the Quebec Federation of Labour argued that the generous federal incentives were helping to perpetuate, not cure, regional disparities by reinforcing the industrial status quo, and were just a pointless giveaway to foreign interests. The report called the Department of Regional Economic Expansion "The Instrument of our Exploitation." How was that possible? Not much later, a study of 31 firms (the Springate report) indicated that the incentive grants often had little or no influence on the investment decision of the companies, so that the grants were "windfall gains," and that companies could and did falsify their applications to receive the money. T. N. Brewis of Carleton University, one of Canada's leading authorities in regional disparity, hazarded the suspicion that "the grants may be of more benefit to industrialists than to workers. . . ."

Did anybody remember the prophecy of the economistic oracle (O. J. Firestone) that the Department of Regional Development, as it was then called, would be productive as long as Pierre Elliott Trudeau and Jean Marchand were prime minister and minister respectively, because both were "eminently sensible" and were good friends?

There were other repercussions. The inclusion of Montreal in DREE incentive programs (discontinued mid-1973) meant that the Atlantic area received a smaller share of total grants. This touched off Atlantic resentment against Ottawa and Quebec, although the Montreal program could be justified, given the premise of incentives. The grants became an unwiting instrument of discord among recipient areas themselves.

Similarly, the designation of Saint John as a special area, more particularly its population projections, was denounced by community spokesmen of the French-speaking north shore. The Acadian community envisaged its young and unemployed being drawn off to the English-speaking south, and its own residual strength languishing even more than it had. The most rewarding, creative achievement of the redistribution culture in Canada would be to create a thriving French-language entrepreneurship and regional life in northern New Brunswick as an economic expression of the Canadian character. Instead, in northern New Brunswick, there was recrimination against the *sudistes*.

But DREE, as it was constituted, was limited anyway. Its reliance on incentives and infrastructure grants gave it an essentially passive role. It could not control where an industry located or initiate and run enterprises on its own. But most of all it was culturally unarmed. It was not meant to work out interregional solidarity which would allow in turn for the kind of exchanges that were required.

Still, in the ideological colony, nobody would think of changing the Department of Regional Economic Expansion into the Department of Indigenous Contradictions. Our governments continue to look at the enigma of regional disparities across the American-ideology-in-Canada, in which the methods of redistributing wealth are taken as fundamental, and to attack the enigma in those terms. Whereas infrastructure and growth centres and rural rehabilitation engaged the earlier explorers in their expeditions up and down the holy dominion of economics and public administration,·now decentralization of DREE, a multi-factor approach and general development agreements are the advance strategies.

But what of the indigenous ideology of redistribution, in which the social relationships among the peoples of the regions are fundamental? And what of the people of the regions themselves, in whom the strength of the redistribution culture lies?

The dullness of the Atlantic Region's economic culture, which is the legacy of their long decline and dependence, can not be measured, only experienced and observed. Harry Flemming of the Atlantic Provinces Economic Council has referred to the "low level of public debate . . . we grasp at the shadows of politics but rarely grapple with the substance," and to the passiveness in economic innovation and planning that it means. Robert Vaison, professor of public administration at St. Mary's University, Halifax, wrote in 1970 of development agencies that "tend to perpetuate socio-economic control by the local establishment," and are "blocking institutions" rather than vehicles for involving the larger public in entrepreneurial commitment and capturing, in economic activity, their potential. But the kind of stirring abroad in Atlantic society to break those limits and to open up new orders of possibilities has yet to happen. Most of the stirring has been all the way to Ontario and British Columbia. Catering to foreign enterprise is no substitute for the inventiveness and resourcefulness that allow a practical society to create new opportunities out of old, and to overcome passivity.

Quebec also has its legacy of dependence (as has the country as a whole). A lot of its stirring has taken place into a separatist party. The West is remote from the great regional concerns of Quebec and the Maritimes. Similarly, the West's particular spirit of resourcefulness, from its settlement past, is cut off from the rest of Canada by cultural blockages. The Ontario minister of industry remarks, "What's good for Ontario has to be good for the rest of the country." Ontario still doesn't understand.

Those are the constraints out of the past, to be added to the constraints of past collidings.

Now imagine these same regions and their peoples partaking of a sense of solidarity with each other from a discovery of the redistribution culture — a culture which not only has something to offer the slow-growth areas in terms of financial backing and economic space (and the methods *are* important), but which is also rich in interrelationships, and which, by the paradox of the contradiction, reinforces their regionalism as it links them to the whole.

You are imagining the release of revolutionary energy.

Note that the culture animates — opens a new vista for — the more prosperous regions as well as the slow-growth ones. Across the American-ideology-in-Canada, it breeds a psychology of "give although the giving hurts" in the one case, and "grab while the grabbing's good (both federal monies and foreign investment)" in the other. Across the indigenous ideology, it breeds enterprising spirits for a new society. Coincidentally, the cultural engagement of a region like Ontario in the entrepreneurship of redistribution will almost inevitably free it, by a process of animation feedback, from its own psychological subjection to foreign enterprise.

Note also that ideological obscurantism, that is, the avoidance of ideological debate (exploring the context of what is being done) does not work at all in the redistribution culture.

The redistribution culture is not a system of auxiliary economic techniques bolstered by idealism and administered by bureaucrats. It is a system of tumultuous social relationships. Ideological elaboration is essential to its psychological binding. Redistribution not only has to happen, but must be seen to be at work, and must be put to work, in terms of interregional solidarity. Otherwise it malfunctions. All parties to the culture are at odds with it. The economic dimension of our regionalism and our dualism is downgraded.

Here we return full circle to the question of identity. This economic dimension of our regional contradiction and our dualist contradiction is large and everywhere with us, but for lack of a lively ideology of redistribution, there is hardly any popular expression of it. Canadian identity is that much more weakly perceived.

The Rowell-Sirois Report — which traces this radical historical devleopment unique unto itself, at loggerheads with America, and which, taken to its logical conclusion, is full of revolutionary implications — is treated, because of its style, as a fusty parochial document. In my university days, when we were assigned a term paper on the report, we did our best to get it over with, and forget it. We did forget it.

Although the American western, with its implicit mystique of equality, American style, has been on our movie screens (and television sets) since the genre was first developed, the regional despair and clamour at the root of the redistribution culture has been ignored on film because there hasn't been a Canadian feature film industry.

The structure of Canadian broadcasting has also checked the full elaboration of the Canadian identity, by not being fully adapted to the interregional structure of the nation. Instead of a second and private English-language television network with its operating headquarters in Toronto alongside the CBC's base of operations — in its Canadian programming, just an imitative descendant of the CBC — an indigenous structure would have located the operational centre of a second network in Winnipeg or Vancouver, also national like the CBC, also publicly owned, to provide real competition and contrast in exploring the Canadian character, and to create a more equal cultural relationship between Ontario and the other English-speaking parts of the country, which would reinforce the solidarity underlying redistribution. It would have created a second publicly owned French-language system, with Radio-Canada more quickly building up interregional links between the cultural heartland in Montreal and the country as a whole, and the second involved in more communication and self-expression from the contiguous French-speaking regions like eastern Quebec and northern New Brunswick.

As for the actual occasion when redistribution was established in principle in Canada in the form of tax equalization payments, it could not be more obscure, although it may come to be seen as one of the great moments in the history of a civilization, equivalent in the magnitude of its implications to the storming of the Bastille or the American Civil War. A reference in an esoteric volume put out by the Canadian Tax Foundation (Canadian Tax Paper No. 43) puts the date for legislative approval of the payments by the House of Commons at July 31, 1956. The payments began in 1957.

Political statements about redistribution ("Many of our policies have to do with helping the have-nots at the expense of those who have") and federal-provincial conferences are ritual, but usually weak ritual. The complex formula for equalization payments rests in a file in the Department of Finance. Funds allocated by the Department of Regional Economic Expansion shuttle into bank accounts. There is no mass Potlach ceremony ritualizing reciprocal obligations. There is no cathartic Athenian theatre, no Munich beer festival, no Quebec winter carnival, to drain away inter-regional rivalries every year and reaffirm solidarity. Canadians don't even roast steer together, and make symbolic exchanges of wood pulp and copper ore.

There is, in fact, an enormous amount of ceremony staged for Canadians in celebration of economic myth, but almost none of it expresses the redistribution ethic in the Canadian psyche. There are daily ritualistic ceremonies associated with hair shampoo and deodorant and fuel oil and jelly and instant coffee and gasoline and chewing gum and automobiles, lavishly mounted and presented in sacrificial consumption.

These ceremonies are recurring and endless. They go on all day and all night, like an East Indian wedding out of control. But there is no ceremonial staging of how part of a B.C. faller's taxes went to liberate a Nova Scotia steelworker from a foreign owner's plant abandonment, by helping to finance its provincial purchase and modernization; or of how taxes on corporate profits made at the expense of a victimized Quebec asbestos worker once somehow, nevertheless, ended up helping to provide sustenance for a Saskatchewan farm family, victims of unequal national policy; and no expression of the kind of solidarity and understanding the ritual might evoke in all of us.

The hair shampoo and deodorant advertisements are the consummate symbolism of the colonial ideology. The missing ceremony of redistribution is the suppressed symbolism of the indigenous ideology. The first is mean and barbaric. The second reflects a rich inclination in man. If we replaced the former with the latter, nobody would make the seemingly incredible mistake that except for the use of French in places, Canadians are more or less Americans, and more rather than less.

Without indigenous ideology, the redistribution culture cannot flourish, and without that, self-perception is impossible. By contrast, when the time comes that tax transfers flow from Nova Scotia to British Columbia, or that a prosperous Quebec feels secure enough in the culture that it participates spontaneously in redistribution to less prosperous Ontario, knowing full well that the situation might reverse itself again in a few years, or months, then Canadians, as Canadians — as psychic bearers of the dualist contradiction and the regional contradiction — will know that they have come into their own.

PART VI

Conclusion

CHAPTER 15

"A Splendid Serendipity"

When I first came across the case of Polymer Corporation, I thought I had found an advanced public enterprise model. It was technologically forward. It was adaptable. It competed in world markets in the most difficult circumstances. It had managed the unexpected by surviving, despite negative predictions by industrial leaders and Canada's habitual deference to American experience. In particular, it reported to Parliament but was never interfered with by Parliament. Everybody applauded this autonomy as the best possible relationship between government and crown enterprise. And for Polymer it was the best possible relationship.

But as I worked my way back into Polymer's history, and then back from that to the origins of the public enterprise culture, which involved, also, tracing out the relationship between the culture and identity (and that was how my investigation proceeded, backwards, from the particular case into the hidden, enduring culture behind it), I discovered, as usual in the ideological colony, that the opposite was the case. The most advanced models, particularly Ontario Hydro in its early days and the CNR in the 1920's, were thickly tied up in our history and politics. Those two experiences were momentous episodes in our practical education and in the expression of our practical character. That's what counts, in economies. On the other hand, when they cease to be practical vehicles of striving by the mass of the people, they lose some of their cultural strength and fall away as models.

The CNR, although still a commendable enterprise, is the best example of such regression.

The late Donald Gordon used to argue that the CNR

was operated with the same profit motives as a private corporation. Under Donald Gordon, it undoubtedly was. "Exhortations from an executive are a poor substitute for the discipline of a profit-and-loss account, without which administrative problems are robbed of both urgency and clarity," Gordon proclaimed.

Maybe he should have accepted those bank presidencies that were offered him. He would have understood them better. An efficient administrator can administer a country into the ground if he chokes off the creative entrepreneur in the process.

Putting administrative problems aside for the moment, the private enterprise administration of a Canadian public enterprise does choke off this creativity because, in such enterprises, that turbulence and imagination come neither from "the discipline of a profit-and-loss account" nor from "exhortations from an executive" — the only two alternatives Gordon conceived of — but from the public enterprise culture nourishing the enterprise, as the private enterprise culture nourishes American enterprise, as China's moral binding nourishes Chinese inventiveness, and so on. That is where our practical genius lies, in the deep wells of our identity.

Has the CNR, since 1933, managed anything as inspired and significant as the development of public radio broadcasting, although the CNR's broadcasting stations were only one expression of the railroad's entrepreneurial liveliness in the 1920's? The depression finished that. We can only speculate, and then with great difficulty, on the innovations that would have come out of the CNR if the early culture in the railroad had been allowed to evolve and to express itself freely all this while.

When Henry Thornton wrote, as he was dying, that "if the country is to be saved, the saviours will not be found in the haunts of capital, nor will they come from the seats of the mighty, but such salvation as may be will find its birth in the hearts and minds of the great mass of the common people of the Dominion," he was referring, in a grandiloquent way, but nevertheless from a long practical experience, to that widespread cultural energy which animates economic life.

The more that politics and history are into it — not directly into the decision-making apparatus of a crown corporation but into the culture in which the corporation is embedded — the more this collective genius can express itself in economic activity. "Social control" describes the classic goal of state enterprise, or workers enterprise, in Europe. "Practical liveliness" or "practical liberation" — the apparent opposite of the idea of control — best describes the entrepreneurial phenomenon of public enterprise in Canada.

But "social control" in Canadian public enterprise has also been too easily maligned. "The discipline of a profit-and-loss account" may, at times, be a useful administrative device — and of course public enterprise can take advantage of that device — but it provides no discipline at all when it comes to saving us from the enormous costs of institutionalized insanity in the form of wasteful production heaped on manipulative marketing heaped on technological arrogance, and of other economic development that exploits man and his environment instead of liberating them. Public enterprise, on the other hand, has the mechanisms of such discipline in itself.

Here is where the great innovations in economic activity are going to take place in the future, and one of the reasons why Polymer's usefulness as a model is limited. The more that a corporation can accommodate public control without sacrificing its own exuberance and imagination, the more advanced it is as an entrepreneurial form. The Polymer experience does not help us too much here. But this control is not simply a parliamentary or legislative matter. And it is not a negative matter. "Discipline" and "control" are misleading descriptions of the ramified historical bent and states of mind which proceed more by giving a public enterprise a certain quality rather than by checking its operations. Internalized in our public enterprise style, and brought to a fine entrepreneurial edge by the storms of public debate, this process works itself out creatively as our character unfolds. The "check" against the unsafe use of electricity in Ontario, for example, came seemingly from the public enterprise process in Ontario Hydro itself, and was part of a constructive attitude to electrical power rather than as a check on an irresponsible attitude.

Had we realized this 20 years ago, the controversies of nuclear energy, and then Atomic Energy of Canada's own technological direction, including Ontario Hydro's participation, would have been openly debated, and both the companies and the country would better understand their implications today.

Had we realized this five years ago, the planning of lower Toronto (Metro Centre), in which the CNR is partner to the CPR, would not have been cut off from the citizenry and have ended up as more of the imitative same, as it has, but would have been an individualist advance on everything that had gone before, as Expo was. Instead of culturally abandoning the CNR, we should have liberated the CPR. In the process, the liberators themselves would have been liberated, or at least animated, and the public enterprise culture in urban development would have had that much more amplitude.

Has the culture of the CNR really regressed that much? In an article on Metro Centre Development, the *Toronto Star* referred to the principals of the CNR and the CPR as "railway barons." The reference was incidental to another description. Could exception be taken to it? Was it noticed by readers? By contrast, would anybody have called Henry Thornton a "railway baron" (except the *Toronto Telegram* and its allies, but they called Thornton anything that was malicious)? Could Adam Beck be considered a utilities baron, although his private enterprise counterparts in the United States were such and were recognized as such? But despite this regression, Canada has openly grappled with the dilemma of how to combine a public consciousness with entrepreneurial autonomy — that is part of our historical formation — which gives us now a cultural leg up on much of the rest of the world.

And of all the public enterprise models, the monopoly model is best. It frees entrepreneurship from the straitjackets of market competition and oligopoly competition. It is the most appropriate of all forms to an entrepreneurship of no-growth (redirected growth, stable state economy), as it was before to situations of stable or declining trade. It does not have to keep on increasing sales and intensifying propaganda in order to maintain its share of the market and to keep up in the oligopoly.

It is also the most suitable of all forms for matching capacity to demand without diminishing service, which is the beginning of an ecological entrepreneurship. (When the ecological implications of world energy use are finally perceived, the Trans-Canada Air Lines domestic monopoly, with its high load factor, its long use of aircraft and its service ethic, will be rediscovered. Such Canadian examples will dominate our economic textbooks. Eventually an earnest American professor will make a local edition for his country, with footnotes on private oligopoly so that U.S. undergraduates will be able to see how their own culture relates to the lessons of the main text.)

While it is not impossible to imagine a stable state economy from inside the American oligopoly culture, the imagining of it is traumatic because expansion (increasing profits and assets) is the mainspring of the American practical life. This is no superficial habit. Reinforced by patriotism and mythology, it is the traditional way that individualist American man has expressed himself. Also, in order to sustain the culture, an artificial syndrome of private consumption has been built up by intensive propaganda over time. That is also America's legacy.

The prospect of no-growth in such a fragile culture is more than just the stabilization of the gross national product. It is the prospect that the heart and soul may go out of the practical life. America would be denied its own dynamic.

No-growth carries with it the horrible vision of stagnation and disintegration.

The classic Canadian public monopoly, on the other hand, with a different tradition, nourished by the politics of community, is not traumatized by the prospect of no-growth. Its dynamic is public service. Such public enterprise expands naturally into an elaboration of the relationship between itself and the public. To Canadians, this would not be an altogether new kind of entrepreneurship, but it would be the release of an entrepreneurial style previously co-opted by the demands of production. The public dimension of public enterprise would blossom. A new, and yet familiar, entrepreneurial type would emerge.

Canada being a public enterprise country, this is the frontier for Canadian economic man. And like the American frontier, which was an expression of the American character and simultaneously reshaped that character, our imminent experience on our own frontier will reshape and confirm our exceptional energy. Until now the Canadian communities have nourished and stimulated public enterprise. On the frontier, public enterprise, and its new generation of entrepreneurs, will nourish and stimulate the Canadian communities.

Am I exaggerating the cultural difference between Canada and the United States, and also the leading role of the public enterprise model for the future, and with it the Canadian aptitude for that role as an expression of our own peculiar history? I don't think so. Try to recall the evocative symbolic descriptions of the American economic culture, in terms of its corporate slogans and imagery. My own mind keeps going back to General Motors, and to its old slogan "body by Fisher," with its appeal to luxurious appearance and the status that goes with the ownership of such a car — a bit outdated but evocative. But we really don't need to search about for hidden clues to the American economic culture. It's on the surface. Now compare that imagery to the slogan of Ontario Hydro — "The gifts of nature are for the people" — and to the slogan of the early CNR, in its passenger days — "Courtesy and Service." Is any economic culture more appropriate to the future than that, and at the same time, does anything better express the best side of the traditional Canadian character, in its practical manifestation?

The gifts of nature are for the people. Courtesy and service.

Although as yet we have few examples to go on, mostly at the level of co-operative technical agreements, we can also envisage new kinds of international corporations that will not be corporations at all but divers configurations of public monopolies, based variously on technology sharing, production agreements or co-operative ventures, and that these groupings, in their sectors, will replace the centralized mercantile configurations of today which are not truly international or multinational and which are becoming culturally destructive.

In the new configurations, no profits would flow from branch plants to head offices in other countries. The world economy, or the regional economy, or however extensive the configurations were, would be freed in those sectors from the barbarities of oligopoly competition and the traumas of free trade. The best of all these configurations, where optimum scale allows, and even perhaps where it doesn't, would likely be technology sharing among autonomous public monopolies in the various nations or regions. Technological variety would flourish because the cultural autonomy out of which such variety flows would be reinforced. The main entrepreneurial task in such configurations would be to put together technology sharing agreements and exchanges of personnel that respect the cultural differences of the participant countries, since it is by those differences that the system generates liveliness and competiton.

As it happens, the Americans, as a people with unique psychic characteristics, are particularly ill-suited to that kind of entrepreneurship. They have been congenitally blind to collective differences. Accordingly, the present centralized mercantile apparatus suits them. Whereas Canadians, who have a long history of dwelling on collective differences, who have also a successful tradition of adapting to them in international projects (which is one of the rare forms of genuine economic internationalism), are especially suited to such a form of international enterprise.

Next to the U.S., colonial Canadians are parochial. Abroad in the world, decolonized Canadians are worldly next to the parochial U.S.

Turning finally to the late Donald Gordon's preoccupation with administrative problems, we discover that "the discipline of a profit-and-loss account," without which such problems are allegedly "robbed of both urgency and clarity," proves to be not such an effective discipline after all. In a disintegrating cultural situation, such discipline crumbles, as in the case of the Penn Central which came to its sorry state amid allegations of managerial profligacy and deception. But generally in an oligopoly culture (as Galbraith has described the American economy), the profit-and-loss account clarifies mostly the level at which the oligopolistic settlement has been made and, in addition, can hide a serious lack of discipline in the participants combined, as it can also in monopoly, private or public. Generally speaking, the profit-and-loss account, no matter what the industrial structure, is only as useful as the culture of the economy around it is rigorous. It is all right in its limited place, but as a discipline for economic activity, it is no substitute for cultural competition.

So the Canadian public enterprise experience, worked on by 150 years of striving, is significant after all. What about that other original aspect of our practical life, the redistribution culture, whose historical roots in the dualist contradiction go back even farther?

As I have already argued, the coming together in one state of two ethnically contrary "nations," and the simultaneous overlapping and coming together of powerful regionalisms, is a significantly instructive experiment in social relationships, and constitutes a civilization proper.

If Canada disappeared tomorrow, that experiment would still be worth the making.

Not the least but its finest expression is the practical culture of redistribution.

Here, too, is where the future lies. Without rough economic equality among the parts, the most elementary level of solidarity of nations in the world is impossible. While the poor are striving to catch up to the rich, and the rich are proceeding even faster in terms of production and the use of resources and energy and the creation of waste, even the ecology of the planet cannot be protected. The mechanics of redistribution — foreign aid, for example — do not help much, just as the mechanics of redistribution in Canada by themselves do not help much. An ideologically vigorous culture of equality among contrary nations has to be brought into being. Canada, in its way, has the roots of this culture in itself.

I say this because such a redistribution culture of heterogeneous, contrary nations would not be a polite, utopian tea party. It would be a profoundly excruciating and turbulent coming together and falling away, just as the Canadian experience has been and is constantly becoming. Nowhere else in the world have such intense cultural contradictions and regional contradictions been sustained and elaborated on for such an instructive time. The more that our contradictory history and politics have been mixed in to redistribution, the richer this culture has become. Also paradoxically, the more we look into ourselves and further work out our redistribution culture — the more we are thoroughly indigenous — the more useful we are to the world. What was always considered our weakness, and still is so considered, is really our strength.

If Canadian history and politics are at the root of this entrepreneurial genius in public enterprise and this nascent genius in redistribution, why have we usually assumed the opposite, namely that politics and culture (the product of history) hinder the spirit of entrepreneurship?

This seemed to be the lesson of economic liberalism in Great Britain, where a market-regulated economy and the attendant upheaval of the Industrial Revolution broke with traditional culture, and also the closer lesson of the United States, where feudalism had simply been left behind. "History is bunk," said Henry Ford. Since American man defined himself, in his Americanism, as economic man, the traditional supremacy of social values (including politics) over economic values also apparently was bunk. The entrepreneur could be taxed and regulated, and harassed and subsidized by government, but in his entrepreneurial function, which was the definitive function in America, he was altogether alone (with his god, in John D. Rockefeller's case, with his board in others). Here was a new man, as he saw himself, with a psychic past that stopped at some shadowy connection with pilgrims, formed above all by the new nation and the frontier, yet believing himself unfettered by culture, throwing off the traces of Europe and the shackles of collectivity, and engaged in the ahistorical, or anti-historical, liberating pursuit of getting ahead.

If, in Great Britain and the rest of Europe, liberal economics broke with tradition, in the United States there was nothing to break from. There was no tradition. Or so it might appear.

The truth is, of course, quite different. All peoples are historical and function in a continuity, except perhaps disjointed primitive groups. Anything else would be absurd. The Industrial Revolution and the simultaneous unfolding of the American spectacular were exceptional historical events, and came into being exactly because of the exceptional historical processes that led to them.

Why, for example, did the Industrial Revolution occur in Europe instead of in China, where administration and technology had the lead on Europe until relatively recently in historical time? Why did such great economic advance arise from an economically primitive 18th century America instead of from the France of Louis XIV which commanded relatively immense resources (R. H. Tawney's question) or from South America where the same rough equality and new country that favoured the United States also prevailed (Tocqueville's question)?

A search for the answer leads us back into a singular, although multilinear, historical current — some of it already explored — made up, among other things, of western religious modes (in particular, Protestantism); the development of the mercantile economy; medievalism before it; the evolution of parliamentary institutions and the idea of individual liberty, in northern Europe, alongside them; and the fragmentation of Europe into nation states anterior to that; and the dawning of empiricism, and its various roots, interrelated with them as well. These were highly particular circumstances, of which the United States in turn was a particular issue. History (cultural inheritance) was thick in the psyche of the American entrepreneur, whether Henry Ford knew it or not.

Tocqueville, although he probably couldn't fit a wheel on an axle, did understand history superbly, and rightly attributed the "prodigious commercial activity of the inhabitants" to the influence of inherited customs as well as to the physical richness of the country. Far from having no continuity, America was "the only country in which it has been possible to witness the natural and tranquil growth of society, and where the influence exercised on the future condition of states by their origin is clearly distinguishable," which, after a perfunctory geographical outline, is where *Democracy in America* begins.

Another related matter Tocqueville noted was that immigrants with no instinctive love of country could take a zealous interest in the affairs of the township and the state. Although on one level Americans were the most individualistic of peoples, and their society the most atomistic of all, on another level and underlying this individualism was a rare propensity for communal institutions, and also "a love of order and law," which was possible because there was a common value system going back beyond the revolution (that wasn't really a revolution) to the British origins combining with the new land.

That tradition, as it happened, was singularly appropriate to the future. "A series of circumstances had conspired to saturate even the revolutionary position of the Americans with the quality of traditionalism," writes Louis Hartz. And: "The past became a continuous future, and the God of the traditionalists sanctioned the very arrogance of the men who defied him." America did dispense with all tradition, except the American one.

Almost all great social inventions and lasting movements for liberation have this paradoxical quality of traditionalism in them, because revolutions cut off from the past are nourished only feebly at the beginning by cultural momentum. They suffer from lack of historical substance. The cultural strains checking and confounding the revolutionary impulse are enormous, so that the chances of success, that is, the blossoming of the forward movement, are slight. Hence the seemingly easy spontaneity of the American revolution, in contrast to the failure of the Russian revolution which did not have the cultural experience of western Europe that Marxist prophecy was based on. Hence also the repeated failures of forward movements in China after the fall of the Empire, until the Communist Party made its historic adjustment to the Chinese peasant past. And hence, in Canada, the exceptional creative capacity of public enterprise and redistribution, because of the cultural past that is already a part of them.

Hartz' description of the United States in 1776 now applies to Canada instead. Our contradictory past now foreshadows a continuous future, and the men who will seem to be arrogantly defying "the God of the traditionalists" by putting together new public enterprises, and pushing forward the public dimension of all such enterprise, and brazenly using the tools of redistribution to create absolute interregional equality, will be sanctioning Canadian tradition by so doing. In the 1970's, it is this tradition which is singularly appropriate to the future.

Where do the Americans stand in all this? They stand as the Europeans stood to America in 1776.

Looking back, Hertz describes two contrasting European attitudes towards the United States at the time, but both based on the conventional European assumption that a liberal revolution being what it was — an upheaval, a transformation — the new American republic had no tradition. In other words, the independent republic, lacking a history as it was assumed, had no identity of cultural substance.

The first of these European groups were the "reactionaries." Blind to the continuity of the American past, they considered the American constitution to be made out of the whole cloth of doctrinaire (liberal) reason, and predicted its demise. In the same way, present-day American conservatives (the vast majority), and their colonial followers in this country (at our universities, also the vast majority!), blind to the continuity of the Canadian past, will almost certainly predict the economy's downfall when our own nationalism explodes in public enterprise and redistribution, just as the few among them who have put their minds to it have already predicted it.

The second European group, in the days of the early republic, were the liberals. They were the "radicals" of the age. They, also, were blind to the continuity of the American past inside the American future. Benjamin Franklin reported how the revolutionary constitutions of 1776 evoked the "rapture" of European liberals everywhere. Not seeing the substantial and unique American identity in it, because Americans weren't supposed to have identity, they saw the constitution as a product of emancipated rationalism, which was the only way in Europe that such constitutions could be promoted. Condorcet commented that American constitutionalism "took no force from the weight of centuries but was put together mechanically in a few years." To which John Adams replied, in his notes, "Fool! Fool!" Hence, also, that contemptuous comment by Gouverneur Morris about the French: "They want an American constitution without realizing they have no Americans to uphold it." In the same way, the American progressives, or "radicals," of today, like Ralph Nader and John Kenneth Galbraith, are — just like their conservative fellow nationals — equally ignorant of the native continuity in Canada's practical life, and misconceive it.

Galbraith, having said that it makes no difference what country owns the Canadian economy (economies being "put together mechanically" rather than culturally, to plagiarize Condorcet), and also having discussed Canadian public enterprise as if it were a product of the emancipated, progressive, socialist mind, as it would have to be in the United States, best illustrates the analogy.

The American economic culture is now decadent. Although it is strong in technique, as the decadent cultures of royalist France and imperial China were before it, it is feeble in social invention. Its parochial traditionalism, once so liberating for all of the world, has now become a cultural trap.

Government spending has removed a large part of the American economy from the free and various forces that animated the America of old, without an equivalent ethic having evolved alongside it. Although the concentration of corporate power is greater than ever, superceding popular control through a free market and weakening the impulses of popular commitment, the individualist, reformist, albeit mostly rhetorical, trust-busting campaigns of an earlier America have not now appeared, as they did before, to check it, or rather to reinforce the old mythology — not excepting Naderism, which is just a last romantic reaching out for an American past left behind by the general trend of the age.

In this decadence, most noticeable in defence spending, urbanism, broadcasting and the husbanding of energy and resources, but also touching on the whole fabric of American society, Galbraith plays the role of the emancipated progressive (played before by the rationalist European liberal). He proposes public enterprise. And just as the 18th century Europeans pointed to American constitutionalism, Galbraith points to public entrepreneurship in Canada and elsewhere.

But in the United States, there is little popular response. How could there possibly be, America being what it is? Their old compulsive doctrine is too much in them. And without an honest-to-goodness social revolution, rather than just the self-confirmation of 1776, would large scale public enterprise do the United States any good, or for lack of a cultural aptitude built up over the years in conflict and striving, as it has been in Canada, would it just get bogged down in bureaucracy and manipulation.

Americans like Galbraith want the Canadian future without realizing they have no Canadians to uphold it.

This explanation of change in terms of cultural aptitude — even revolutionary change as in China, or revolutionary proclamation as in the United States — is only another way of underlining the importance of indigenous ideology.

Such cultural aptitude is a function of identity, formed by the working out of particular contradictions over time. As we have seen in the cases of the United States and China, only indigenous ideology, drawn from those contradictions, discerns and brings out this aptitude, whereas non-indigenous ideology discounts it or ignores it, and colonial ideology actively suppresses it; and as long as the colonial ideology holds, it suppresses it indefinitely. In Canada, a remarkable aptitude exists, as we have also seen. We are already on the frontier, whereas some other peoples, like the Americans, because of their own particular contradictions, are in the parish.

What we have now finally to accomplish is our own Ideological Declaration of Independence, or our own Declaration of Ideological Independence, if you will, and the most startling innovations in public enterprise and redistribution will not only work, but they will not seem startling at all to Canadians, only to everybody else. The future will link up to the past as naturally and as felicitously as the future of the U.S. republic linked up to the past of the American colonies.

The righteous philosopher had things the wrong way about, then, when he wrote that "ideological and historical commitments . . . normally close off the possibilities for radical change" and when he applauded the Canadian consciousness for not having any. That is sheer escapism. All peoples are ideological. All peoples are participants in history. Ideological liveliness, and with it historical awareness, *open up* the possibilities for radical change. Without an indigenous ideological consciousness, a people are the prisoners of other ideology — they are grievously lacking in self-perception — and are capable of hardly any inventiveness at all. They are no less susceptible to dogma and to the backward uses of ideology and history. They are, in fact, quite likely to be afraid of undertaking change, because they are afraid of themselves.

But public enterprise and redistribution are only the most concrete expressions of this forward-looking identity which Canada's peculiar contradictions have formed. If we are "the first truly 20th century nation," as the novelist claims, if our reaction to life seems "a strictly contemporary one," as it appears to the poet, if, also, "when we do arrive at a mature or highly developed awareness of ourselves, it will be . . . an identity suited to the age we are entering rather than the one we are leaving behind," as the newspaper columnist perceives it, it is not because we have no identity or continuous history, as they all seem to have assumed, but because of the very opposite — our forceful continuous history and our peculiarity.

The American anthropologist, Conrad Arensberg, offers some illuminating precisions on this process of cultural evolution which occurs by "combining new and old" or by the "emergence of the new out of the old."

Such evolutionary innovation has a "two-stepped" character, in human cultures as in paleontology.

The first is the conservation of the old in the face of change, and is clearly conservative. Innovations are made to fit existing custom. They are used to bolster old ways. They contribute to continuity by reinforcing the past and also by being reworked and enriched by the past.

The second effect is quite different. It is a "splendid serendipity," a "lucky and unexpected opening of new possibilities of greater dimensions than the old," an opening up of a "vast new door" to change that was never intended and never imagined. This second effect may come years or centuries after the original innovations.

So it has been in Canada.

First, to conserve the old in the face of American progress, we innovated in government enterprise from canals to railroads to hydro power to broadcasting to air transport and beyond. The construction of the CPR was the boldest, and also the most culturally tangled, of these undertakings. The use of tariffs to create a National Policy was another part of it. Confederation, and the attendant statutory payments to provinces which were the forerunners of redistribution, were themselves such defensive innovations.

Taken alone, as technique, they were brilliant devices. Taken as a whole (the Canadian scheme of things), in relation to the United States, they were in reaction. No matter what the inspired social inventiveness in them, Canada always seemed vaguely a backward kind of a place. "Defensive expansionism," after all, is defensive. Not unnaturally, the originality of public enterprise was discounted, and redistribution produced as much friction as it did solidarity. The underlying market contradiction and regionalist and dualist contradictions were taken as a kind of curse Canadians had to learn to live with. Canada was a second-best country. We suffered it, and mistakenly took our suffrance for our essential selves.

This is not to say that Canada, as a distinct culture, was sluggish or stagnant in those years. The first step, in Arensberg's schema, is a period of constant application:

"Reaching a frontier for new cultural advance is hard evolutionary work; it requires human thought; it is no automatic, biological response; it takes culturally creative, inventive effort."

Defensiveness makes for its own alertness and imagination, and occasionally for great doings, as it has in Canada.

Then, 150 years after the construction of the Lachine Canal, and 200 years after the Conquest and the American War of Independence, a second effect becomes discernible. Innovations in public enterprise and redistribution are still made defensively. But at the same time, our experience in these two cultural modes reaches a point where suddenly it opens up vast new possibilities — an unsuspected frontier beyond the ken, perhaps also against the grain, of its largely conservative originators. *The Canadian public enterprise culture and the redistribution culture coalesce into a momentous aptitude for egalitarianism (the underpinning of democratic community) and for practical liberation.*

There is more to it than that. Our much-abused habituation to the tariff now is illuminated as a fine sensitivity to the relationship between nations. Our long coming to grips with Canada's small domestic market opens us up to the nature of community. The regional and dualist contradictions give us an educated awareness of collective differences, and a rare relative insight into our own condition. What was backward before is now forward. Not through any particular wisdom, quite by historical accident, in no small way because there has been so much reaction in Canada, a "splendid serendipity" is now upon us.

It is exactly because we were the losers of the American Revolution that we can now become winners of a Canadian one.

Selected References

Aside from the books listed below, there were others from which I drew the odd reference but which are not generally related to the subject. I have left these out.

Newspapers were a basic source, primarily the *Vancouver Sun*, the *Toronto Star* and *Le Devoir*, which were clipped for items in the areas concerned. *Maclean's, Le Maclean, Saturday Night* and *Canadian Dimension* were also followed. The Vancouver Public Library's clipping files cover, in addition to the *Vancouver Sun*, the *Financial Post*, the *Vancouver Province* and the *Globe and Mail*. The library's business and economics department also has the *Province* indexed. Additional useful sources include crown corporation and other company annual reports, correspondence, the *Financial Post* annual business surveys (also the FP corporate card service) and *Moody's Industrial Manual*, Statistics Canada publications, other government and departmental publications and information circulars, plus miscellaneous periodical, reference book, crown corporation and newspaper items.

On the theoretical side, Karl Polanyi's *The Great Transformation*, a basic document in itself, has bibliographical notes on related works in economic anthropology and history which interested readers might want to explore (see his Notes To Chapter 5). George Dalton, in his introduction to the collection of Polanyi essays, provides an additional reference list. See also Polanyi, Dalton, Weber, Easterbrook, *et al*, below.

The references have been divided into chapters, with some chapters grouped together. Many books, however, provide background for several sections. Polanyi is of importance on almost every major question — ideology, economic anthropology, economic motivation, tariffs and free trade, redistribution, comparative economic history. Tocqueville and Hartz on America come up in different contexts. Fitzgerald provides general background on China. Reflections on identity from the collections by Russell and Wainright are cited in several places. Some of the material on American economic history, under the Chapter 7 heading on promotions, also provides comparative background for comments elsewhere on railways, bankruptcy and consolidation. The chapter number within square brackets at the end of a listing indicates another reference to the same material.

[CHAPTER 1. The Old Identity Riddle]
Grant, George. *Lament for a Nation.* Toronto: McClelland and Stewart, 1965. [11]

Kilbourn, William, ed. *Canada: A Guide to the Peaceable Kingdom.* Toronto: Macmillan, 1970.

Lipset, Seymour Martin. *Revolution and Counterrevolution.* New York: Basic Books, 1968.

Russell, Peter, ed. *Nationalism in Canada.* Toronto: McGraw-Hill, 1966. [2]

Wainright, Andy, ed. *Notes for a Native Land.* Ottawa: Oberon, 1969. [2,3,15]

[CHAPTER 2. Canada as a Series of Contradictions — CHAPTER 3. The Importance of Being Ideological]

Bell, Daniel. *The End of Ideology.* Glencoe, Ill.: The Free Press, 1960.

Fitzgerald, C. P. *The Birth of Communist China.* Harmondsworth: Penguin Books, 1964.

Hartz, Louis. *The Liberal Tradition in America.* New York: Harcourt, Brace and World, 1955. [4,11,15]

Kilbourn, William. *The Firebrand.* Toronto: Clarke, Irwin, 1956.

Lévesque, René. *Option Québec.* Montreal: Editions de l'Homme, 1968. (*An Option for Quebec.* Toronto: McClelland and Stewart, 1968.) [4-6]

Mackenzie, William Lyon. *The Selected Writings of William Lyon Mackenzie.* Edited by Margaret Fairley. Toronto: Oxford University Press, 1960.

Mackenzie, William Lyon. *Sketches of Canada and the United States.* London: E. Wilson, 1833.

Madariaga, Salvador de. *Spain: A Modern History.* New York: Frederick A. Praeger, 1958.

Sawer, Geoffrey. *Modern Federalism.* London: Watts, 1969.

Tocqueville, Alexis de. *Democracy in America.* 2 vols. New York: Vintage Books, 1945. [1,11,13,15]

Trudeau, Pierre Elliott. *Le Fédéralisme et la société canadienne-française.* Montreal: Editions HMH, 1967. (*Federalism and the French Canadians.* Toronto: Macmillan, 1968.)

Snow, Edgar. *The Other Side of the River.* New York: Random House, 1961.

[CHAPTER 4. The Formative Years — CHAPTER 5. The Culture at Work — CHAPTER 6. Public Enterprise and Identity]

Aitken, Hugh G. J. "Defensive Expansionism: The State and Economic Growth in Canada," in W. T. Easterbrook and M. H. Watkins, eds., *Approaches To Canadian Economic History.* Toronto: McClelland and Stewart, 1967.

Aitken, Hugh G. J. *The Welland Canal Company.* Cambridge, Mass.: Harvard University Press, 1954.

Aitken, Hugh G. J., ed. *The State and Economic Growth.* New York: Social Science Research Council, 1959.

Ashley, C. A. and R. G. H. Smails. *Canadian Crown Corporations.* Toronto: Macmillan, 1965. [8]

Berton, Pierre. *The Last Spike.* Toronto: McClelland and Stewart, 1971.

Berton, Pierre. *The National Dream*. Toronto: McClelland and Stewart, 1970.

Bourgault, Pierre L. *Innovation and the Structure of Canadian Industry*. Science Council of Canada, Special Study No. 23. Ottawa: Information Canada, 1972. [9,10]

Brown, J. J. *Ideas in Exile*. Toronto: McClelland and Stewart, 1967. [10,12]

Canada. Statistics Canada. "Analysis of Control of Selected Canadian Industries, Year Ends, 1960-67," *Canada's international investment position*. Ottawa: Information Canada, 1971. Table XIX, p. 152.

Canada. Statistics Canada. *Federal Government Enterprise Finance*. Ottawa: Information Canada, annual.

Canada. Statistics Canada. *Provincial Government Enterprise Finance*. Ottawa: Information Canada, annual

Clark, S. D. *The Developing Canadian Community*. Toronto: University of Toronto Press, 1968.

Creighton, Donald. *The Empire of the St. Lawrence*. Toronto: Macmillan, 1956.

Dales, J. H. *Hydroelectricity and Industrial Development: Quebec 1898-1940*. Cambridge, Mass.: Harvard University Press, 1957.

Denison, Merrill, *The People's Power*. Toronto: McClelland and Stewart, 1960.

Easterbrook, W. T. "The Climate of Enterprise," in Hugh G. J. Aitken, ed., *Explorations in Enterprise*. Cambridge, Mass.: Harvard University Press, 1965.

Easterbrook, W. T. "Long-Period Comparative Study: Some Historical Cases," *The Journal of Economic History*, XVII, 4 (Dec. 1957), 571-595.

Easterbrook, W. T. and Hugh G. J. Aitken. *Canadian Economic History*. Toronto: Macmillan, 1967. [8]

Eggleston, Wilfrid. *Canada's Nuclear Story*. Toronto: Clarke, Irwin, 1965.

Eggleston, Wilfrid. *Scientists at War*. Toronto: Oxford University Press, 1950.

Glazebrook, G. P. deT. *A History of Transportation in Canada*. 2 vols. Toronto: McClelland and Stewart, 1964. [8]

Goodspeed, D. J. *DRB (A History of the Defence Research Board of Canada)*. Ottawa: Queen's Printer, 1958.

Hodgetts, A.B. *What Culture? What Heritage?* Toronto: Ontario Institute for Studies in Education, 1968.

Hodgetts, J.E. "The Public Corporation in Canada," in W.G. Friedmann and J. F. Garner, eds., *Government Enterprise*. New York: Columbia University Press, 1970.

Hunter, W. D. G. "The Development of the Canadian Uranium Industry: an Experiment in Public Enterprise," *Canadian Journal of Economics and Political Science*, XXVIII, 3 (Aug. 1962), 329-352.

Innis, Harold. "Government Ownership in Canada," Part II, *Problems of Staple Production in Canada*. Toronto: Ryerson, 1933.

Lipset, Seymour Martin. *Agrarian Socialism*. Berkeley: University of California Press, 1967.

Lundberg, Ferdinand. *The Rich and the Super-Rich*. New York: Lyle Stuart, 1968.

Marsh, D'Arcy. *The Tragedy of Henry Thornton*. Toronto: Macmillan, 1935. [8,15]

Mavor, James. *Government Telephones*. Toronto: Maclean, 1917.

Morton, W. L. *Manitoba*. Toronto: University of Toronto Press, 1957.

Musolf, Lloyd D. "Canadian Public Enterprise: A Character Study," *American Political Science Review*, 50 (1956), 405-421.

Musolf, Lloyd D. *Public Ownership and Accountability: The Canadian Experience*. Cambridge, Mass.: Harvard University Press, 1959.

Myers, Gustavus. *A History of Canadian Wealth*. Toronto: James Lewis and Samuel, 1972. [8]

Newman, Peter. *Flame of Power*. Toronto: Longmans, 1959.

Perry, Robert L. *Galt, U.S.A.* Toronto: Maclean-Hunter, 1971. [9]

Plewman, W. R. *Adam Beck and the Ontario Hydro*. Toronto: Ryerson, 1947.

Polanyi, Karl. *The Great Transformation*. Boston: Beacon Press, 1957. [3,9.12,15]

Polanyi, Karl. *Primitive, Archaic and Modern Economies*. Edited and introduction by George Dalton. Garden City, N.Y.: Anchor Books, 1968. [13-15]

Ramsey, Bruce. *PGE: Railway to the North*. Vancouver: Mitchell Press, 1962.

Rea, K. J. and J. T. McLeod, eds. *Business and Government in Canada*. Toronto: Methuen, 1969.

Sauriol, Paul. *La Nationalisation de l'électricité*. Montreal: Editions de l'Homme, 1962.

Scott, Otto. "Polymer of Canada," *Rubber World*, March, 1966.

Stevens, G. R. *Canadian National Railways*. 2 vols. Toronto: Clarke, Irwin, 1960 and 1962. [8]

Trudeau, Pierre Elliott. *Approaches to Politics*. Toronto: Oxford University Press, 1970.

[CHAPTER 7. Mining Promotions]

Allen, Frederick Lewis. *Only Yesterday*. New York: Bantam Books, 1959.

Ashton, T. S. *The Industrial Revolution 1760-1830*. London: Oxford University Press, 1968.

Bradley, H. W. "End of Reconstruction and Rise of Industry," *Encyclopædia Britannica*, 1972, vol. 22, 649-660. [9]

Brooks, John. *Once in Golconda*. New York: Harper and Row, 1969.

Broude, Henry W. "The Role of the State in American Economic Development, 1820-1890," in Hugh G. J. Aitken, ed., *The State and Economic Growth*. New York: Social Science Research Council, 1959. [4]

Canada, *Report of the Royal Commission on Banking and Finance.* Porter Commission. Ottawa: Queen's Printer, 1964. See also E. K. Cork.

Conway, G. R. *The Supply Of, and Demand For, Canadian Equities.* Toronto: Toronto Stock Exchange, 1970.

Cork, E. K. *Finance in the Mining Industry.* Study prepared for the Royal Commission on Banking and Finance. Ottawa: Queen's Printer, 1962.

Doherty, John G. and Timothy Pritchard. *Bulls, Bears and Sheep.* Toronto: McClelland and Stewart, 1971.

Goulden, Joseph C. *Monopoly.* New York: Pocket Books, 1970.

Graebner, N. A. "Civil War and Reconstruction, 1850-1876," *Encyclopædia Britannica,* 1972, vol. 22, 637-649. [9]

Hofstader, Richard. *The American Political Tradition.* New York: Anchor Books, 1954. [3]

Holbrook, Stewart H. *The Age of the Moguls.* Garden City, N.Y.: Doubleday, 1954.

Josephson, Matthew. *The Robber Barons.* New York: Harcourt, Brace, 1934. [4,9]

Myers, Gustavus. *The History of the Great American Fortunes.* New York: Modern Library, 1937.

National Bureau of Economic Research. *Capital Formation and Economic Growth.* Princeton, N.J.: Princeton University Press, 1955. [5]

Ontario. *Report of the Attorney General's Committee on Securities Legislation in Ontario.* Kimber Report. Toronto: 1965.

Ontario. *Report of the Royal Commission to Investigate Trading in the Shares of Windfall Oils and Mines Limited.* Kelly Commission. Toronto: 1965.

Shaffer, Ivan. *The Stock Promotion Business.* Toronto: McClelland and Stewart, 1967.

Sharp, Paul F. *Whoop-Up Country.* Minneapolis: University of Minnesota Press, 1955. [9]

Smith, A.D.H. *John Jacob Astor.* New York: Blue Ribbon Books, 1929.

Sobel, Robert. *The Big Board.* New York: The Free Press, 1965.

Sobel, Robert. *The Curbstone Brokers.* New York: Macmillan, 1970.

Thomas, Dana L. *The Plungers and the Peacocks.* New York: Putnam, 1967.

Weber, Max. *The Protestant Ethic and the Spirit of Capitalism.* Foreword by R. H. Tawney. New York: Charles Scribner's Sons, 1958. [5,15]

[CHAPTER 8. The Canadian Monopoly Culture]

Galbraith, J. K. *The New Industrial State.* Boston: Houghton Mifflin, 1967. [9]

International Air Transport Association. *World Air Transport Statistics.* Montreal, annual.

Wheatcroft, Stephen S. *Airline Competition in Canada.* Ottawa: Department of Transport, 1958.

See also Myers *(A History of Canadian Wealth)* and Easterbrook, Aitken on the fur trade; Marsh, Stevens and Glazebrook on railways; Ashley, Smails on air transport.

[CHAPTER 9. The Colonial Oligopoly Culture]

Canada In The Atlantic Economy. Published for the Private Planning Association of Canada. 13 vols. Toronto: University of Toronto Press, 1967-

Daly, D. J., B. A. Keys and E. J. Spence. *Scale and Specialization in Canadian Manufacturing.* Economic Council of Canada, Staff Study No. 21. Ottawa: Queen's Printer, 1968.

Eastman, H. C. and S. Stykolt. *The Tariff and Competition in Canada.* Toronto: Macmillan, 1967.

English, H. E. *Industrial Structure in Canada's International Competitive Position.* Montreal: Private Planning Association of Canada, 1964.

Fullerton, D.H. and H.A. Hampson. *Canadian Secondary Manufacturing Industry.* Study prepared for the Royal Commission on Canada's Economic Prospects. Ottawa: Queen's Printer, 1957.

Godfrey, Dave and Mel Watkins, eds. *Gordon to Watkins to You.* Toronto: New Press, 1970.

Harnetty, Peter. "The Imperialism of Free Trade: Lancashire and the Indian Cotton Duties, 1859-1862," *Economic History Review,* 2nd series, XVIII (1965), 333-349.

Harnetty, Peter. "The Imperialism of Free Trade: Lancashire, India and the Cotton Supply Question, 1861-1865," *Journal of British Studies,* VI, 1 (Nov. 1966), 70-96.

Hobsbawm, E.J. *Industry and Empire.* Harmondsworth: Penguin Books, 1968.

Hunter, Alex, ed. *Monopoly and Competition.* Harmondsworth: Penguin Books, 1969.

Johnson, Brian. *The Politics of Money.* London: John Murray, 1970.

Lamb, Helen B. "The 'State' and Economic Development in India," in Simon Kuznets, W. E. Moore and J. J. Spengler, eds., *Economic Growth: Brazil, India, Japan.* Durham, No. Carolina: Duke University Press, 1955.

Levitt, Kari. *Silent Surrender.* Toronto: Macmillan, 1970.

Moore, Milton. *How Much Price Competition?* Montreal: McGill-Queen's University Press, 1970.

Myrdal, Gunnar. *Asian Drama.* Vol. 1. New York: Pantheon, 1968.

Rotstein, Abraham and Gary Lax, eds. *Independence: The Canadian Challenge.* Toronto: McClelland and Stewart, 1972.

Schumpeter, Joseph A. *Capitalism, Socialism and Democracy.* New York: Harper and Brothers, 1950.

Wonnacott, Ronald J. and Paul Wonnacott. *Free Trade Between the United States and Canada: The Potential Economic Effects.* Cambridge, Mass.: Harvard University Press. 1967.

[CHAPTER 10. Some Other Examples of Economic Masochism]

Buckler, E. J. "Canadian Case History—Polymer Corporation Limited," *Research Management*, VI, 4 (July 1963), 289-304.

Canada. *Report of the Senate Special Committee on Science Policy: A Science Policy For Canada.* 3 vols. Ottawa: Information Canada 1970, 1972 and 1973.

Cordell, Arthur J. *The Multinational Firm, Foreign Direct Investment, and Canadian Science Policy.* Science Council of Canada, Special Study No. 22. Ottawa: Information Canada, 1971.

Defries, R. D. *The First Forty Years (1914-1955).* History of Connaught Medical Research Laboratories. Toronto: University of Toronto Press, 1968.

Jacobs, Jane. *The Economy of Cities.* New York: Random House, 1969. [14]

Kennedy, John de Navarre. *The History of the Department of Munitions and Supply.* Ottawa: King's Printer, 1950.

Organization for Economic Co-operation and Development. *Reviews of National Science Policy: Canada.* Paris: 1969.

Thistle, Mel. *The Inner Ring.* Early History of the National Research Council. Toronto: University of Toronto Press, 1966.

[CHAPTER 11. Historical Roots—CHAPTER 12. The Expo Experience]

Barris, Alex. *The Pierce-Arrow Showroom is Leaking.* Toronto: Ryerson, 1969.

Brown, Les. *Television: The Business Behind the Box.* New York: Harcourt Brace Jovanovich, 1971.

Friendly, Fred W. *Due to Circumstances Beyond Our Control.* New York: Random House, 1967.

Johnson, Nicolas. *How to Talk Back to Your Television Set.* Boston: Little, Brown, 1970.

Minow, Newton N. *Equal Time.* Edited by Lawrence Laurent. New York: Atheneum, 1964.

Opotowsky, Stan. *TV The Big Picture.* New York: E. P. Dutton, 1961.

Peers, Frank W. *The Politics of Canadian Broadcasting 1920-1951.* Toronto: University of Toronto Press, 1969.

Spry, Graham. "The Costs of Canadian Broadcasting," *Queen's Quarterly*, LXVII, 4 (Winter 1961), 503-513.

Spry, Graham. "The Decline and Fall of Canadian Broadcasting," *Queen's Quarterly*, LXVIII, 2 (Summer 1961), 213-225.

Watson, Patrick. *Conspirators in Silence.* Toronto: McClelland and Stewart, 1969.

Weir, E. Austin. *The Struggle for National Broadcasting in Canada.* Toronto: McClelland and Stewart, 1965.

[CHAPTER 13. Redistribution and Identity—CHAPTER 14. The Social Relationships count]

Atlantic Provinces Economic Council. *Fifth Annual Review.* Review of the Department of Regional Economic Expansion. Halifax: 1971.

Atlantic Provinces Economic Council. *Seventh Annual Review*. Review of the Provincial Development Corporations. Halifax: 1973.

Bédard, Roger-J. *L'Essor économique du Québec*. Montreal: Beauchemin, 1969. [4-6]

Brewis, T.N. *Regional Economic Policies in Canada*. Toronto: Macmillan, 1969.

Buckley, Helen and Eva Tihanyi. *Canadian Policies for Rural Adjustment*. Economic Council of Canada, Special Study No. 7. Ottawa: Queen's Printer, 1967.

Canada. *Report of the Royal Commission on Dominion-Provincial Relations*. Rowell-Sirois Report. Book 1 abridged. Edited by D. V. Smiley. Toronto: McClelland and Stewart, 1963. See also W. A. Mackintosh.

Jones, Richard. *Community in Crisis*. Toronto: McClelland and Stewart, 1967.

Mackintosh, W. A. *The Economic Background of Dominion-Provincial Relations*. Study prepared for the Royal Commission on Dominion-Provincial Relations. Toronto: McClelland and Stewart, 1964.

Mathias, Philip. *Forced Growth*. Toronto: James Lewis and Samuel, 1971.

Moore, Milton A., J. Harvey Perry and Donald I. Beach. *The Financing of Canadian Federation*. Toronto: Canadian Tax Foundation, 1966.

Simeon, Richard. *Federal-Provincial Diplomacy*. Toronto: University of Toronto Press, 1972.

Smiley, D. V. *Canada in Question: Federalism in the Seventies*. Toronto: McGraw-Hill Ryerson, 1972.

[CHAPTER 15. "A Splendid Serendipity"]

Arensberg, Conrad M. "Cultural Change and the Guaranteed Income," in Robert Theobald, ed., *The Guaranteed Income*. Garden City, N.Y.: Doubleday, 1966, 206-230.